MEMORY AND BRAIN

MEMORY
AND BRAIN

LARRY R. SQUIRE

Veterans Administration
Medical Center
and
University of California

San Diego

New York   Oxford
OXFORD UNIVERSITY PRESS
1987

Oxford University Press

Oxford   New York   Toronto
Delhi   Bombay   Calcutta   Madras   Karachi
Petaling Jaya   Singapore   Hong Kong   Tokyo
Nairobi   Dar es Salaam   Cape Town
Melbourne   Auckland

and associated companies in
Beirut   Berlin   Ibadan   Nicosia

Library of Congress Cataloging-in-Publication Data
Squire, Larry R.
Memory and brain.
Bibliography: p.   Includes indexes.
1. Memory—Physiological aspects.   2. Brain.   I. Title.
[DNLM: 1. Brain—physiology.   2. Memory—physiology.
3. Neurophysiology.   4. Neuropsychology. WL 102 S774m]
QP406.S66   1987   153.1′2   86-28614
ISBN 0-19-504207-7
ISBN 0-19-504208-5 (pbk.)

4 6 8 9 7 5

Printed in the United States of America
on acid-free paper

To
H. W. S., J. R. S., M. J. S.,
M. F. S., R. F. S.

Preface

One hundred years ago, a remarkable series of publications appeared that would stand as landmark work in the field of memory research. My colleague Paul Rozin once called that period, the 1880s, the golden decade of memory research. It began in 1881 with the publication of Theodule Ribot's *Les Maladies de la Memoire* (translated into English in 1882 as *Diseases of Memory*). This was the first comprehensive and systematic compilation of human amnesic cases and the first attempt to develop from the facts of amnesia general principles about the organization of normal memory. In 1885 Hermann Ebbinghaus published *Uber das Gedachtnis (On Memory),* which described the first systematic laboratory studies of memory. These showed that learning, remembering, and forgetting had lawful properties and that they could be studied with scientific methods. In 1887, Sergei Korsakoff, a Russian psychiatrist, published the first descriptions of the syndrome of amnesia that would bear his name—now the best known and most widely studied example of the amnesic syndrome. Then in 1890 William James published his famous *Principles of Psychology,* which contained among many other things his distinction between primary and secondary memory, a distinction that was later linked to the organization and function of brain systems.

Though one is hard pressed to identify another decade like the 1880s, work on memory has progressed since then in many fruitful directions. One major development has been the emergence of neuroscience and the possibility of investigating brain mechanisms subserving memory functions. In the 1930s Karl Lashley established a laboratory of neuropsychology—literally the joining of neurology and psychology. (The term seems to have first appeared in the literature in 1937.) Lashley's important experiments showed that many ideas about brain function, derived from early-century stimulus–response theory, were naive and simplistic. In fact, the neural basis of memory in particular and cognition in general seemed almost beyond reach at that time. Then, in 1949, Hebb's famous book *The Organization of Behavior, A Neuropsychological Theory* convinced many that it was possible after all to think seriously about the brain processes underlying perception, memory, and other higher cognitive functions.

The last few decades have seen an explosion of technology and data. Some even say that there is no theory in neuroscience, so great has been the ascendancy of method and techniques over ideas. In any case, an abundance of facts and observations have accumulated. One could say that the work of Lashley and Hebb inaugurated the modern era of memory research. What has happened since then?

We still know relatively little about how the brain learns and remembers. Yet remarkable progress has been made, especially in the last two decades. Much of this newer work is quite specialized. Narrow subdisciplines study small pieces of the problem. Those studying memory include psychologists, neurologists, biologists, mathematicians, and computer scientists. Work is being done at many levels of analysis—from neurons to brain systems and whole behavior. Can the pieces be fit into any coherent, larger picture?

The purpose of this book is to provide a step in that direction. It tries to bring together many separate threads of recent psychological and neurobiological work on memory, to lay out the main ideas and important facts, and to create as complete a picture as possible. Such a project runs some risks. Neuroscience is a fast-moving field, a discipline of journal articles, not books. The specialist may find my treatment of his or her subject superficial. Undoubtedly, significant material is omitted. Yet, it seems worthwhile to begin, if only because the accumulation of facts may soon outpace our ability to understand their significance. Explicit statements about the broader hypotheses guiding contemporary work might make it possible to design better, more direct experiments. And just providing a sensible organization for the facts can help. To the extent that we can tie what we know to other relevant facts, understanding runs deeper and the chance for insight is greater. In this book, I have tried particularly to join two traditions of work on memory that have not always seemed to recognize the relevance of the other: psychology and neuroscience. We want to understand both the organization and formal structure of memory as well as its neural basis. I have tried to show how these enterprises work hand in hand.

Some have expressed the hope that this book will be useful as a textbook. If it turns out that way, that is fine, though this was not the original intention. The intention was simply to take stock of what has been learned and to try to identify the outlines of a larger picture with the hope that my friends and colleagues would find the result useful and interesting. At the same time, I would hope that scientists from other disciplines, as well as advanced undergraduates and graduate students, will find the material accessible. Much of scientific writing is too specialized, and students are often not the only audience excluded. For newcomers to this area, I have included a glossary of terms. However, there is no substitute for good introductory textbooks in neuroscience and psychology.

The book grew out of a chapter prepared originally for the *Handbook of Physiology* (Squire, 1987). Neal Cohen contributed to the first draft of that chapter, and my editor Fred Plum provided numerous valuable suggestions. I thank Shelley Reinhardt and Jeffrey House at Oxford Press for their encouragement to revise and expand this into a book and for their expert counsel at all stages of the work. The work of my research laboratory during this period has been generously supported by the Veterans Administration, the National Institute of Mental Health, the National Institutes of Health, and more recently the Office of Naval Research. The fact that the research work has proceeded smoothly, despite the distractions of this project, is owed to my extraordinarily capable senior research assistant, Joyce Zouzounis.

I am lucky to have been in an ideal research environment for many years, among many fine colleagues in neuroscience and psychology. Two persons have been especially important in shaping and sustaining that environment. Lee Henderson, Associate Chief of Staff for Research at the San Diego Veterans Administration Medical Center, has been enormously helpful to my research group; and his staff, under the expert direction of Darlene Whorley, has provided efficient and sympathetic administrative support. My departmental Chairman, Lewis Judd, Professor of Psychiatry at the University of California School of Medicine, San Diego, has consistently given the strongest possible support to basic reseach within our department. He has provided a happy and productive academic home.

In writing this book, I benefited greatly from conversations with many persons, especially Ted Bullock, Nelson Butters, David Cohen, Neal Cohen, Francis Crick, Max Cowan, Joaquin Fuster, Roland Giolli, Peter Graf, Irwin Levitan, Gary Lynch, George Mandler, David Rumelhart, Pedro Pasik, Larry Swanson, Robert Thompson, and Robert Terry. I am additionally grateful to a number of persons who generously read and commented on drafts of individual chapters: David Amaral, Adele Diamond, Steven Foote, Michela Gallagher, Bill Greenough, Simon LeVay, Jim McGaugh, Mort Mishkin, Carla Shatz, and Dick Thompson. Lynn Nadel, Ken Paller, and Dan Schacter read an entire early draft, offering many useful comments. Most especially, I thank my two principal collaborators, Art Shimamura and Stuart Zola-Morgan, who read the complete text and offered many helpful comments and much encouragement. Their suggestions immeasurably improved the book, as did their contributions to the frequent and stimulating interchanges that have become a mainstay of our laboratory group. I also thank Donald Goldsmith for his excellent editorial help and my dedicated assistant Anne Kelley for her untiring help with the manuscript. Finally, I thank my wife Mary, who also helped with editing and who abided this project with grace and good humor.

Del Mar   L. R. S.
October 1986

Contents

CONTENTS

CONTENTS

MEMORY AND BRAIN

1

Definitions:
From Synapses to Behavior

Most organisms can change in response to the events that occur during their lifetimes. Because of this capacity, the experiences that an animal has can modify its nervous system, and it will later behave differently as a result. This adaptive capacity gives organisms the ability to learn and to remember. Neuroscientists and psychologists have generally preferred broad definitions of learning and memory. One can begin with well-studied examples of learning, such as the conditioned reflex (Pavlov, 1927), or with familiar examples of rat laboratory behavior, such as bar pressing. Yet it has always been recognized that a complete account of learning and memory must accommodate many different kinds of behavioral change. Memory includes not only the conditioned reflex but also the ability to remember one face out of a thousand that have been seen, the ability to memorize a poem, the ability to demonstrate an improved throwing arm, and the ability to find one's way around an old neighborhood.

The concepts of learning and memory are closely related. Learning is the *process* of acquiring new information, while memory refers to the *persistence* of learning in a state that can be revealed at a later time. Memory is the usual consequence of learning. Hilgard and Marquis (1940), in what is perhaps the best-known review of the psychological principles

3

of conditioning and learning, defined learning as a "change in the strength of an act through training procedures (whether in the laboratory or the natural environment) as distinguished from changes in the strength of the act by factors not attributable to training" (p. 347). McGeoch (1942), in an early, comprehensive review of human learning, wrote, "Learning as we measure it is a change in performance as a function of practice. In most cases, if not in all, this change has a direction which satisfies the current motivating conditions of the individual" (pp. 3, 4).

Neal Miller (1967), wishing to exclude ambiguous cases of learning, wrote that "Learning is a relatively permanent increase in response strength that is based on previous reinforcement and that can be made specific to one out of two or more arbitrarily selected stimulus situations" (p. 644). Miller called this "Grade-A Certified Learning." But, Miller (and others) recognized that some types of behavioral change do not conform to such a restrictive definition, even though they could provide insight to understanding both the capacity of organisms to change and the neural basis of this capacity. One wants to exclude from consideration the effects of factors like fatigue or injury, which, though resulting from experience, are not at all what is meant by memory. At the same time, other relatively simple forms of behavioral adaptation, such as habituation and sensitization, deserve close attention. They do not depend on association, but they can be long-lasting and might well constitute building blocks for classical conditioning and other forms of learning (Hawkins and Kandel, 1984).

Biologists believe that the capacity for memory provides a special case of a more general phenomenon: neuronal plasticity. Many neurons exhibit plasticity, that is, they can change structurally or functionally, often in a lasting way. Plasticity is evident in such diverse phenomena as drug tolerance, enzyme induction, sprouting of axon terminals after a brain lesion, and strictly synaptic events such as facilitation and depression. The discovery of just how the nervous system performs these and other examples of plasticity would be likely to provide important clues to the problem of how the nervous system accomplishes learning and memory. Kandel and Spencer (1968) made this point in their comprehensive review of the neurophysiological basis of learning. "Since persistence is one of the most distinctive features of learning, we believe that analysis of the plastic properties of neurons is a prerequisite for the neuro-

4

Figure 1 *Left.* Santiago Ramon y Cajal (1852–1934), Spanish neuroanatomist. *Right.* Ivan P. Pavlov (1849–1936), Russian physiologist. (Left, from Ramon y Cajal, 1952; Right, from Hearst, 1979.)

physiological study of learning'' (p. 65). No matter how learning and memory are defined, at present we understand them so poorly that we cannot afford to discard any phenomenon that might yield clues about their neural basis.

Reflection on the physiological basis of memory led most early writers to consider some type of growth or change in the existing structure of the nervous system. William James (1890) wrote, ''The only impressions that can be made upon them [brain and spinal cord] are through the blood, on the one hand, and through the sensory nerve-root on the other . . . The currents once in, must find a way out. In getting out they leave their traces in the paths which they take. The only thing they can do, in short, is to deepen old paths or to make new ones'' (p. 107). By the late nineteenth century, biologists had learned that most mature nerve cells have lost their capacity to divide. The hypothesis that existing nerve cells can grow therefore appeared to be a reasonable way of accounting

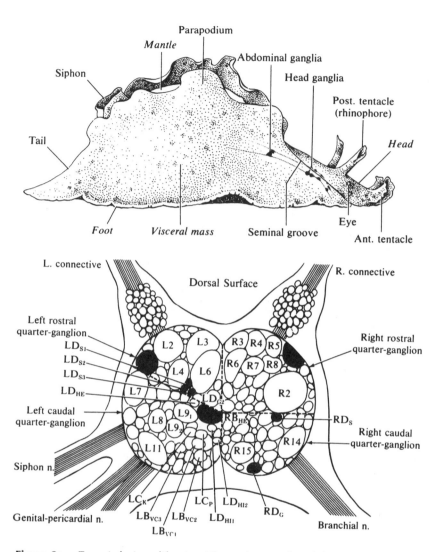

Figure 2a. *Top. Aplysia californica.* The major ganglia of the nervous system are shown in the position they occupy inside the animal. The animal's nervous system contains about 18,000 nerve cells, distributed among nine ganglia. A full-grown animal is about the size of a human hand. *Bottom.* Map of identified cells in the abdominal ganglion. Many of the cells are large enough to be seen by the naked eye, and they can be identified from animal to animal. (From Kandel, 1976.)

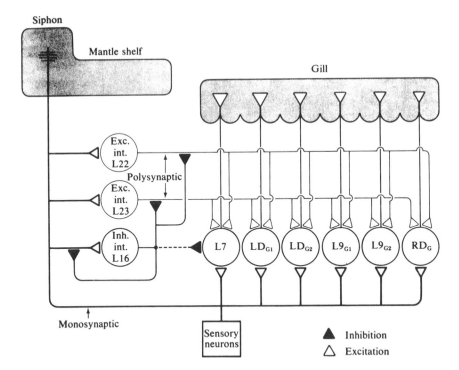

Figure 2b. Neural circuit of the gill withdrawal reflex. The sensory neurons, consisting of a population of about 24 cells, make direct, monosynaptic connections from the siphon skin to the gill motor neurons. They also make indirect, polysynaptic connections to the motor neurons via three interneurons. During habituation of the reflex with repeated stimulation, the excitatory synapses from the sensory neurons onto motor neurons and interneurons undergo depression. (From Kandel, 1976.)

for the persistence of memory. Such a concept was first introduced by Ramon y Cajal (1894) and independently by two of his contemporaries (Tanzi, 1893; Lugaro, 1900). During the past century, this basic idea has been restated several times, making explicit the hypothesis that the synapse is the critical site of plastic change (Konorski, 1948; Hebb, 1949; Eccles, 1953; Kandel, 1977). The idea is that memory involves a persistent change in the relationship between neurons, either through structural modification or through biochemical events within neurons that change the way in which neighboring neurons communicate.

Advances in neurobiology have produced two significant and relevant discoveries since synaptic change was first proposed to explain memory. The first of these discoveries is that neurons show many kinds of plasticity. Application of electrical stimulation, neuronal disuse, and more natural treatments such as enriched rearing conditions have all been shown to produce synaptic change: presynaptic changes in the economics of transmitter release (depression, facilitation, and post-tetanic potentiation), postsynaptic changes in receptor sensitivity, and morphological alterations in synaptic structure. These results demonstrate that neurons can change in a functionally significant way, and they provide possibilities concerning the actual processes that occur during behavioral learning. The second important discovery is that in favorable invertebrate preparations, alterations in synaptic efficacy can be correlated directly with behavioral learning—most clearly in the cases of habituation, sensitization, and classical conditioning. For example, habituation in the sea hare *Aplysia* depends on a decrease in the tendency of neurons to release neurotransmitter as a function of repeated stimulation (Figure 2).

Prior to the recent technological developments of neuroscience, memory was a problem studied primarily by psychologists. Today, both memory and the broader topic of neural plasticity are major areas of interest within neuroscience itself, and they can be approached in several ways. Although one important and fruitful focus of recent interest has been an understanding of the molecular and cellular facts of synaptic change, the problem of memory raises other types of questions as well. There are many steps between synaptic change and behavioral memory. Do the particular molecules synthesized during learning contain an information code? Does the pattern of synaptic pathways that are changed during learning code for information? What is the code? What happens during forgetting: an irreversible erasure of what occurred during learning, or only a change in accessibility, which is potentially reversible? Where is memory localized in the nervous system? Is it widely distributed, or do restricted loci store specific memories? Are there memory centers?

Many important questions about memory address a more global, psychological level of organization. Is memory one thing or many things? If more than one kind of memory were to exist, then the neural foundations discovered for one kind of memory might not apply to the others, and principles of organization developed for one kind might not generalize to the others. Is it useful or necessary to distinguish between short-lasting and long-lasting memory or between memory for one kind of material (e.g., faces) and memory for other kinds (e.g., words, numbers)? What brain systems participate in information processing, storage, and retrieval? What is the flow diagram of information-processing events, and how can the flow diagram be related to anatomy?

Questions about memory must be addressed at several different levels of analysis, ranging from the molecular events that underlie synaptic change to the broader problems of the organization of memory within the brain and the organization of whole behavior. Answers to these questions have been sought in the analysis of simple preparations, in model systems, and in behavioral studies of experimental animals. Such studies bring to bear all the techniques of modern behavioral neuroscience: lesions, recording of neural activity, biochemical and anatomical measurement, electrical stimulation of brain, and administration of drugs. Clinical procedures or accidents of nature sometimes allow significant studies to be carried out with human subjects. The pages that follow attempt to summarize what is now known about memory. Specific molecular and intracellular events involved in neuronal plasticity will not, for the most part, be discussed. While it is recognized that the molecular biology of synaptic change is of great interest, here the synaptic change itself is considered as the elementary component of memory. The focus is on the links between synaptic change and behavioral memory: neurons, neural systems, and the problem of how memory is organized in the brain.

2

Memory as Synaptic Change

Since the first description of synapses, the concept that synaptic change is the critical event in information storage has dominated neurobiological work on memory. However, strikingly dissimilar ideas have been expressed concerning how synaptic change actually represents information. The most prevalent view has been that the specificity of stored information is determined by the location of synaptic changes in the nervous system and by the pattern of altered neuronal interactions that these changes produce. This idea is largely accepted at the present time, and will be explored further in this and succeeding chapters in the light of current evidence. However, this view of memory has not always been so popular as it is now. Science rarely progresses through the smooth accretion of knowledge. Although textbooks often depict an orderly process of information gathering, digressions and blind-alleys are commonplace. A significant component of scientific work consists of serious, extended exploration of possibilities that later turn out to be incorrect. The recent history of the neurobiology of memory includes an episode of this sort. The story is itself a digression, but it forms a recent part of the history of memory research and will be briefly told here. A useful and important aspect of scientific work is to understand alternative possibilities and why they are wrong.

Connections versus Molecular Codes

One possible hypothesis about memory and information storage is that acquired information is specified by the type of molecule synthesized by the involved neurons. The molecule—for example—a protein, is information-carrying: Its structure both depends on experience and contains a code that represents experience (e.g., a particular amino acid sequence). This view of memory was proposed in the 1960s. "It seems reasonably certain that the chemical correlates of learning do not represent merely a non-specific stimulation of protein synthesis necessary for the increased production of synaptic transmitters or for neuronal growth. The results of bioassay clearly indicate that the molecules whose increased synthesis has been shown . . . do actually take part in the coding of acquired information" (Ungar, 1971, p. 47). According to this view, each neuron in the brain has its own individual molecular label. New combinations of these molecules are formed during learning, and the new combinations code for the acquired information.

These ideas were stimulated by two different traditions of biological work. The first was the elucidation of the genetic code and the central dogma of molecular biology, which holds that species memory is coded in the base sequence of DNA, which in turn serves as a template for the synthesis of RNA and protein. It seemed attractive to some that the structure of RNA and protein produced by a neuron could be specific to the kind of stimulus in the environment that triggered the synthetic events, or specific to the location in the nervous system at which the events occurred. In support of this possibility, some investigators reported qualitative changes, i.e. altered base ratios, in rat brain RNA following training experiences (Hyden and Lange, 1965).

The second tradition lay in several years of work on conditioning in animals having relatively primitive nervous systems, especially the flatworm *Planaria*. Although there was disagreement as to whether this organism could exhibit classical conditioning at all (Bennett and Calvin, 1964), one branch of work in this area proceeded from the demonstration of classical conditioning (Thompson and McConnell, 1955) to the demonstration that worms cannibalizing "trained" worms thereby acquired the conditioned reflex (McConnell, 1962), to reports that the conditioned

11

reflex could be transferred between animals by injecting RNA from trained worms into naive worms (Jacobson, Fried, and Horowitz, 1966).

In 1965, four different laboratories reported almost simultaneously that memory could be transferred from trained to naive rats by injection of brain homogenates or extracts (Reinis, 1965; Babich, Bubash, and Jacobson, 1965; Fjerdingstad, Nissen, and Roigaard-Petersen, 1965; Ungar and Oceguera-Navarro, 1965). Within a few years, approximately 100 publications appeared, many of them reporting positive effects (for reviews, see Ungar, 1970; Fjerdingstad, 1971; Zippel, 1973). Great controversy existed from the beginning about these findings. The original report that acquired food-seeking behavior to a signal could be transferred between rats by injection of brain homogenates (Babich et al., 1965) could not be replicated (Gross and Carey, 1965). In 1966, 23 different investigators representing seven laboratories signed a letter to the journal *Science* reporting their combined failures to demonstrate transfer of memory in mammals by brain extract (Bryne et al., 1966).

Krech and Bennett concluded a few years later, based on 17 separate experiments involving more than 2,000 animals, ''Although an occasional significant difference in the expected direction was obtained between the trained and naive recipient groups, we were not able to reproduce these findings in a satisfactorily consistent manner'' (Krech and Bennett, 1971, p. 162). Another reviewer catalogued all studies published through 1970, counting 133 successful independent demonstrations of transfer of memory, 115 failures, and 15 ambiguous cases (Dyal, 1971). The successes appeared to have come from 24 different investigative groups, 13 of whom also tallied some failures.

In the 1970s, work in this area slowed considerably. Except in a few laboratories where the work continued, the phenomenon proved elusive and could not form the basis for cumulative experimental work. Perhaps just as important was the reluctance of neuroscientists to believe that transfer of memory was in principle possible. Whereas it is now widely believed that development of neural connections requires chemical recognition between neurons (Sperry, 1963), it is supposed that this is accomplished by concentration gradients rather than by different molecules labeling different neurons. If neuronal differentiation and formation of connections during development can be accomplished without neuron-specific molecular labeling, then there is no necessity to suppose that

Figure 3. Cover drawing from *The Worm Runner's Digest,* a publication of the 1960s and 1970s, which featured the flatworm *Planaria.* Many of its articles argued that memory was stored as a molecular code that could be transferred between animals. (From *The Worm Runner's Digest,* IX, 1967, no. 1.)

this kind of labeling occurs during learning. Specificity of acquired information can be achieved by where in the nervous system synapses change. There is no additional need for coding of information within neurons by molecular rearrangement; and if no such coding occurs, then transfer experiments cannot succeed (Barondes, 1972).

In any case, some work on information coding in molecules continued into the 1970s. Ungar and his colleagues (1972) isolated and sequenced a 15-amino acid peptide, which was named scotophobin. This peptide was found in the brains of rats trained in a dark-avoidance task; when injected into naive rats, it conferred upon them a tendency to avoid the dark. Considerable work in the 1970s was directed toward the effects of scotophobin and other apparently behavior-specific peptides. It is not a simple matter, however, to prove that the behavioral effects of a given peptide, hormone, or drug are so specific that they produce a fear of the dark. The difficulty arises from the fact that when an animal is placed in a specific environmental situation, it may behave in a specific way even if it is under only a general sort of influence. Synthetic scotophobin was found to alter locomotor activity, but studies were not done using other behavioral situations to determine what other effects scotophobin might exert. Studies were also not conducted to determine whether other peptides or hormones might in fact mimic the behavioral effects claimed for scotophobin.

These studies never reached a clear conclusion. A few reports of successful transfer studies appeared in the mid-1970s, together with reports of failures to replicate as well as claims that the so-called successful experiments could be explained without assuming transfer of information by injection. Georges Ungar died in 1977, and studies involving transfer of information by injection do not appear after 1979. *The Worm Runner's Digest,* the unofficial journal of this era, published its last issue in 1979, after 21 years of continuous publication.

In any event, the hypothesis that RNA or protein molecules code for acquired information by rearrangement of their structure must now be regarded as ill-founded. This was a concept made popular by the great discoveries of molecular biology, including the elucidation of the genetic code. Although never accepted by the majority of scientists working on the biology of memory, the hypothesis was taken seriously for a time by some; and it competed for several years with the traditional idea that memory is stored by changes in synaptic efficacy and that these changes are brought about by cellular events common to all neurons that change.

Neurons versus Synapses

Discussions of synaptic change as a basis for information storage often ignore an important question: Do all the synapses made by a neuron change together, or do some of the synapses made by a neuron change, while others do not? The fact that all cellular constituents (except DNA) are replaced at regular intervals implies that very long-lasting changes in connectivity between neurons (of the kind needed to subserve memory that lasts for years) require some mechanism that can survive this turnover. One obvious possibility is that changes in gene expression underlie long-term memory, and a sizable literature on the effects of protein synthesis inhibitors on memory is consistent with this idea (for review, see Davis and Squire, 1984). If memory involves changes in neuronal gene expression mediated by protein synthesis, the simplest hypothesis is that *all* the synapses made by a neuron are altered. But it would be advantageous from the standpoint of information processing if experience altered some synapses in a stable and long-lasting way, while leaving unchanged other synapses made by the same neuron. If a neuron must make simultaneous and equivalent changes at all of its 10^3-10^4 synapses, it would lose considerable potential information-processing power.

At present, little data are available to show which of these scenarios is correct, or even how a synaptic change can become long-lasting. However, some mechanisms have been proposed, which allow changes at specific synapses to perpetuate themselves so as to survive molecular turnover (Crick, 1984; Lisman, 1985). For example, neuronal input at one dendritic spine could activate a protein kinase localized to that spine by phosphorylating it; this kinase could then phosphorylate other kinases in the same spine (Lisman, 1985). With appropriate concentrations of the kinase and phosphatase, which reverses the phosphorylation reaction, this reaction would continue indefinitely. Hence, phosphorylation acts like a switch. As turnover occurs, newly synthesized kinase molecules would be phosphorylated, and they in turn would phosphorylate other inactive kinases. Activated kinase molecules could perform some specific intercellular function and could thereby modify synaptic connectivity.

Such a proposal, by itself, is neutral with respect to the hypothesis that the formation of memory also depends on *de novo* protein synthesis at the time of training. Both local synaptic events and protein synthesis in the cell body, initiated at the time of learning, could be involved in producing long-term stability. For example, protein synthesis could supply enzymes or structural material needed for synaptic change, which would be transported to all the synaptic endings of a neuron. Locally organized, self-perpetuating activity at some subset of these synaptic endings could make use of transported material to first establish the synaptic change and then to maintain it so that it would survive molecular turnover.

The Nature of the Synaptic Change

Questions about synaptic change lie at the heart of many contemporary research programs, which aim first to enumerate the control points where plastic changes can occur between neurons and then to specify what changes actually occur when behavior is modified. Three types of changes can be hypothesized to underlie altered synaptic connectivity: sustained electrical activity, stable biochemical/biophysical changes that alter transmitter release or receptor characteristics, and morphological changes in neurons that alter the geometry of intercellular contact. The hypothesis that sustained electrical activity in closed reverberating circuits could underlie stable, long-lasting memory has not been seriously considered since Konorski (1948) and Hebb (1949) wrote critically of the idea.

> In fact, if we hold that the whole body of interneural connexions acquired by the organism during its individual life is due to the incessant activity of self-re-exciting chains of neurons, once thrown into activity, it is incomprehensible how they can be preserved after such states of complete inactivity of the brain as are produced by a very profound narcosis, a cerebral ischemia, and so on . . . yet it is well known that the whole body of "engrams" is as a rule completely preserved after such states . . . (Konorski, 1948, pp. 88–89).

Hebb (1949) included the concept of sustained electrical activity in formulating his dual trace mechanism, according to which activity in reverberatory circuits furnishes a temporary, short-term form of memory.

> . . . some memories are both instantaneously established and permanent. To account for the permanence, some structural change seems necessary, but a structural growth presumably would require an appreciable time. If some way can be found of supposing that a reverberatory trace might cooperate with the structural change, and carry the memory until the growth change is made, we should be able to recognize the theoretical value of the trace which is an activity only, without having to ascribe all memory to it. The conception of a transient, unstable reverberatory trace is therefore useful, if it is possible to suppose also that some more permanent structural change reinforces it (Hebb, 1949, p. 62).

This formualtion was widely recognized as a useful, and even plausible, mechanism; and the concept continues to appear in contemporary

Figure 4. *Left.* Jerzy Konorski (1903–1973), Polish psychologist. *Right.* Donald O. Hebb (1904–1985), Canadian psychologist. (Left, from Rosvold and Zernicki, 1975; Right, from Hearst, 1979)

textbooks of psychology and neurology. However, sustained electrical activity of the particular sort that Hebb originally proposed is unlikely to provide a basis for temporary memory. It should first be noted that reverberating activity has never been observed. Secondly, it is now known that neurons have available a far simpler mechanism for short-term, plastic modifications, a mechanism actually used by neurons to store experience in some cases. The best-studied example of this mechanism comes from the invertebrate mollusc *Aplysia* (Kandel 1976; Kandel and Schwartz, 1982), and the same principle has been demonstrated in other invertebrates, such as the crayfish. The neuronal modification accompanying behavioral habituation or sensitization includes presynaptic changes in the ability of sensory neurons to release transmitter. The key result of

17

these studies is the recognition that neurons themselves are plastic elements. A neuron's readiness to release transmitter can be temporarily increased or decreased without requiring either activity (action potentials) *in* the neuron or synaptic communication *between* neurons during the time the change persists. So exotic a mechanism as reverberatory circuits is not needed to sustain temporary memory. Individual neurons can themselves hold information.

With respect to more stable, long-lasting memory, the dominant hypothesis until perhaps the mid-1970s (despite Hebb's proposal) was that synaptic change depends on biochemical or biophysical events, but without any accompanying morphological change in neuronal structure. Before then, hypotheses concerning long-term memory mechanisms were primarily discussions of how new protein synthesis and/or other macromolecules might establish long-lasting changes in synaptic efficacy. These hypotheses rested on two types of experiments, those demonstrating that inhibitors of brain protein synthesis block the formation of long-term memory (Davis and Squire, 1984) and those demonstrating that training experiences lead to increased incorporation of radioactively labeled precursors of RNA or protein into brain (Dunn, 1980; Rose, 1977).

Biochemical mechanisms alone could be supposed sufficient to support sustained changes in synaptic efficacy, but recent work has revived the classical idea that the response of neurons to experience leads to structural change. Three kinds of evidence exist. First, the work of Rosenzweig and his colleagues (Rosenzweig and Bennett, 1978) and of Greenough (1984a) have shown that the brain's architecture is plastic— i.e., it can be changed by experience. A considerable list now exists of structural changes that can be linked correlatively to behavioral experience (Figure 5). For example, rats reared in enriched environments, in comparison to rats reared in the standard laboratory environment, show an increase in gross cortical weight and thickness, in the size of neuronal somata, in the number and length of dendritic branches, and in synapse diameter. Changes have also been observed in the number and shape of dendritic spines as a result of rearing in enriched environments.

More recent studies have demonstrated that an enriched environment increases the number of synapses ending on individual cortical neurons (Turner and Greenough, 1985). Taken as a whole, the results show that the neurons of rats reared in an enriched environment, at least in visual

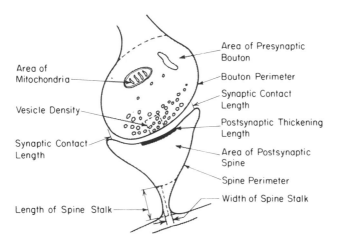

Figure 5. Schematic diagram of a synapse onto a dendritic spine showing measures of synaptic morphology that have been used to study experience-dependent structural alterations at synapses. Experience can increase the number of synapses, presumably either by forming them outright or by selectively preserving some synapses from a population that is continuously being replaced. (From Chang and Greenough, 1984.)

cortex, have more extensive dendritic fields and a greater number of synapses on these dendrites. Such dendritic effects appear not only in young animals but also in adult and middle-aged animals who are exposed to an enriched environment. Although these neuronal changes are small arithmetically (less than 10% for most measures), they have proven reliable. It now appears that anatomical changes are a likely substrate for enduring increases in synaptic connectivity, just as Hebb originally proposed.

To produce changes in morphology requires less extreme conditions than an enriched rearing environment. In experiments using 3–4 weeks of daily maze training sessions, adult rats revealed more extensive apical dendritic fields in pyramidal neurons of occipital cortex. In rats with corpus callosum section who were monocularly trained, these changes were lateralized to the hemisphere that received input from the exposed eye (Chang and Greenough, 1982). In these cases, 20 to 30 days of maze training, administered for 1 hour each day, produced measurable changes in brain anatomy. It must be emphasized, however, that all the observed changes are *correlative*. It has not been demonstrated that these changes reflect directly the storage of information as opposed to other processes that occur at the same time. For example, they could reflect the less specific effects of arousal and attention-giving that must accompany any learning process. One useful study of this issue would be to determine the fate of the changes in brain architecture as memory for the maze training weakens, and whether these changes are either more short-lived or more long-lasting than the memory.

Studies of long-term potentiation (LTP) (Bliss and Lomo, 1973; Swanson, Teyler, and Thompson, 1982) provide a second source of evidence for structural modification in the nervous system. LTP describes a long-lasting increase in the strength of a synaptic response following electrical stimulation of a neural pathway. LTP can be produced by brief, high-frequency stimulation of the perforant path (connecting entorhinal cortex to the dentate gyrus of the hippocampal formation) or similar stimulation of the Schaffer collaterals that project from the CA3 region of hippocampus to CA1. LTP can also be elicited in neocortex and possibly at other sites; it can persist for days and even months. Two laboratories have shown independently that LTP in CA1 of hippocampus results in two kinds of structural change in dendrites (Chang and Greenough, 1984; Lee, Schottler, Oliver, and Lynch, 1980). First, there is an increase in the number of one type of synapse: those situated between axon terminals and the shafts (or branches) of dendrites. Because most axon terminals from the stimulated pathway end on dendritic spines, not on the main dendritic branches themselves, this change is very small in terms of the total number of synapses in the area. The second kind of structural change is that the dendritic spines become rounder. Both synapse formation and dendritic spine modification can occur within a few minutes of stimulation. The change in spine shape appears temporary, disappearing within 8 hours, but the increase in synaptic number persists (Figure 6).

Because of the rapidity with which it can be established and because of its longevity, LTP is a good candidate for a memory mechanism. Although its role in behavioral memory is not yet clear, the magnitude of LTP does correlate with the speed of maze learning in rats (Barnes, 1979). Considerable work has been carried out to elucidate the biochemical events that lead to LTP and structural synaptic change (Lynch and

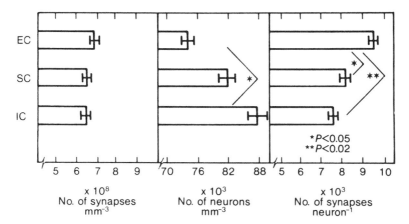

Figure 6. Morphological plasticity of synapses dependent on behavioral experience *(top)* or long-term potentiation (LTP) in hippocampus *(bottom)*. *Top.* Density of synapses and neuronal nuclei were determined in upper occipital cortex (layers I–IV), and these values were used to derive an estimate of the number of synapses per neuron. Rats were reared from 23 to 55 days of age in a complex environment (EC), in pairs in social cages (SC), or in individual cages (IC). Enriched rearing conditions resulted in an increased number of synapses per neuron. Neuronal density was decreased in EC animals, due to a greater volume of neuronal somata, neuronal processes, and glia. *Bottom.* Brief bursts of high frequency stimulation (100 Hz for 1 second or 200 Hz for .5 second) produced LTP of the Schaffer collateral-CA1 system in rat. In the CA1 zone, LTP increased the number of shaft synapses (synapses onto dendritic shafts) and also the number of sessile spine synapses (synapses onto stubby, headless spines). Density of the much more common spine synapse was not affected. (From Greenough, 1984b.)

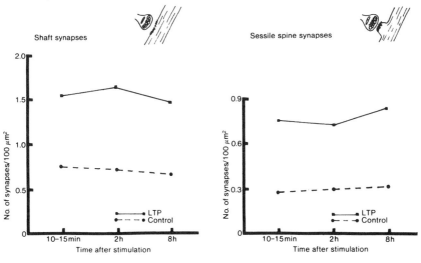

Baudry, 1984). It has been suggested that calcium concentrations increase in dendritic spines following intense synaptic activity, thereby activating a membrane-associated proteinase, calpain. This enzyme functions by degrading a structural protein in the membrane, fodrin, which causes shape changes and reveals previously hidden receptors to which neurotransmitter can bind. The possible role of these events in synapse formation, as opposed to the more transient dendritic shape changes, has not yet been explored. In any case, increased synaptic activity is considered to recruit a novel sequence of intracellular events, which operate only when long-lasting synaptic modifications are to be made. Interestingly, this biochemical process appears to be available only in phylogenetically recent brain regions, and not in brain stem or cerebellum. Because the cerebellum is one place where neural changes related to learning may occur (Thompson et al., 1983; see Chapter 7), this last observation raises the intriguing possibility that more than one cellular mechanism exists for learning and memory.

Study of habituation and sensitization in *Aplysia* (Bailey and Chen, 1983) provides a third source of evidence for morphological change. Behavioral training produced anatomically observable alterations both in the number and size of active zones on presynaptic terminals of sensory neurons and also in the number of vesicles associated with the active zones. Previous studies had shown that the presynaptic terminals of the sensory neurons are the critical locus of plasticity for habituation and sensitization. The active zones on these terminals presumably are the sites of transmitter release. In sensitized animals, all anatomical measures were markedly increased (by 79% for active zone area and 69% for vesicle number), but for habituated animals, the measures were decreased (33% decrease for active zone area and 54% for vesicle number). This result directly links a morphological change in neuronal structure to behavioral memory. These findings, together with the evidence that mature neurons show considerable capacity for morphological growth and change, and that artificially induced synaptic plasticity (LTP) involves morphological change, make it plausible that long-lasting behavioral memory itself generally has a morphological basis.

3

Memory and the Developing Nervous System

The fundamental concept that neuronal growth and change occur during the formation of permanent memory brings the neurobiological study of memory into contact with developmental neurobiology. This chapter shows how study of the developing nervous system is relevant to the neural basis of memory. In particular, the problem of memory can be illuminated by considering the competitive events that occur during development.

The growth and development of the nervous system proceed in a characteristic sequence. Carefully studied cases include the retino-geniculate pathway, the geniculo-striate projection, the vertebrate submandibular ganglion, and the superior cervical ganglion. In each case there is an initial oversupply of cells and axons, and a greater number of axon terminals form functional connections on their target cells in the developing animal than in the adult. Three major events produce the adult pattern of connectivity (Figure 7); namely, neuronal death (Hamburger, 1975; Cowan, 1973), the elimination of collateral branches of neurons (Cowan, Fawcett, O'Leary, and Stanfield, 1984), and the elimination of synapses by surviving neurons (Purves and Lichtman, 1980). The examples that follow emphasize the roles of cell death and, particularly, of synapse elimination in development.

23

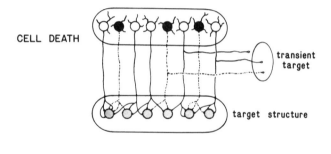

CELL DEATH

transient
target

target structure

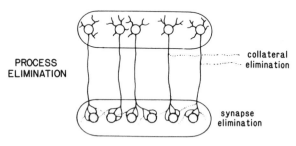

PROCESS
ELIMINATION

collateral
elimination

synapse
elimination

Figure 7. Three events in the development of specific connections in the vertebrate nervous system: cell death, elimination of axon collaterals, and synapse elimination. It is estimated that 50% of the nerve cells that are initially formed die before postnatal life. Process elimination by the surviving neurons involves both the removal of whole pathways and the elimination of functional synapses within remaining pathways. In this way, specific connections and networks are sculpted out of the initially formed nervous system. (From Cowan and O'Leary, 1984.)

Each rhesus monkey fetus has 2.85 million retinal axons, but each adult has only 1.2 million axons (Rakic and Riley, 1983). Most of the retinal axon loss occurs during a 30-day interval within the gestation period (embryonic day 90 to 120 within a total gestation period of 165 days). During the same time that retinal axons are lost, the axon terminals from each eye segregate into their appropriate layers within the lateral geniculate. Thus, even though each eye initially sends axons to the full expanse of the lateral geniculate, each lateral geniculate ends up with three layers of input from each eye. The temporal correspondence between these two events, laminar segregation within the lateral geniculate

24

and the disappearance of axons, suggests that cell death is an important event in the developing visual system.

If cell death were the sole mechanism used by the retino-geniculate pathway to achieve the mature pattern of synaptic connectivity, two kinds of axons should exist early in development: axons that originate in each eye and then terminate in those zones of the lateral geniculate that will later be appropriate for each eye, and axons that originate in each eye and terminate in inappropriate zones. In this case, cell death could re- move those axons terminating in inappropriate places; and only those that terminate in appropriate places would remain. This idea is consistent with the finding that when techniques are used that sample many axons at the same time, inputs from the two eyes are found initially to termi- nate throughout the lateral geniculate in an intermixed fashion.

However, studies in the cat show that axons initially terminating in- appropriately do not necessarily die. Instead, they can alter their pattern of terminal arborization. Thus, the elimination of synapses among *sur- viving* axons, in addition to cell death, must be significant (Shatz and Kirkwood, 1984; Sretavan and Shatz, 1984). When individual axons were examined at different developmental stages, it was found that during the period of segregation in the lateral geniculate, axons lost short side branches in some zones while arborizing more fully in others. Separate physiolog- ical studies revealed that some of the synapses lost during this period had already become functional. Taken together, the monkey and cat studies show that adult connectivity in the retino-geniculate pathway arises both through cell death and through a combination of synapse elimination and synapse proliferation among the surviving retino-geniculate axons. Cell death, synapse elimination, and synapse proliferation together produce the mature, segregated pattern of axons.

In the projection from lateral geniculate to visual cortex, synapse elim- ination is especially important in achieving the adult pattern of connec- tivity. In the cat and monkey, the axons from each eye initially terminate in an intermixed manner within the cortical layer IVC (Rakic, 1977; LeVay, Stryker, and Shatz, 1978). These axons then segregate into ocu- lar dominance columns during postnatal development (Wiesel, 1982), and synapse on neurons within these columns, such that each column contains cells especially responsive to one or the other eye. A selective

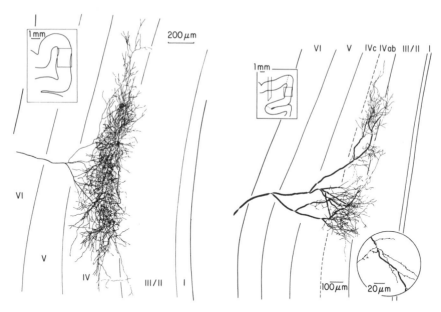

Figure 8. Pattern of arborization of a single geniculo-cortical afferent axon in the visual cortex of a 17-day-old kitten *(left)* and an adult cat *(right)*. Prior to the segregation of cortical inputs into alternating left-eye and right-eye columns, the arborization of individual afferents extends uniformly over a disc-shaped area more than 2 mm in diameter. This area is destined to be segregated into at least four columns. In the adult, after column formation is complete, individual afferents do not arborize uniformly. The arborization is divided into a number of clumps, separated by gaps, whose dimensions correspond to the size of individual ocular dominance columns. The gaps are filled with afferents serving the other eye. The insets show the region of visual cortex from which the reconstructions were made. The inset to the right (top) also shows the injection site. (From LeVay and Stryker, 1979.)

loss then occurs from the terminal arborizations of geniculate neurons that remain in inappropriate columns (Figure 8). ''As the axon matures, there appears to be a selective loss of branches, so that ultimately it innervates ocular dominance columns serving one eye and leaves gaps for the columns serving the opposite eye'' (Wiesel, 1982, p. 591).

Synapse elimination has been followed more directly in the rat submandibular ganglion. At the time of birth, about five axons terminate on each ganglion cell; by adulthood, the ratio of axons and target cells is 1:1 (Lichtman, 1977). Furthermore, electron microscopy revealed that during development the number of synaptic profiles per ganglion cell increases. Apparently, the axon that remains on each cell increases its terminal field and makes more synapses. Purves and Lichtman (1980) developed a principle of competition that applies to this and other cases of synapse elimination. As development proceeds a large number of axons compete for target cells. In this competition, as a result of the selective elimination of some axons, and possibly through relocation of others, the number of axons terminating on each ganglion cell is reduced. Thus, there is loss of some of the original connections; but at the same time, the axons remaining in appropriate locations increase their terminal arborization.

Competition

The idea that the principle of competition is relevant to learning and memory comes from the fact that competition not only occurs during normal development; it also occurs after birth as a result of an individual animal's experience. In a famous series of experiments kittens were deprived of vision in one eye early in life (Wiesel and Hubel, 1965). In later life the kittens had abnormal visual systems. Their cortical cells became unresponsive to the deprived eye. Further work showed that the axon terminals bringing input from the normal eye to neocortex now occupied a large portion of the cortical space that ordinarily would have been filled by terminals from the deprived eye. This change did not arise as a straightforward consequence of disuse, because binocular deprivation did not result in unresponsive cortical cells to the extent that would have occurred after monocular deprivation. These experiments produced an important insight. Inputs from the lateral geniculate, representing each of the two eyes, must compete for control of the postsynaptic, potentially binocular neuron. A reduction in the use of one pathway in relation to the other allows the more highly used pathway to gain control (Figure 9).

These changes that result from visual experience are reflected directly in the morphology of the terminal fields of the competing axons. If visual deprivation in one eye occurs early in life before the ocular dominance columns have been fully formed, the axon terminals that receive input from the deprived eye become abnormally withdrawn or trimmed.

27

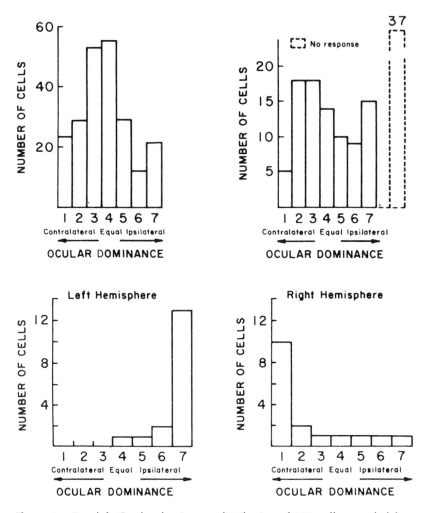

Figure 9. *Top left.* Ocular dominance distribution of 223 cells recorded from striate cortex of normal adult cats. Cells in groups 1 and 7 could be driven by only one eye. In groups 2–3 and 5–6, cells were driven better by one eye than the other. In group 4, cells were driven about equally by each eye. *Bottom.* Ocular dominance distribution of 34 cells recorded from the left and right striate cortex of a cat without visual experience in the right eye from 9 weeks to 6 months of age. The majority of cells responded only to visual stimulation from the experienced eye. *Top right.* Ocular dominance distribution of 126 cells recorded from cats without visual experience in either eye from about 1 week to about 3 months of age. Thirty-seven cells did not respond to visual stimulation. In contrast to the effects of unilateral eye closure, after bilateral eye closure both eyes could drive cortical cells. (Adapted from Wiesel and Hubel, 1963, 1965.)

At the same time, the terminals from the normal eye do not vacate the territory that they would ordinarily have yielded to the other eye. Competition also occurs in monkeys deprived of vision in one eye after the ocular dominance columns have been fully formed (at 6 to 10 weeks of age). Thus, a period of time exists after the formation of columns during which axons from the territory of the experienced eye will sprout terminals into the territory of the deprived eye (Wiesel, 1982).

The competition that occurs in the visual system in response to experience can be described in the following way: When an axon or a tract of axons loses its influence over a target area, the remaining axons increase their influence over the same area. The principles that guide these events are not understood, although the suggestion has been made that innervating axons compete for a trophic factor or other factors that could stabilize axon terminals and promote their growth. According to such an idea, competition is influenced by the relative amount of neural activity in the innervating populations of axons, such that the more active inputs take up more trophic factor, and as a result form stronger and more effective synapses on target neurons.

Competition most likely is a prominent event in the adult nervous system, long after development is complete. Thus, competition may always be possible whenever axons from different neurons have overlapping terminal fields, not just during development when connections are being formed and sorted out. In the monkey, detailed studies have been done of the cortical map formed by sensory projections from the hand and fingers (Merzenich, Kaas, Wall, Sur, Nelson and Felleman, 1983). This map consists of an area of approximately 3×5 mm on the sensorimotor cortex of the parietal lobe, within which the dorsal and ventral surface of each digit and the dorsal and ventral surface of regions of the hand are separately represented. Light mechanical stimulation of one digit or an area of the hand reliably drives cortical units within one particular zone of that map; and units within neighboring zones are driven by tactile stimulation of other fingers and other parts of the hand. Together these zones make up the total map.

The detailed structure of this map is not static. For example, following section of the median nerve, a sensory nerve which innervates the thumbward half of the palm side of the hand, cortical zones that would have responded to stimulation of that part of the hand initially fall silent. Yet by 22 days after nerve section, all these cortical zones could be driven by new inputs, mostly from the dorsal skin surface. The reorganization occurred in most cases because other parts of the skin expanded their areas of cortical representation. However, sometimes the region representing a dorsal skin area did not simply expand its territory but completely moved into an initially silent and denervated zone of cortex.

This capacity for reorganization reflects the normal dynamism of cortical organization, which is dependent on experience. In another study, monkeys were given 2.5 hours of light skin contact per day, arranged so that only the distal parts of one or two digits were stimulated (Jenkins, Merzenich, and Ochs, 1984). Stimulation continued for several weeks. Maps of the hand representation in somatosensory cortex before and after this procedure showed that experience had expanded the cortical areas corresponding to the stimulated digits, at the expense of surrounding cortical zones. Thus, in the adult animal the cortical representations of the hand can expand, shift, or contract, depending on the particular experiences of the animal. It is not clear whether these changes depend on actual growth of synaptic terminals into new zones, or whether a large number of potential synaptic connections exist from the beginning, only some of which are strong enough to be effective. In both cases, morphological growth and change in axon terminals or dendritic spines could be involved. Whatever the mechanism, it seems very likely that differential neural activity in the axons that innervate sensorimotor cortex plays a determining role in bringing about changes in the map. That is, competitive effects caused by differential activity in two converging inputs may initiate the reorganization.

One example of competition that suggests the importance of neural activity appears in additional data from experiments on the developing visual system of kittens. The competition for cortical neurons occurs not only after monocular deprivation, but also after severing an eye muscle to render kittens cross-eyed (Hubel and Wiesel, 1965). Such kittens have fewer than the ordinary number of binocular cells. This finding shows that the neural activity that originates in each eye and converges on prospective binocular cells in the cortex must be synchronous. When synchronous input does not occur, one input or the other is able to dominate the postsynaptic cell. The input that does not compete successfully loses some control of that cell.

The activity or responsiveness of the postsynaptic target cell seems to play a role in competitive events in cortex (Rauschecker and Singer, 1979). Hence plasticity both in development and in adulthood might follow rules similar to those proposed for the Hebb synapse (Hebb, 1949; Marr, 1969; Stent, 1973). That is, synaptic efficacy would increase between an input cell and a postsynaptic cell in situations where the input successfully fires the postsynaptic cell. In addition, synaptic efficacy would decrease for those inputs to the same postsynaptic cell that are inactive when the postsynaptic cell fires.

A further example of the importance of neural activity in competition appears in developmental studies of the visual system of frogs and toads. The development of binocularly responsive cells in optic tectum depends on the pattern of neural activity that originates in the two eyes. The individual binocular neurons in tectum receive input from two sources: a direct tectal projection originating in the contralateral retina and an indirect, polysynaptic pathway, originating in the other retina and reaching the tectum via the nucleus isthmi. Surgical rotation of one eye in Xenopus larva before the retinal axons have reached the tectum results in an inversion of the direct retino-tectal projection. At the same time, the projection to the same tectum from nucleus isthmi adjusts in a manner that maintains binocularly driven cells (Gaze, Keating, Szekely, and Beazley, 1970; Udin and Keating, 1981). The adjustment occurs because cells in nucleus isthmi come to drive cells located in a part of the tectum different from the location of the cells they would ordinarily drive. In other words the axons from the nucleus isthmi make effective contacts on different cells than the ones they would usually find. The particular trajectories taken by axons actually change as they near their target sites, so that the nucleus isthmi cells can reach their new target cells (Udin, 1983). Thus, the final pattern of functional connectivity in development includes physical rearrangement of terminals as they approach their tectal targets.

In this case, it appears unlikely that the final pattern of connectivity—either during normal development or during the abnormal development caused by experimental manipulations—is dependent on various other mechanisms that have sometimes been suggested, such as the silencing of structurally normal synapses or the construction of local inhibitory circuitry. Instead, it appears that the axons from nucleus isthmi actually *move* in order to terminate on tectal cells that receive synchronous neural activity from the same visual field of the other eye. This rearrangement requires neural activity carrying visual information, because the adjustment does not arise in animals reared in the dark (Keating and Feldman, 1975).

To summarize, the existence of competition in the developing nervous system appears beyond doubt, and competition shows itself as well in the effects of experience after completion of the intrinsic developmental program (Wiesel, 1982; Jenkins et al., 1984). The effects of experience on the functional connectivity of neural pathways are reflected in morphological change, which depends upon the degree of activity and synchrony in the inputs converging on common targets. Morphological change seems to be triggered most effectively by asynchronous input, and it results in more effective synaptic connections for the active inputs and less effective connections for the inactive ones.

The earliest speculations concerning memory proposed that memory might reflect the continuation into adulthood of the same processes that led to the formation of neuronal connections during development. At present, the evidence is still insufficient to demonstrate a definite parallel between the effects of experience on the developing nervous system and processes of memory formation in the adult. Even if one accepts that synapse elimination and competition are dominant events during the initial development of connections, it remains unproven that the same events are always important when the mature nervous system learns and remembers. It is possible that in learning the emphasis should be placed separately either on synaptogenesis (Greenough, 1984b) or on the elimination of synapses (Changeux and Danchin, 1976). Alternatively, one can consider increases and decreases in synaptic strength together, as has been done above, and hypothesize that increases in synaptic strength in the mature nervous system are typically accompanied by decreases in the strength of competing connections.

Remembering and Forgetting

The preceding section led to a connectionist view of memory storage that depends on competition between axon terminals and morphological changes in neurons. This point of view also leads to some ideas about human memory that have traditionally been discussed only at the behavioral level. Consider the familiar question as to whether everything that is learned remains preserved in memory or whether some things are irretrievably lost. One school of thought holds that nothing is ever lost from storage, and that forgetting represents only the loss of access to memory. The other school holds that memory is not completely preserved, and that forgetting is a true loss of information from storage.

Although little direct evidence on this point exists, both the connectionist view developed above and the principle of competition provide a strong case for supposing that forgetting involves actual loss of some of the neural connections that originally represented acquired information. Consider once again the studies of monocular deprivation in monkeys (Wiesel, 1982). Monocular deprivation in 6-week old monkeys leads to competition and an actual loss of connectivity between the deprived eye and visual cortex. Competition changes the existing circuitry: It increases the efficacy of the used pathway and decreases the efficacy of the unused pathway. At least part of this altered efficacy arises from morphological change in the relevant pathways, namely a trimming of terminals from the deprived eye and the sprouting of terminals from the experienced eye.

If performed sufficiently early, opening the deprived eye and covering the initially experienced eye can induce gradual recovery of normal ocular dominance columns or even a reversal of the effects of deprivation (Blakemore and Van Sluyters, 1974). This suggests that the original deprivation weakened some of the originally existing connections between the deprived eye and the visual cortex. When the side of eye closure was switched sufficiently early, this connectivity could be regained, but now there was an accompanying loss of connectivity between the other, newly deprived eye and visual cortex. Axon terminals from the originally deprived eye must not have completely atrophied. The initial deprivation weakened the strength of the synaptic connections between these axon terminals and visual cortical neurons, but this strength could be regained.

These results deserve consideration in any attempt to establish the probable basis of forgetting. Monocular deprivation studies in young cats and monkeys suggest that new experiences affect the nervous system by directly strengthening or weakening connections. If memory does in-

33

volve morphological changes that increase connectivity, it seems natural to suppose that forgetting depends in a symmetrical manner on the regression of these changes. Of course, forgetting need not involve a *complete* reversal of synaptic changes. Any decrease in the alterations established during learning would represent *some* forgetting in the biologic sense. However, because any representation is redundant to some extent and because memory involves the representation of many features of an event, we need not suppose that forgetting involves an irretrievable loss of all synaptic changes that represent a memory. Nevertheless, loss of connectivity can be expected to lead to diminished speed, efficiency, or completeness of recall.

In the case of the visual system, monocular experience strengthens some connections while weakening others. This finding not only suggests how literal forgetting could occur, but also how forgetting could occur in conjunction with normal learning and remembering. The formation and use of memory is a dynamic process: The content of memory should change as interfering information is acquired and as rehearsal and subsequent learning episodes affect pre-existing memory. Some of what is stored in memory is forgotten; others parts may become stronger. As time passes after learning, representations of events should lose detail, while remaining elements of the same representations become more highly organized and more strongly connected (Squire, Cohen, and Nadel, 1984). As a result, losses in connectivity are associated with gains in connectivity in other parts of the same ensemble. Rehearsal or additional learning leads to the reorganization of what remains in memory, including the weakening of some elements (Figure 10).

This account of forgetting suggests why the debate as to whether memories really ever disappear has continued for so long. New information-storage episodes constantly occur, resculpting previously existing representations. Such events, and perhaps the passage of time itself, change the structure of memory. In other words, forgetting occurs continuously. Yet however much a representation loses its detail and features, it should keep some similarity to the original representation for a very long time. Indeed, behavioral experiments show that when material is relatively well learned initially, forgetting can occur gradually and continuously for many years, after which an appreciable amount of memory still remains (Figure 11; also see Bahrick, 1984).

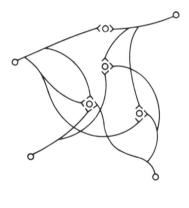

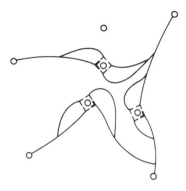

Figure 10. Hypothetical scenario showing how remembering and forgetting could be affected by the same competitive events that occur during development. *Top.* Initially after learning, the assembly of neurons and synaptic contacts representing an item or event in memory is richly interconnected, with one neuron making contact with many other neurons. *Bottom.* Later, there has been a reduction in the number of different neurons making contact with any given neuron, but there has also been an increase in the number of synapses onto some neurons and an increase in the size of some synaptic endings. Thus, there is change within the representation with time. This change could account for forgetting, because there has been a reduction in the number of neurons in the representation as well as a reduction in the number of different neurons which each neuron in the representation can be influenced by. The same change could also provide for reorganization and strengthening of what remains, because there has been an increase in the number of synapses made by the remaining inputs as well as an increase in the synaptic surface for some of the remaining contacts.

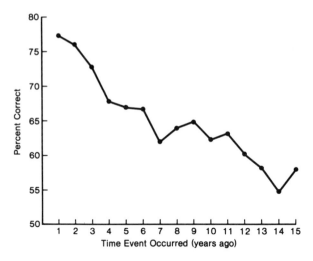

Figure 11. Gradual forgetting in long-term memory. A test of remote memory was administered annually for 8 years (1978–1985) to groups of approximately 25 persons (total-205 persons, mean age-41.4 years). The test, which was multiple-choice with four alternatives, asked subjects to recognize the names of television programs that had broadcast for no more than one season during the past 15 years (Squire and Slater, 1975). The results of these eight test administrations have here been superimposed on each other, so as to obtain an average measure of memory for events that had occurred 1 to 15 years prior to test administration. Thus, the data point for events that occurred one year ago is based on television programs broadcast during one year from 1977 to 1984, and tested one year later (1978 to 1985). The data point for events that occurred two years ago is based on television programs broadcast during one year from 1976 to 1983, and tested two years later (1978 to 1985). Forgetting occurs gradually over the years, but even after 15 years considerable information remains (chance performance = 25 percent). Information in long-term memory eventually becomes resistant to forgetting.

The debate as to what actually happens during forgetting has had a long tradition in psychology. Does true forgetting occur, or is forgetting simply a loss of accessibility? Each of us has had the experience of retrieving successfully from memory some apparently forgotten and previously inaccessible detail of an event from the remote past. Such experiences have apparently convinced the majority of persons that *all* memory remains preserved, and that forgetting simply reflects inaccessibility. Loftus and Loftus (1980) asked 169 laypersons and persons with graduate training in psychology to choose one of two statements to describe how memory works:

> 1. Everything we learn is permanently stored in the mind, although sometimes particular details are not accessible. With hypnosis, or other special techniques, these inaccessible details could eventually be recovered.
>
> 2. Some details that we learn may be permanently lost from memory. Such details would never be able to be recovered by hypnosis, or any other special technique, because these details are simply no longer there (Loftus and Loftus, 1980, p. 410).

Eighty-four percent of the psychologists and 69% of the nonpsychologists chose statement 1.

The belief that memory is permanent apparently arises from personal experience and from popular notions about hypnosis and psychoanalytic theory. The popular view corresponds to Freud's statement that ''in mental life nothing which has once been formed can perish'' (Freud, 1930, p. 69). Freud's interpretation was that repression is a major cause of slips of the tongue, common lapses of memory, and (to a large extent) forgetting in general (Freud, 1901).

However, none of the behavioral data prove that all memory storage is permanent (Loftus and Loftus, 1980). When special circumstances or reminder cues can elicit recall of memories that are otherwise apparently unavailable, this demonstrates only that the brain stores more memories than are readily accessible; it does not prove that all past experiences are permanently represented. It is a truism of intellectual history that so-called classic views often achieve an exaggerated or simplified form. Although Freud did consider most forgetting to be psychologically motivated, he also explicitly recognized the possibility of literal or biologic forgetting.

> Perhaps we have gone too far in this. Perhaps we ought to content ourselves with asserting that what is past in mental life may be preserved and is not necessarily destroyed. It is always possible that even in the mind some of what is old is effaced or absorbed—whether in the normal course of things or as an exception—to such an extent that it cannot be restored or revivified by any means or that preservation in general is dependent on certain favorable conditions. It is possible, but we know nothing about it. We can only hold fast to the fact that it is rather the rule than the exception for the past to be preserved in mental life (Freud, 1930, p. 74).

Psychological and behavioral arguments cannot conclusively establish the nature of forgetting. Indeed, decades of competent behavioral experiments have not settled this issue. The nature of forgetting is in part a biological problem, and to settle the question of forgetting will require additional biological facts. One wants to know whether the particular synaptic changes that initially represent information do or do not disappear with time. Whereas direct evidence on this question is not yet available, a good deal is known about how deprivation and experience affect the neural organization of sensory systems. This work makes the idea of literal or biologic forgetting a reasonable possibility. To state this idea explicitly: All forgetting, whether it occurs in a few hours or over a period of years, reflects in part an actual loss of information from storage and a corresponding regression of some of the synaptic changes that originally represented the stored information. Tests of this idea will ultimately rest on neurobiological evidence.

4

Modulation of Memory

Learning and memory do not occur in isolation from other cognitive processes. To a large degree, exactly what is remembered and how much is remembered depend on factors such as the alertness level at the time of learning and the nature of the events occurring just after information has been registered. For example, punishment and reward influence what is learned by signaling the importance of immediately preceding events. Once learning has occurred, the conditions that later exist when remembering is attempted will influence how well remembering succeeds. Memory can be influenced in many different ways. Pathways or systems that themselves are not sites of plastic change can and do affect the development, maintenance, and expression of plasticity at memory storage sites (Krasne, 1978). Thus, memory storage can be amplified or dampened by neural events that occur after an experience.

> If the physiological consequences of an experience are considerable, the organism would best retain that experience for long periods of time. If the consequences are trivial, the experience is best forgotten quickly. Thus [there might have developed] a mechanism with which organisms select from recent experiences those that should be permanently stored" (Gold and McGaugh, 1975, p. 375).

Behavioral studies of the effects of drugs or hormones have demonstrated that many different agents given shortly after a training experience can disrupt or facilitate memory (see Squire and Davis, 1981; McGaugh, 1983a). If a drug is given after training, but long before a test that assesses retention of what was learned, that drug must affect processes operating after training. It cannot influence the registration process itself, or processes specific to memory retrieval, or sensory and motor functions necessary for behavioral performance. It therefore seems reasonable to conclude that a post-training drug treatment found to affect performance on a later retention test must be revealing something about memory processes themselves. What one then wants to know is *which* neurotransmitter systems are involved in mediating the effects on memory, *how* these systems exert their effects, and whether pharmacological treatments affecting memory might mimic the action of endogenous neural systems whose usual function is to influence the strength of memory. Many neurotransmitter systems are in fact organized so that it is possible in principle for them to influence memory through this kind of modulatory action. Several of these systems are considered next, followed by discussion of what sorts of modulatory influences such systems might exert on memory.

Modulatory Systems

In the past two decades a major new principle of brain organization has emerged: The forebrain in general and the neocortex in particular are innervated *extrinsically* and by several separate, widely projecting ascending fiber systems, each of them linked to a particular neurotransmitter. These fiber systems are to be distinguished from the classical sensory projection systems, which (except for olfactory input) influence neocortex only via the thalamus. Perhaps the best-studied example of such a system is the widely branching norepinephrine projection. Cortical norepinephrine (NE) originates in the locus coeruleus, a small nucleus in the brain stem at the level of the pons that contains only 1,600 cells in the rat and an estimated 9,000 to 16,000 cells in the adult human (Foote, Bloom, and Aston-Jones, 1983). From the locus coeruleus, small-caliber, slow-conducting NE axons connect with a number of regions in the brain, notably amygdala, hippocampus, hypothalamus, and thalamus. The locus coeruleus is believed to be the only source of NE fibers for most of the forebrain (Figure 12). The extensive and widespread neocortical projection from locus coeruleus connects to all cortical regions and to all six cortical layers.

A second extrinsic system begins with dopamine (DA)-containing cells in the mesencephalon, especially in substantia nigra. The substantia nigra forms two organized projections to the forebrain: the nigrostriatal projection to the caudate-putamen and globus pallidus, and the mesocortical projection from substantia nigra and ventral tegmentum to specific cortical areas including mesial frontal, anterior cingulate, and entorhinal cortex. Although these projections are not so widespread as the other extrinsic systems discussed in this chapter, they are notable because they give subcortical cells an opportunity to influence neural activity in several cortical regions.

A third extrinsic system has its origin in the raphe nuclei of the midbrain (particularly in the median and dorsal nuclei), and it supplies about 80% of the forebrain's serotonin (Azmitia, 1978). The raphe nuclei project widely, through six distinct pathways, to a variety of forebrain structures. The dorsal raphe nucleus and, to a lesser extent, the median raphe nucleus project directly and extensively to the neocortex, especially to layer IV of visual cortex. The serotoninergic system is therefore in a favorable position to modulate sensory input.

A fourth extrinsic system arises in the nuclei of the basal forebrain, particularly in the nucleus basalis of Meynert, and also in the adjacent diagonal band and medial septum. The nucleus basalis was discovered only recently to be a source of neocortical afferent projections. It was subsequently shown that projections from nucleus basalis provide the primary source of neocortical acetylcholine (ACh) (Mesulam and Van Hoesen, 1976; Lehmann, Nagy, Atmadja, and Fibiger, 1980). These projections from nucleus basalis to neocortex and amygdala, together with the well-known cholinergic projection from the adjacent medial septum and diagonal band of Broca to hippocampus, are a source of widespread cholinergic innervation.

A fifth extrinsic system, for gamma-aminobutyric acid (GABA)-con-

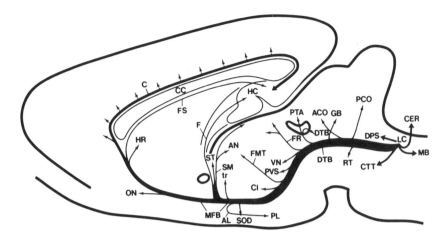

Figure 12. *Top.* Schematic representation of the course and primary branchings of the dorsal tegmental bundle (DTB), which originates in the catecholaminergic cell bodies of the locus coeruleus (LC) and widely innervates the forebrain. C, cingulum; CC, corpus callosum; F, fornix; FS, fornix superior; HC, hippocampus; HR, hippocampal rudiment; MFB, medial forebrain bundle; ON, olfactory nuclei; ST, stria terminalis. (From Lindvall and Bjorklund, 1978; refer to their paper for identification of more caudal loci.) *Bottom.* Later it was appreciated that LC neurons reach neocortex by a trajectory that passes through the frontal lobe and then caudally within neocortex through the full longitudinal extent of each hemisphere. M, medial axons innervating medial cortex; L, lateral axons innervating lateral cortex. (From Morrison, Mollivar, and Grzanna, 1979.)

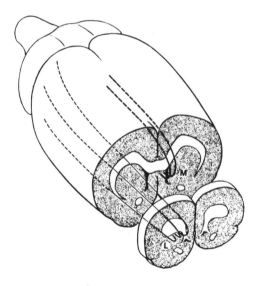

taining neurons, has also been described (Vincent, Hokfelt, Skirboll, and Wu, 1983). Groups of magnocellular cells in the mammillary region of the hypothalamus contain glutamate decarboxylase, a specific marker for GABA neurons. These cells project diffusely to several neocortical sites, which include frontal cortex, motor cortex, and occipital cortex. In addition to this extrinsic, ascending GABA system, a substantial source of GABA also exists intrinsic to cortex. Nevertheless, the extrinsic source of GABA provides another way that a population of neurons distant from neocortex can have widespread and presumably rather nonspecific effects on its activity.

Examples of widely projecting, potentially modulatory systems are not limited to neocortical inputs. For example, a diffuse projection has been identified to the hippocampal formation from the lateral hypothalamic area (Kohler, Haglund, and Swanson, 1984). The projecting neurons contain the opiate peptide alpha-melanocyte-stimulating hormone and terminate nonspecifically in all subfields of the hippocampal formation.

The organization of these brain systems means that, quite apart from the classical thalamo-cortical projections, discrete subcortical regions have the opportunity to exert widespread, modulatory effects on neuronal activity in neocortex and other forebrain structures. One interesting case where the subcortex modulates forebrain activity occurs in subcortical projections to hippocampus. Neuronal transmission from the perforant pathway to the hippocampal formation, which originates in the entorhinal cortex, depends on an animal's behavioral state. For example, transmission from the perforant pathway to dentate gyrus proceeds more effectively during slow-wave sleep than at times when the animal is quiet and alert (Winson and Abzug, 1978). This effect of behavioral state on neural transmission depends on NE innervation of the dentate gyrus (Dahl, Bailey, and Winson, 1983), serotonergic innervation, and a third input of unknown origin (Winson, 1980; Srebro, Azmitia, and Winson, 1982). It is therefore evident that modulation from a subcortical area can change the functional wiring of the hippocampus, presumably to make its operation optimally appropriate to the state of the animal. This result shows clearly that modulatory influences on brain function can occur in the context of normal behavior. A natural next question is whether they play any role in learning and memory.

Norepinephrine and Memory

Locus coeruleus neurons, the source of the forebrain NE system, fire in relation to an animal's level of vigilance, and they can be phasically activated by stimuli such as lights, tones, and mild skin contacts (Foote, Bloom, and Aston-Jones, 1983). This suggests that the locus coeruleus helps alert the forebrain for the processing of important external stimuli. NE might therefore be expected to influence learning and memory, insofar as increased vigilance or attention at the time of learning can make information processing more efficient. Moreover, because memory is not fully formed at the instant of learning, it is possible at least in principle that NE might influence learning and memory shortly after the moment of learning by also producing a vigilant or attentive-like state. The evidence for such modulatory influences are considered next.

Studies of visual development have suggested a possible direct link between forebrain norepinephrine and neural plasticity (Kasamatsu, 1983). If a normal kitten is denied vision through one eye early in life, neurons in primary visual cortex are later unresponsive to the eye that was closed, and the experienced eye is more effective in driving cortical cells than it ordinarily would be. This shift in control of cortical neurons, induced by monocular deprivation, will not occur if forebrain norepinephrine is depleted during the monocular rearing period by injections of 6-hydroxydopamine. Furthermore, in older cats, who are beyond the several-week critical period when monocular deprivation is ordinarily effective, local perfusion of norepinephrine into visual cortex restores neural plasticity. The older cats then show shifts in ocular dominance characteristics after monocular deprivation. Similarly, plasticity can be re-established in adult cats, who are beyond the critical period, by electrical stimulation of locus coeruleus during daily periods of monocular deprivation. That is, stimulation of locus coeruleus produces shifts in ocular dominance as a result of monocular deprivation, shifts that ordinarily would not be observed in adult animals.

The role that NE plays in inducing these effects has been questioned, primarily because the same results were not obtained by methods for depleting NE other than 6-hydroxydopamine (Daw, Robertson, Rader, Videen, and Coscia, 1984). It is possible that the 6-hydroxydopamine used in the original studies affects more than NE alone. Also, develop-

44

mental studies in the monkey have shown that NE fibers are relatively sparse during the first days of life in primary visual cortex (Foote and Morrison, 1984). This calls into question how much NE innervation of neocortex actually exists during the critical period, when NE would have to exert its modulatory effects on plasticity. However, it is still an intriguing concept that some kind of extrinsic, modulatory input to cortex, perhaps something other than NE alone, plays a fundamental role in neural plasticity. One possibility is that NE and ACh together modulate cortical plasticity, or that cortical plasticity can be modulated by NE, ACh, and also by other excitatory inputs to visual cortex that originate outside the thalamus (Bear and Singer, 1986).

Modulatory action of NE on neural plasticity has also been reported in hippocampus. In rat hippocampal slices treated with NE, the duration of synaptic change was increased after high-frequency stimulation of the mossy fibers. The half-decay time of the synaptic change increased from about 1 hour to about 1 hour and 40 minutes (Hopkins and Johnston, 1984). The effects of other neurotransmitters have not yet been evaluated.

Considering only cases where the effects of NE on neural systems and behavior have been studied in vertebrates, no direct role for aminergic systems in learning has yet been demonstrated. A study of classical conditioning (McCormick and Thompson, 1982) showed that rabbits with bilateral locus coeruleus lesions, which removed the source of forebrain NE, had normal acquisition of a tone-airpuff, classically conditioned nictitating membrane response. Because the NE system can exhibit remarkable recovery during the weeks following a partial surgical or pharmacological lesion (Acheson and Zigmond, 1981), it is significant in this case that behavioral testing followed surgery by 1 week or less. At the same time, in other studies, the finding that NE depletion has no effect on learning is often difficult to interpret because training is scheduled several weeks after treatment.

Many studies have attempted to evaluate the role that the NE fiber system plays in learning and memory, following the strategy used in classical conditioning work. Some early reports suggested that locus coeruleus lesions impaired learning, but subsequent experiments have yielded largely negative results. For example, electrolytic lesions of locus coeruleus that depleted more than 80% of forebrain norepinephrine failed to impair the learning of a T-maze or the learning of other appetitively and aversively motivated tasks (Mason, 1981). Studies using this and other techniques have also found little support for the notion that norepinephrine modulates memory by mimicking the central effects of reward (Fibiger, 1978). That is, there seems little reason to suppose that learning deficits should occur indirectly following NE depletion because of an impairment in an NE-mediated reward mechanism.

A different approach to the same question about NE and its possible role in memory is to study patients in whom the NE fiber system has been damaged. One study involved amnesic patients with Korsakoff's syndrome. These patients develop a severe memory disorder, and often other cognitive deficits, after many years of alcohol abuse (Chapter 13). As evidenced by metabolite studies, the patients can also have a depletion of NE. Nevertheless, general intellectual status as measured by conventional IQ tests can be normal or close to normal. In a group of nine such patients, the reported severity of the memory deficit (the score on the Wechsler Adult Intelligence Scale [IQ] minus the score on the Wechsler Memory Scale) correlated with lumbar spinal fluid concentrations of MHPG, the primary brain metabolite of norepinephrine (McEntee and Mair, 1978). That is, the degree of dysfunction of the NE system correlated with a measure of the memory deficit. However, the score used to calculate this correlation (IQ minus MQ) may not reflect the severity of the memory impairment itself. The MQ is sensitive to cognitive changes other than memory, and the IQ-MQ difference score could therefore reflect the severity of cognitive impairment other than memory impairment. In a related study, the NE alpha-receptor agonist clonidine improved performance slightly on two subtests of the Wechsler Memory Scale, memory passages and visual reproduction (McEntee and Mair, 1980). However, no patient approached normal levels of function, and performance on several other memory tests was not affected at all (paired-associate learning, remote memory, short-term recognition of faces). Finally, on a visual reproduction test, amphetamine and methysergide improved performance as much as clonidine did. A connection between NE and memory has not yet been established.

46

Acetylcholine

Acetylcholine is an additional neurotransmitter that may have a role in learning and memory. One early proposal in this regard was that cholinergic synapses were themselves the site of memory storage (Deutsch, 1971). Drugs such as physostigmine and scopolamine affected retention if administered to rats at any of several different intervals after brightness discrimination training, ranging from 30 minutes to 28 days. Retention was always tested about 30 minutes later, while the drug was active. A drug's specific effect—impairment, facilitation of retention, or no effect, depended in a systematic way on the strength of initial training, the dose of drug, and the age of the habit. To explain these results it was hypothesized that synaptic changes representing stored information develop gradually over many days and then recede during the course of normal forgetting. Thus, at the time of maximal synaptic "strength," 14 days after training for some of the tasks studied, the acquired habit could be disrupted by a dose of physostigmine. Yet the same dose had no effect 1 day after training, when synaptic "strength" had not yet developed, and it facilitated retention 28 days after training when memory in untreated animals was weak.

The subsequent discovery that most of the acetylcholine in neocortex has its origin in the basal forebrain makes the hypothesis that cholinergic synapses themselves store memory implausible. The ascending, widely projecting cholinergic pathways seem better suited as a modulatory system than as an information-containing, information-storing system. However, exactly what kind of modulatory role might be exerted by acetylcholine is not yet clear. One key finding from the early work with animals should be kept in mind in any case, because it seems to set the effects on memory of cholinergic drugs apart from the behavioral effects of other drugs that have been studied. Cholinergic drugs are the only ones that have been reported to exert opposite effects, either facilitating or impairing, depending simply on how long after training the drug is administered. Moreover, cholinergic drugs affect performance for a long time after training, virtually as long as memory for the original training persists. For most drugs, the sensitive period during which they affect behavior is during a short period just before and after learning and immediately before retest.

Several years after these animal studies, autopsy studies of patients with Alzheimer's disease revealed lesions in the cholinergic neurons of the nucleus basalis (Whitehouse, Price, Struble, Clark, Coyle, and Delong, 1982). This new finding furnished a rationale for attempting to treat the cognitive impairment in Alzheimer's disease, and in particular the memory impairment, with cholinergic agonists. This attempt has not yet yielded notably successful results (Bartus, Dean, Beer, and Lippa, 1982). Nevertheless, the possible therapeutic utility of cholinergic drugs is an important avenue to explore thoroughly. The idea that cholinergic agonists might be of value has also been encouraged by the finding that scopolamine can produce some signs of dementia in normal subjects (Drachman and Leavitt, 1974; but see Beatty, Butters, and Janowsky, 1986). In addition, when cholinergic-rich neurons from fetal septal tissue were implanted into the hippocampus of aged rats, or into the hippocampus of rats with fornix-fimbria lesions, their performance on tasks requiring learning and memory was restored to some extent (Gage, Dunnett, and Kelley, 1984; Dunnett, Low, Iversen, Stenevi, and Bjorklund, 1982).

It was subsequently found that patients with Alzheimer's disease exhibit specific and selective pathology in the entorhinal cortex and hippocampal formation (Hyman, Van Hoesen, Damasio, and Barnes, 1984). In addition, the olfactory system is prominently involved, and the pattern of neuropathological findings follows the known anatomy of cortico-cortical connections (Pearson, Esiri, Hiorns, Wilcock, and Powell, 1985). Thus, it seems doubtful that the cholinergic projections themselves are a primary focus of the disease process. Pathological change in the entorhinal cortex, that is, in medial temporal lobe structures known to be linked to memory functions (Chapter 12), could provide a rather direct explanation of the memory deficit in Alzheimer's disease. At the same time, known projections from cholinergic neurons in basal forebrain to structures in the medial temporal lobe that are themselves important in memory functions leave open the possibility of a modulatory role for the cholinergic system.

For those neurotransmitters that have been linked to memory it is possible that the specific neuroanatomical circuitries served by the neurotransmitters deserve as much emphasis as the nature of each transmitter substance. Acetylcholine, for example, might owe its importance in memory to the fact that this neurotransmitter exerts unique synaptic actions. Alternatively, acetylcholine might owe its importance in memory functions simply to the fact that it is located at synapses in neural structures, such as the hippocampus and amygdala, which are themselves important in memory. By this account, the other neurotransmitters found in these neural structures and their anatomical connections are just as important to memory functions as acetylcholine.

Hormones

The subcortical neurotransmitter systems that project to forebrain provide for one kind of potentially modulatory effect on learning and memory. Hormones also exert modulatory effects, in some cases by initiating their actions on memory peripherally. For example, epinephrine, which is released from the adrenal medulla, can influence the degree of retention, at least when training involves some stress. Subcutaneous administration of epinephrine immediately after training in a one-trial, shock avoidance task affected retention in a dose-dependent way (Gold and van Buskirk, 1975). An optimal dose (.01 to .1 mg/kg) facilitated retention, but a larger dose impaired it (Figure 13). The amount of the optimal dose shifted when the intensity of footshock was altered. A higher intensity footshock caused the dose that was facilitating at low footshock levels to impair retention (Gold and van Buskirk, 1976). Similar data for the administration of ACTH show that the optimal dose for producing memory facilitating effects, and even the direction of the effect, can be shifted by varying the intensity of the training footshock.

Such results stimulated the proposal that many peripherally administered drugs and hormones affect memory by modulating the action of endogenous hormones released by training (Gold and McGaugh, 1975). Such effects may be mediated peripherally, at least in part. The drug syrosingopine, an analogue of reserpine that primarily depletes peripheral catecholamines, produced as much amnesia as reserpine did (Walsh and Palfai, 1979). Systemic injections of norepinephrine or dopamine, which do not cross the blood-brain barrier in appreciable amounts, blocked the amnesia associated with syrosingopine.

Intraperitoneal injection of amphetamine immediately after training can

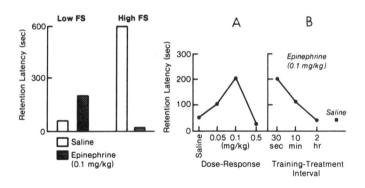

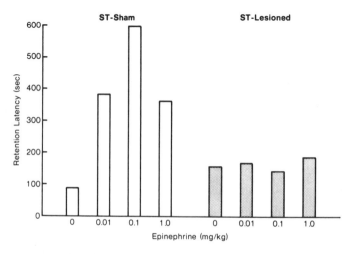

Figure 13. *Top left.* The effect of epinephrine on memory is influenced by the motivational conditions of training. Rats were trained using either a weak or strong footshock (FS) and given epinephrine immediately after training. The same dose that facilitated retention in the low footshock condition was disruptive in the high footshock condition. *Top right.* Rats were trained on a one-trial passive avoidance task with a weak footshock. A. The most effective dose (.1 mg/kg, given subcutaneously) significantly facilitated retention performance. B. As the injection of the best dose was delayed after training, its effect on memory decreased. *Bottom.* Epinephrine facilitated retention of control animals (ST-sham) but had no effect on animals with lesions of stria terminalis. (Top from Gold and McGaugh, 1975; bottom from McGaugh, 1983b.)

facilitate retention (McGaugh, 1973). Until recently, the idea that such an effect depends on direct effects of amphetamine on the brain seemed reasonable and was widely accepted. However, amphetamine is a particularly well-studied example of a drug that has its effects on memory through actions initiated on peripheral hormones (Figure 14). Direct injection of amphetamine into the lateral ventricles did not affect memory (Martinez, Jensen, Messing, Vasquez, Soumireu-Mourat, Geddes, Liang, and McGaugh, 1980). Nonetheless, the systemic injection of dl-4-OH amphetamine, which primarily affects peripheral catecholamines, did facilitate retention. Furthermore, adrenal demedullation blocked the facilitatory effects of both 4-OH amphetamine and d-amphetamine (Martinez, Vasquez, Rigter, Messing, Jensen, Liang, and McGaugh, 1980).

In order to affect memory, peripherally released hormones must have some ultimate effect on the central nervous system. The amygdala appears to be one brain area through which the effects of catecholamines are exerted (Figure 13), as shown by the fact that facilitatory effects of epinephrine on memory were blocked by lesions of stria terminalis, a major output pathway of the amygdala (McGaugh, 1983b). In addition, electrical stimulation of amygdala through an indwelling electrode produces amnesic effects, and these have been linked to actions of peripheral hormones. The stimulation exerts its amnesic effects centrally, via stria terminalis, but stimulation disrupts memory only if epinephrine is present. How epinephrine's action reaches the amygdala and how the amygdala modulates memory remain unknown. It is possible that epinephrine activates norepinephrine receptors in the amygdala (Liang, Juler, and McGaugh, 1986), because direct pharmacological manipulation of NE in the amygdala after training improves retention. The amygdala has widespread connections to neocortex (Amaral, 1987), and it may be important in establishing affective associations to events and in making information available across modalities (Murray and Mishkin, 1985).

Hormones that are released by the pituitary, such as ACTH, vasopressin, and oxytocin, also have an influence on learning and memory. Based on pioneering studies with ACTH by de Wied and his colleagues (de Wied, 1964), it was suggested that some hormones could act specifically either as memory-facilitating or as amnestic agents. The present view is that hormones have less specific effects. For example, whether ACTH facilitates or impairs memory depends on the dose and level of footshock

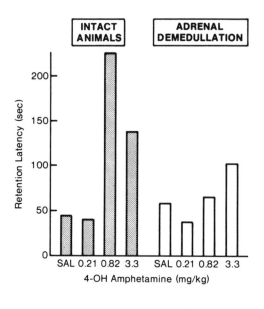

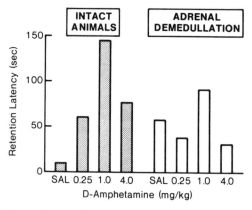

Figure 14. Evidence that amphetamine facilitates memory at least in part via the peripheral nervous system. Both 4-OH amphetamine *(top)*, which does not readily cross the blood-brain barrier, and D-amphetamine *(bottom)* facilitated retention. Both effects were attenuated by removal of the adrenal medulla. Sal = saline control. (Redrawn from Martinez et al., 1980a; Martinez et al., 1980b.)

(Gold and Delanoy, 1981). Furthermore, lesions of amygdala blocked the effects on memory of both ACTH and vasopressin (van Wimersma, Greidanus, Croiset, Bakker, and Bowman, 1979), just as they block the effects of epinephrine. This implies some commonality in the actions of ACTH, vasopressin, and epinephrine.

Endogenous opioid peptides (the endorphins and enkephalins) and their antagonists form another class of hormones that can influence learning and memory (Martinez, Jensen, Messing, Rigter, and McGaugh, 1981; Riley, Zellner, and Duncan, 1980). Naloxone, an opiate antagonist, facilitates retention of both aversive and appetitive tasks (Gallagher, King, and Young, 1983; Izquierdo, 1979). Recent experiments with rats (Arnsten and Segal, 1979) and with humans (Arnsten, Segal, Neville, Hillyard, Janowsky, Judd, and Bloom, 1983) suggest that naloxone improves selective attention. Perhaps naloxone's effects on memory depend on changes in attentional processes.

Modulation of Memory: One or Many Effects?

Just how the neurotransmitters and hormones that have been linked to memory affect brain systems involved in memory is still unclear. Some of these agents may have direct effects on the brain, whereas others may initiate their effects peripherally. Moreover, the hormones and neurotransmitters seem either to facilitate or impair memory, depending on specific circumstances, rather than to convey any absolute facilitating or amnestic effect. Finally, the hormones and neurotransmitters may mimic a normal modulatory function, e.g., attention, reward mechanisms, or affect.

What does any particular modulatory effect reveal about the endogenous role of the affected system in normal learning and memory? For example, if adrenal medullary hormones and ACTH, which are known to be released during stress, can facilitate or impair retention when they are given to animals after training, what is the endogenous role of these hormones in normal learning and memory? One possibility is that hormones participate in the formation of peculiarly vivid recollections, those that develop when a stressful event punctuates an experience. Such memories have acquired the name "flashbulb memories" to denote their unusual character and vividness (Brown and Kulik, 1977). For example, nearly everyone born before the mid-1950s can recall where they were and what they were doing when they heard the news of President Kennedy's assassination. Information concerning ongoing personal activity at that time and the source of the news has no obvious use, yet memory of such things is enduring. The tendency to retain such memories might have developed out of more ecologically natural circumstances, where ongoing behavior might be suddenly interrupted by the arrival of a predator. In such a case, remembering the events immediately preceding, as well as where the events occurred, would be highly adaptive in that it would help avoid visiting the same place later. Livingston's proposal (1967) of a "Now Print" mechanism that allows for the storage of events immediately preceding reinforcement represents a similar suggestion.

The hypothesis is that peripheral hormones play a role in establishing particularly vivid memories because a stress-producing and hormone-releasing signal often follows events that will later be well remembered. But many memories are formed without obvious stress, such as when one remembers the basic facts of a casual conversation, or recalls the events of a relaxing weekend, or recounts the plot of a film recently seen. The role played by modulatory systems in such everyday learning and memory remains unclear. Our ability to recall previous events clearly does not always depend on those events having produced marked autonomic consequences.

It has been suggested that certain hormones and neurotransmitters exert relatively nonspecific, modulatory effects on memory. Some effects may be exerted through specific brain structures that have been directly linked to memory functions. It is also possible that such effects operate on many different brain structures, through widespread ascending anatomical connections such as those identified for the NE system. Finally, it is possible that these effects, which are obtained in most cases by giving drugs during or shortly after the time of learning, should not always be interpreted in terms of memory. They may have some broader action: For example, they could exert a motivational or attentional effect, or could play on some other dimension of brain activity, so that "memory" defines their modulatory action on the nervous system too narrowly.

One way to clarify the nature of modulatory effects on memory would be to study in more detail those cases where modulatory effects of drugs on synaptic efficacy can be demonstrated rather directly. Better information about how drugs actually modulate synaptic connectivity could make discussions of memory modulation more specific and could help identify the different types of modulation that are possible. This experimental strategy seems most promising with the invertebrate and with examples of long-lasting synaptic efficacy, such as long-term potentiation.

5

Localized and Distributed Memory Storage

The set of changes in the nervous system that represents stored memory is commonly known as the *engram,* a term introduced by the German biologist Richard Semon at the beginning of this century (Semon, 1904; Schacter, 1982). Just *where* memory is localized in the brain is a beguilingly simple question. If one begins with the dominant theme of contemporary neurobiological approaches, that learning and memory depend on alterations in the connectivity between synapses, then it is obvious and straightforward to ask where in the nervous systems these synapses are located. Yet only a beginning has been made at illuminating this fundamental problem.

History of the Problem

Two contrasting ideas can be identified in the history of the brain sciences concerning where the engram is located. One tradition is the connectionist, deterministic, and localizationist view of memory forcefully advocated by Ramon y Cajal (1911), Konorski (1948), Hebb (1949), Eccles (1953), and more recently by Kandel (1976). From the early nine-

56

teenth century (Gall, 1825), one view was that the nervous system is composed of identifiable, localized parts, and that behavioral functions can be localized to particular components. This school of thought persisted in the experimental work of Broca (1861) and Ferrier (1876) and achieved considerable success by demonstrating that localized brain lesions or stimulation produce highly specific effects on language, vision, and motor movements (Luria, 1966); Zangwill, 1963). This tradition views memory as coded by the activity of specifiable neural connections.

The second tradition arose in opposition to the extreme and sometimes absurd localizationism advocated by Gall. The view developed out of this other tradition was that behavior and mental activity arise from the integrated activity of the entire brain. Flourens (1824) and Goltz (1876–1884) supported this idea with experiments showing that behavior seemed to be affected similarly no matter where cortical lesions were placed. In this century, the anti-localizationist viewpoint appears in the writings of Gestalt psychology (Koffka, 1935; Kohler, 1940), in the work of Lashley (1929; 1950), and in the work of John and his colleagues (John, 1972).

In the case of Gestalt psychology, the anti-localizationist position was expressed as a field theory. Field theory denied the importance of individual synaptic connections, proposing instead that the pattern of electrical activity over large cortical areas determines perception and mental function. In field theory, the pattern of electrical activity is the prime currency of cerebral function. Characteristics of perception directly correspond to how electrical current is distributed on the cortex, and not to any specific set of neural connections activated by the current. Field theory posited, for example, that the percept of a closed figure is associated with continuous current on the cortex, whereas the percept of an open, discontinuous figure is associated with an interruption in current flow.

Not all anti-localizationist positions are field theories. In fact, it would be more accurate to represent the anti-localizationist position with the more empirically grounded ideas developed by Lashley and John than to identify this position with Gestalt field theory. It was Lashley himself (Lashley, Chow, and Semmes, 1951), together with Sperry (Sperry, 1947; Sperry and Miner, 1955; Sperry, Miner, and Myers, 1955) who led the experimental attack in the early 1950s that conclusively refuted field the-

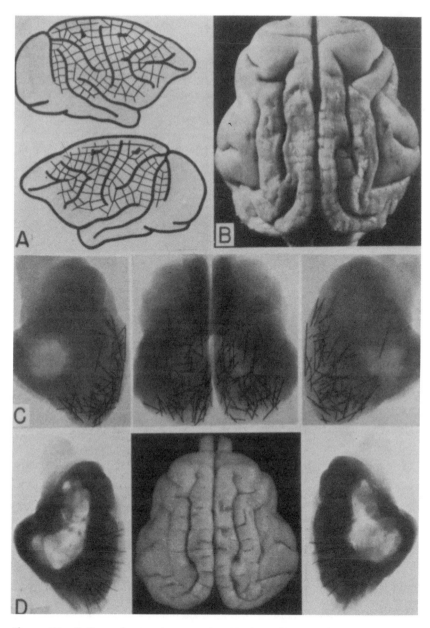

Figure 15. Failure of several types of cortical insult to produce major functional disruption. These results were difficult to reconcile with electrical field theory or any hypothesis of cerebral organization based on horizontal intracortical conduction. *A.* Multiple subpial knife cuts through the depth of the gray matter in sensorimotor cortex of monkey. *B.* Similar knife cuts in visual cortex of cat. *C.* Lateral and dorsal X-ray views of tantalum wire insertions in visual cortex of cat. *D.* Lateral X-ray and dorsal surface views of mica plate insertions in visual cortex of cat. (From Sperry, 1958.)

ory (Figure 15). Neither Lashley nor John were field theorists, although they did reject a localizationist view of memory storage.

> It should be emphasized that this is not a "field" theory, nor does it deny the highly organized structure of the brain. . . . We consider representation of information by statistical features of temporal patterns of ensemble behavior more likely than by the localized activity of specific cells (John, 1972, p. 854).

John's fundamental concept was that memory must be widely and equivalently distributed throughout many areas of brain; any particular neuron or synapse can participate in the storage and recall of particular memories in a probabilistic manner and not in a deterministic way.

The Nonlocalizing Brain Lesion

Among the influential experimental findings, perhaps the most significant was Lashley's failure to identify any particular brain region in the rat as special or necessary in the storage of memory for the maze habit (Lashley, 1929; 1950). In a series of famous experiments rats were trained by giving them five trials per day until they ran through a maze on ten consecutive trials without entering any of eight blind alleys. Cortical lesions of various sizes were made either prior to original learning or prior to the retesting of preoperatively acquired learning. When surgery was scheduled to occur after learning, rats were retrained to the initial criterion 10 days after learning the maze, then operated on and retrained to this same criterion starting 10 days after surgery.

Cortical lesions retarded both original learning and retention of the preoperatively acquired habit. The extent of the cortical lesion was found to be correlated with the impairment in original learning (.75) and also with the impairment in relearning after surgery (.69). But most significantly, Lashley found no relationship between these deficits and the locus of the lesion (Figure 16).

> It is certain that the maze habit, when formed, is not localized in any single area of the cerebrum and that its performance is somehow conditioned by the quantity of tissue which is intact. It is less certain, though probable, that all parts of the cortex participate equally in the performance of the habit and that lesions of equal size produce equal loss of the habit, irrespective of their locus (Lashley, 1929, p. 107).

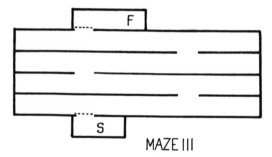

Figure 16A. Ground plan of Maze III, used extensively by Lashley in his efforts to localize the engram. S = starting compartment, F = food compartment. Rats were given 5 trials per day until 10 consecutive errorless trials were recorded. Normal animals required 19 trials and 47 errors to learn the maze and 40 days later relearned it in 2 trials and 7 errors (From Lashley, 1929.)

Lashley considered but rejected alternative hypotheses and concluded that the reduction in learning ability is "the same, quantitatively and qualitatively, after equal lesions to diverse areas" (p. 123); and "in all tests upon learning subsequent to the brain operation the effects of injuries to different areas seemed to be qualitatively identical" (p. 122). Thus, he saw his evidence "pointing to the equivalence of function of all parts of the cerebral cortex for learning" (p. 122).

Lashley conceded that more restricted regions may indeed play an essential role in the learning and retention of certain tasks, as the striate cortex does for visual discrimination habits. But in such cases, all parts of the functional area are equivalent, that is, *equipotential,* in storing information.

> Somehow, equivalent traces are established throughout the functional area. . . . within a functional area the cells throughout the area acquire the capacity to react in certain definite patterns, which may have any distribution within that area (Lashley, 1950, p. 502).

Current views of the brain emphasizing its high degree of anatomical specificity and specialization are not entirely incompatible with this notion of equipotentiality and distributed memory. Zangwill (1963) argued that Lashley's views are compatible with localization of function in the sense that his notion of functional equivalence could apply within any of

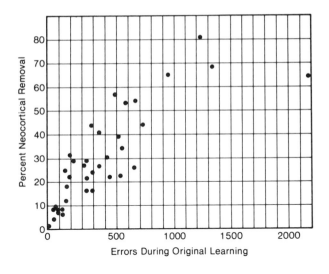

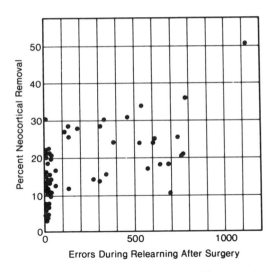

Figure 16B. Relationship between extent of neocortal lesion and errors in learning or relearning the Lashley III maze. *Top.* Original learning (*N* = 37). The ordinate indicates for each animal the percentage of cortex removed, and the abscissa indicates the number of errors made during learning. *Bottom.* Relearning of the same maze task in rats with lesions made about 2 weeks after original learning (*N* = 59). The ordinate indicates the percentage of cortex removed, and the abscissa indicates the number of errors made during the postoperative retention test. (From Lashley, 1929.)

Figure 17. Karl Lashley (1890–1958), American psychologist. (Beach, Hebb, Morgan, and Nissen, 1960.)

the specialized areas of cortex that have been and will likely continue to be discovered.

The resolution of the debate over the localization of memory hinges on the size of the functional area under consideration, that is, on the size of the region that is asserted to demonstrate functional equivalence. Lashley's units were almost surely too large. Indeed, critics immediately reinterpreted his findings, noting that the correlation between retention score and lesion size could reflect progressive encroachment upon specialized cortical areas devoted to sensory analysis of the multiple stimuli essential to maze performance (Hunter, 1930). Experiments later demonstrated that the maze learning deficits observed after cortical lesions in rats do depend on damage to functionally distinct brain regions. For example, an anterior (prefrontal) area is important for alternation behavior, and a posterior (striate or prestriate) area is important for visually guided behavior (Gross, Chorover, and Cohen, 1965). A fairer statement of the situation would be that many different parts of the brain contribute to learning, but each part contributes in a different manner (Young, 1979). Thus, Lashley's proposed functional unit for the maze habit, the whole brain, did not survive experimental test.

During the last 30 years, studies of nonhuman primates have provided strong support for the idea that the brain has numerous specialized functional areas, some of them extremely small. Even in Lashley's time, damage to the prefrontal cortex of monkeys was known to impair learning and retention of the delayed alternation habit (Jacobsen and Nissen, 1937). Later studies narrowed the critical locus, first to the sulcus principalis of the prefrontal region (Blum, 1952) and eventually to the middle third of the principal sulcus (Butters and Pandya, 1969). Lesions in other regions of the prefrontal cortex affected performance on the task, but the most severe deficit was associated with a small bilateral lesion 9 mm in length. It should be noted that even this small area of cortex contains more than one million neurons. Functional equivalence, that is, equivalent distribution of memory, could be an important principle of how memory is organized, but the principle must apply to very restricted brain loci.

Nonlocalizing Signs from Neurophysiology

A second line of evidence, which has been used to support a probabilistic and distributed view of memory, came from electrophysiological recordings taken from discrete brain regions during learning (John, 1972; Bartlett and John, 1973). These experiments showed that evoked responses and multiple unit activity, triggered during learning by auditory or visual conditioned stimuli (CS), could be found in widespread brain regions. An important aspect of these studies was the marked indeterminancy and probabilistic nature of the neuronal responses (John and Morgades, 1969). Averaged activity showed far less variance than cellular activity, and many anatomical regions presented similar evoked responses to the same CS.

Later studies developed a differential generalization procedure to rule out nonspecific factors. Two conditioned stimuli (visual flickers CS1 and CS2) were employed to train two different conditioned operant responses (CR1 and CR2); and a neutral stimulus, a visual flicker (V3) halfway between CS1 and CS2 in frequency, was presented intermittently (Bartlett and John, 1973; John et al., 1973). The neutral stimulus typically resulted in the animal's performing one or the other of the CRs. In this situation, the evoked responses recorded in a dozen or more brain regions, including hippocampus, substantia nigra, and lateral geniculate, were related to the way in which the stimulus was interpreted. When the neutral stimulus (V3) led to performance of the operant response (CR1) that had been conditioned to CS1, the evoked responses to V3 resembled the evoked response that had been observed during presentation of CS1. In contrast, when the neutral stimulus (V3) led to the CR that had been conditioned to CS2, then the evoked response to V3 resembled the evoked response that had been observed during presentation of CS2. In this sense the evoked responses, rather than being driven directly by the stimulus, reflected endogenous processes (at least in part) related to how the stimulus was interpreted. Accordingly, the evoked responses were considered to reflect the readout of specific memories. Similar studies were performed using an indwelling chronic microelectrode to record from single cells in thalamus, visual cortex, and medial suprasylvian cortex (Ramos, Schwartz, and John, 1976). Twenty-nine percent of the cells exhibited properties similar to those described above for evoked responses: Their firing characteristics varied in a manner that depended on the meaning attributed to a presented stimulus, not on the physical nature of that stimulus.

These studies suggested that memory must be coded by the statistical activity of neural elements within widespread collections or ensembles of cells. The crucial event in learning is the development of a characteristic spatiotemporal pattern of neural activity in different parts of the brain. Individual neurons in such an ensemble participate in a purely probabilistic manner. In addition, a single ensemble can encode more than one item of information, each of which has its own characteristic pattern of coherent activity.

This tradition of work holds that statistically configured ensembles, rather than single neurons, provide the appropriate level of analysis to study memory storage in vertebrates. However, the tradition does not specify just how large and widespread these ensembles must be. Although the initial statements of this theoretical approach emphasized the distributed and widespread nature of memory storage, later proposals stated that some regions of the brain are more important for memory storage than others (Bartlett and John, 1973). In addition, it is difficult to interpret the evoked responses unambiguously. When an animal performs a previously established CR to a neutral stimulus and thereby behaves toward the neutral stimulus as it would have behaved toward the original CS, the animal does more than simply "read out" the memory associated with the original CS. The animal also processes a new stimulus, organizes a response, and performs other, perhaps less specific cognitive operations required for information processing and motor expression. Even though any one of these factors might be ruled out as the whole explanation for the distribution and appearance of the evoked responses, the contribution to the evoked waveforms produced by all the factors in combination cannot be assessed with certainty. This makes it difficult to know which of the recorded waveforms, or which aspect of the waveforms, has a specific relationship to memory.

The experimental results thus leave one with quite a range of possibilities when trying to estimate either the number of neurons involved in memory storage or the number of participating brain regions. Indeed, without distorting the concepts of either Lashley or John, one can note that their conclusions are in many ways compatible with the connectionist, deterministic view of memory that derives from work with invertebrates and from cellular studies of synaptic plasticity. The unreliability and indeterminancy of mammalian neurons, in terms of the storage and expression of stored memory, is an issue only at the level of the single cell. The same neurons prove to be more reliable and deterministic when considered as a group, in terms of collections or ensembles.

Cortical sensory systems process different sensory modalities, and within these cortical systems there are different areas specialized for different aspects, features, or components of information processing within a modality (Ungerleider and Mishkin, 1982; Mishkin, 1982). Cortical regions also exist for performing specialized, but amodal computations, such as those involving language and spatial layouts. To the extent that memory is tied to the operation of these highly specialized processing areas, the connectional specificity of these areas provides a framework for memory much like that observed in invertebrates. In short, the behavior of neuronal *ensembles,* as opposed to single neurons, preserves the connectionist specificity that plays such a prominent part in descriptions of invertebrate memory.

In the end, the debate over how memory is stored is not between localizationist and anti-localizationist positions, nor between deterministic versus statistical theories. The crucial issue is the *size* of the ensembles, that is, the size of the functional units that contain equivalently distributed information. Their size must not be so large as to deny the potential informational specificity offered by the precision of anatomical specialization in the brain, nor so small that the activity of individual neurons plays too significant a role. Before exploring this point further to find a compromise between the two extremes, two other traditions will be examined, which have usually been associated with the anti-localization position.

Memory as a Hologram

A much-discussed model of nonlocalized, distributed memory is based on the idea that memory is stored as holograms. Holography is an optical information storage process (Gabor, 1948). Interference patterns are formed when two beams of coherent light are reflected from an object. The permanent record of the interference patterns is a hologram, and it contains the information necessary to reconstruct an image of the object (Leith and Upatnicks, 1962). Holograms provide attractive memory systems because they have enormous storage capacities: A hologram can store a multitude of different interference patterns in a single medium with no loss of retrievability. Furthermore, the representation of the interference patterns is stored in a distributed manner throughout the storage medium, such that small segments of the storage medium can reconstruct the entire representation. As the segment size decreases, there is a progressive loss of detail. Note that this mechanism of distributed storage would be particularly resistant to disruption. It is therefore compatible with the results of Lashley's lesion experiments.

The specific idea that biological memory storage is holographic has been advanced (Van Heerden, 1963; Pribram, 1971). However, the application of the holographic concept to brain function and to the problem of memory storage has so far been examined in only a general, metaphorical manner. Just *how* interference patterns, filters, and coherent beams of light might be realized in the neural hardware of physiological activity of the brain has not been discussed. Likewise no one has stated just how

66

large a brain region would be involved in a particular hologram. If holograms are meant to occupy a large region of brain, and if they are intended to represent information in a qualitatively equivalent way throughout the region, then the holographic concept duplicates Lashley's error. However, the holographic model of distributed memory can be made more compatible with the available data, and with localizationist views, if the principle operates only within anatomically defined functional regions that process particular aspects, components, or classes of information.

Distributed Models of Memory in Cognitive Psychology

Several recent approaches have made use of the holographic principle to provide explicitly distributed models of memory (Edelman and Reeke, 1982; Eich, 1982; Hinton and Anderson, 1981; Murdock, 1982; Rumelhart and McClelland, 1986). These approaches hypothesize that items in memory are represented by different patterns of activity among the *same* neural elements rather than by occupying different loci that can then be linked together to form associations. By supporting different patterns of activity, a group of probabilistic elements could represent many different memories. Each different memory would later be retrieved by re-evoking the particular pattern representing that memory. For a clear discussion of these and other distributed models of computation, see Churchland (1986); for related discussions of computing with neural networks, see Hopfield and Tank (1986), Kohonen (1977), and Grossberg (1982).

These ideas are compatible with the localizationist position, if it is supposed that the elements across which function is equivalently distributed constitute specialized, differentiated processing systems of limited size, which deal with specific aspects of information. Distributed models of memory appear to satisfy this condition, although they seldom address the point explicitly. The models typically focus on a specific problem such as how to represent the meanings of words, concepts, and their interrelationships. Thus, the models deal with the representation of a particular kind of information, and the same models do not consider memory for faces, spatial position, pictures, or music. Furthermore, even

67

within a single narrow domain of information (words and concepts), one finds the suggestion that a particular item in memory may be represented by a pattern of "microfeatures" (Hinton, 1981), that is, by a particular set of active units.

The hypothesis of microfeatures implicitly allows for the important concept that not all elements in a representation are equivalent. Because of anatomical and functional specialization some units are more active, some less active, and some not involved at all in representing a particular item of information. Accordingly, some neurons and brain regions are more involved in representations than others. If one supposes in this way that different sets of neurons in different brain regions make qualitatively different contributions to a particular representation, one avoids Lashley's error, and distributed accounts of memory become in principle compatible with the localizationist position. Parallel and distributed models of memory are currently being discussed, which are based on neurobiological data, rather than purely formal, mathematical considerations (Cooper, Lieberman, and Oja, 1979; Lynch, 1986; Rolls, 1986). These approaches recognize that neurons have dissimilar and distinctive properties, they consider that different brain regions are specialized for different kinds of operations, and they assume that particular memories are stored over limited areas.

Localizationist and Distributed Accounts of Memory Reconciled

The key issue is one of emphasis: Is memory localized to particular units and regions, or is memory distributed equivalently over a collection of units or regions? The answer is that both are true. Representation *is* highly localized. For example, representation of acquired language is organized in discrete regions of the left cerebral hemisphere, as demonstrated by lesion data from aphasic patients and also by the effects of punctate electrical stimulation in the left cerebral cortex of human patients studied with their consent during neurosurgery (Ojemann, 1983). Localized stimulation in bilingual patients can cause naming errors in one language but not in another; and frequently only one of several language functions, e.g., naming, reading, or phonetic identification, is altered by stimulation at a particular site. On the other hand, representation does seem to be distributed across a large collection of common neurons. For example, in the case of the words and concepts of a single language, stimulation of the peri-Sylvian area of the posterior frontal, superior temporal, and inferior parietal lobes can produce anomia, but stimulation has not been found to cause isolated naming disturbances affecting only one particular word or category.

The same point can be made for the visual system. Widely different regions of the brain make separate contributions to the representation of visual information. Whereas the inferotemporal region (area TE) is specialized for the analysis of visual pattern information (Mishkin, 1982), the inferior parietal lobe (areas PE, PEm, PG, and PF; commonly termed areas 5 and 7) is specialized for the analysis of information about the location of a perceived object in visual space (Ungerleider and Mishkin, 1982). Even within area TE, single neurons are specialized to respond to different features of the visual world (Fuster and Jervey, 1981; Gross, Bender, and Gerstein, 1979). Thus, analysis and representation would seem to depend on specific and localized brain areas and on specialized neurons within these areas.

Yet the concept of distributed memory is also appropriate here, if an appropriately sized functional unit can be identified. Such a region would be smaller than area TE itself. The indeterminancy and probabilistic nature of neural firing need not imply diffuseness, nonspecificity, or redundancy of memory storage. Indeterminancy is a characteristic of the individual elements in an ensemble of functionally equivalent elements. Individual elements code features or components of memory, and the ensemble to which they belong operates deterministically and reliably.

The apparently conflicting approaches to memory storage with which this chapter began prove entirely reconcilable. The conflict turns on two issues seldom addressed explicitly in formal models: The size of the functional area across which memory is equivalently distributed; and how broad a class of information can be equivalently represented in the same set of neural elements. Anatomical specialization suggests that the functionally equivalent areas of brain must be rather small, and that the class of information represented in the same elements is relatively narrow. Memory is widely distributed, but different loci store different aspects of the whole. Each differentiated component of memory must be both localized and dependent on specific connections. The principle of distributed, holographic memory is valid within an appropriately small functional unit and within an appropriately narrow domain of function, that is, for specific components or microfeatures of information processing.

Searching for Functionally Equivalent Neural Units

It follows from the preceding discussion that the identification of functional units of neural organization is a major question for contemporary neuroscience. Knowing the functional units would clarify the problem of memory by suggesting a unit device within which information could be equivalently distributed. The functional units would constitute devices for the analysis and storage of microfeatures of information. According to classical neuroanatomy, mammalian neocortex divides into some 50 to 100 regions, each uniquely defined in terms of cytoarchitecture, patterns of extrinsic connections, and function. Studies of the intrinsic organization within these cortical regions have suggested that vertical columns of cells arranged perpendicularly to the cortical surface are the basic mode of organization (Eccles, 1981; Mountcastle, 1979; Szentagothai, 1975).

Lorente de No (1938) was perhaps the first to note the vertical organization of cortex. The vertical organization of sensory areas of mammalian cerebral cortex into functional physiological units, called columns, was discovered in the landmark studies of Mountcastle (1957) and Hubel and Wiesel (1962). In the visual cortex of monkey these functional units, the ocular dominance columns, have a diameter of about 400 um. This same principle of organization has been extended to auditory cortex (Imig and Brugge, 1978) and to the barrel fields of mouse somatosensory cortex, which contain barrel-shaped groupings of cells representing individual vibrissae (Woolsey and Van der Loos, 1970). Columnar organization has likewise been found outside the sensory areas of cortex, most notably in the prefrontal region of monkey (Goldman and Nauta, 1977). These columns are 200–500 um wide, and they extend vertically through all six cortical layers (Figure 18).

These units of organization have been termed macrocolumns (Mountcastle, 1979). About one million of them are estimated to exist in the human brain, with perhaps 10^3–10^4 cells in a single column. The con-

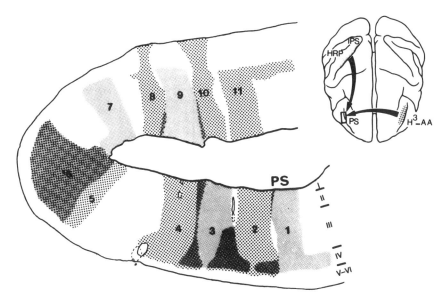

Figure 18. Columnlike organization of interdigitating projections to frontal lobe in monkeys. *Upper right.* Tritiated amino acids [3H] AA were injected into principal sulcus (PS) of the left hemisphere to label callosal projections to the PS in the right hemisphere. Horseradish peroxidase pellets (HRP) were implanted into the posterior bank of the intraparietal sulcus (IPS) in the right hemisphere to label projections to the right PS. In this way, convergent projections to PS, located in the rectangle, were labeled in the same animal. *Left.* A composite of two coronal sections through the convergence zone in the principal sulcus of the right hemisphere. Labeled termination zones for callosal fibers (2, 4, 5, 8, 10, and 11) are indicated by coarse stipple; termination zones for the parietal-frontal projection (1, 3, 5, 7, and 9) are shown in fine stipple. Although the organization of the two projections is irregular and sometimes overlapping, the two inputs are distributed in approximately alternating columns that extend across all six cortical layers. (From Goldman-Rakic and Schwartz, 1982.)

nectivity among the estimated cells within a single macrocolumn is primarily vertical. Connectivity between columns occurs by U-shaped fibers that exit from the cortex and then re-enter ipsilaterally or contralaterally.

. . . the general proposition [is] that the processing function of neocortical modules is qualitatively similar in all neocortical regions. Put shortly, there is nothing intrinsically motor about the motor cortex, nor sensory about the sensory cortex. Thus the elucidation of the mode of operation of the local modular circuit anywhere in the neocortex will be of great generalizing significance (Mountcastle, 1979, p. 9).

The concept of the macrocolumn is to some extent idealized, and the existence of the macrocolumn as a basic computational unit should be regarded as tentative. The width of the columns can vary from 100–1000 um, and they can vary in their cross-sectional area from layer to layer. In the case of the barrel fields of somatosensory cortex, the vertical organization extends only through layer IV. The cross-sectional shape of the macrocolumn can vary from oval, to slab-like, to swirled. In other words, they are often not column-shaped. Furthermore, not every input to a cortical region appears to respect the column boundaries. For example, in the monkey, cells in parietal cortex send an ipsilateral corticocortical projection to the same region of sulcus principalis in the frontal lobe that is also the target of a second projection from the opposite frontal lobe (Figure 18). Despite the apparent segregation and interdigitation of these two projections at their common target site, overlap between the two projections can be found, and the neatness of the interdigitation is frequently broken (Goldman-Rakic and Schwartz, 1982). Thus, although the two projections terminate in a discontinuous and patchy pattern, just as the column concept requires, the term column may not accurately describe the pattern of interdigitation. Knowledge of the exact nature of organization must wait until all the inputs to a particular cortical region can be reconstructed.

Column will probably prove too rigid a concept, because it implies both a specific shape and the existence of distinct boundaries. One possibility is that there is a repeating element of cortical organization, but one which (like a crystal or like wallpaper) has only arbitrary boundaries between repeating segments (Hubel and Wiesel, 1979). Nevertheless, the column concept introduces the significant idea that some relatively small area of cortex, containing perhaps 10^3–10^4 neurons, may prove to be a basic unit of organization. Even if correct, this idea does not require that each modular unit is functionally homogenous. In the visual cortex each macrocolumn includes cells with all grades of eye preference and all grades of preference for lines of different orientation. In addition, each column is interpenetrated with cells sensitive to color (Livingstone and Hubel, 1984). This strongly implies that the search for functionally

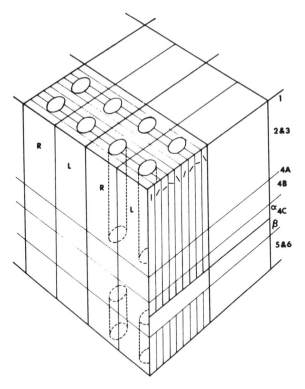

Figure 19. Functional parcellation of cortex beyond the macrocolumn. The schematic diagram proposes a modular organization of macaque striate cortex. Each ocular dominance column (L and R) contains cells sensitive to all orientations and is interpenetrated as well by cells that are sensitive to color but not orientation. Layer 4C, the site of termination of afferents from the lateral geniculate, is also insensitive to orientation. (From Livingstone and Hubel, 1984.)

equivalent neural elements must look to a set size even smaller than the macrocolumn (Figure 19).

Bullock (1980) attempted to answer the question, how many neurons in the nervous system are of the same type? Put another way, how many different sets of neurons exist, if a set consists of virtually indistinguishable neurons? And how many neurons are there in these sets? Although Bullock rightly emphasizes that no firm data exist to answer these questions, he proposes equivalence classes containing no more than 100 neurons, perhaps even fewer. Others (Mountcastle, 1979; Shaw, Harth, and

Scheibel, 1982) have also suggested that an irreducible unit of functional organization exists within the cortical macrocolumn, a unit the size of the orientation column of Hubel and Wiesel. It is proposed to be about 30 um in diameter, to be arranged vertically within a macrocolumn, and to contain 30 to 100 neurons. Such an ensemble would constitute a basic computational unit of functionally equivalent neurons.

At present no compelling anatomical or functional evidence can be adduced for the idea that such a subdivision exists as a general organizing property of neocortex. Nevertheless, the idea remains plausible. Indeed, the number of neurons in an equivalent set must be smaller than the 1,000 or 10,000 contained in a macrocolumn, because the macrocolumns of the visual cortex contain various types of neurons. Moreover, the number of neurons in a cooperative ensemble of equivalent elements must be far smaller than the number typically proposed in more global, statistical approaches to neural function. Small ensembles or assemblies of neurons could contribute informational specificity to the total set of ensembles involved in information storage by coding specific microfeatures or components of information.

The view presented here divides memory into small, functionally homogenous assemblies of neurons. No separate memory centers exist where an entire memory is stored. It is simplistic and misleading to refer to "the engram" as if it were a single entity, rather than a collection of entities. Instead, different microfeatures or components of information are processed and stored by small, functionally specialized assemblies of neurons. On each occasion that recall or recognition occurs, information is expressed by the activity of the same assemblies. Within each contributing assembly, the individual elements are equipotential and behave probabilistically. Memory for whole events is widely represented in the sense that many areas of the brain are involved, but there is no redundancy or reduplication of function across these areas.

6

The Penfield Studies

The preceding chapter has furnished a framework to consider the problem of memory localization in the brain. For example, the concept that small neuronal ensembles can contain particular components of information suggests that memory storage can be localized but that complex memory should require the participation of several brain areas, each contributing in a different way to storage of the whole. However, such a framework provides only a general guide to experimental work, and it tells us nothing about the location of memory storage in any particular case. The question of *where* memory resides remains very much an empirical problem, and several specific examples of learning and memory must be thoroughly studied in order to illuminate it. Before examining those cases that form the focus of contemporary experimental work on the problem of memory storage, another significant part of the history of this problem needs to be told.

Any modern treatment of memory localization must consider the findings of Wilder Penfield's pioneering studies, done more than a quarter century ago. In the course of neurosurgery to relieve focal epilepsy in 1,132 patients, Penfield and his colleagues had the opportunity to explore most of the cortical surface with stimulating electrodes (Penfield and Jasper, 1954; Penfield and Perot, 1963). Because the brain contains

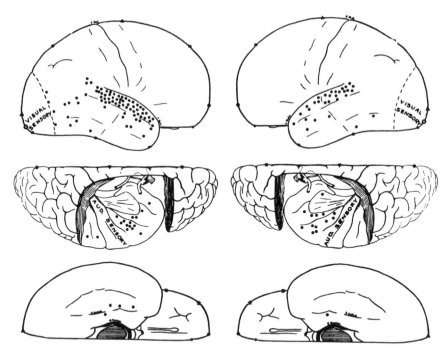

Figure 20. Summary maps from Penfield's series of patients, showing where in each hemisphere experiential responses were produced by electrical stimulation. *Top.* Lateral view. *Middle.* Dorsal view. The frontal and parietal opercula have been removed to expose the plenum temporale. *Bottom.* Ventral view. Experiential responses were obtained during 40 operations on 40 different patients, out of the entire series of 1132 patients. Experiential responses were obtained only in the temporal lobes, in 7.7% of the 520 cases in which the temporal lobe was stimulated. (From Penfield and Perot, 1963.)

no pain receptors, patients received only a local anesthetic and remained fully conscious during surgery. Electrical stimulation of the cortical surface sometimes induced images, which patients described as coherent perceptions or experiences (Figure 20).

Penfield interpreted these experiential hallucinations as veridical reproductions of past experience. Moreover, he supposed that either the record of these experiences, or neural connections allowing access to them, must be close to the location of the stimulating electrode. In Penfield's view, the experiences that were elicited by stimulation reproduced the stream of consciousness from a previous episode of past life: The stimulating electrode drew the reproduction from its place of storage, much as if a tape recorder were switched on at some arbitrary position.

From the advantage of a contemporary perspective it can be said that Penfield's famous observations no longer require their traditional interpretation. However, the observations are well known, and their traditional interpretation is still widely told. It therefore seems worthwhile to consider them here in some detail. Indeed, Penfield's observations can be understood in terms of quite a different set of ideas, which are based on more recent experimental findings: Memory for whole events is stored widely, not in a single location; literal or biologic forgetting can occur, so that recollection of past events is a reconstruction from fragments, not a veridical playback of past events. These themes recur frequently throughout this book.

The Observations

Penfield divided the experiential responses produced by electrode stimulation into four categories: auditory (voices, music, or a meaningful sound), visual (people, a scene, or a recognizable object), combined visual-auditory (scenes with appropriate sounds), or unclassified experiential responses (a thought, a memory, or a flashback). Auditory experiences proved somewhat more common than the other types. The experiences most frequently elicited involved watching or hearing another person's action and speech, and hearing music. It is noteworthy that many sorts of possible experiences were not elicited at all; these included episodes in which the patient was speaking, eating, engaging in skilled behavior, or thinking and reflecting.

Electrical stimulation elicited images only during stimulation of the right or left temporal lobe. For 612 patients who underwent exploration of other areas of the brain, no experiential responses were ever observed. All categories of experiential response were elicited by both right and left temporal lobe stimulation, but right temporal lobe stimulation was slightly more likely to elicit each category of experience. Not all stimulation in the temporal lobe elicited experiential responses. Indeed, only 40 patients (7.7%) out of a total of 520 patients who received temporal lobe stimulation had any experiential responses. Twenty-four of the 40 patients (60%) who reported experiential responses also reported that hallucinations were a part of their habitual seizure patterns. For 16 of *these* 24 patients (67%), the stimulation-invoked experiences included a mental experience identical to that associated with the seizure pattern.

The evoked mental experiences had certain common features. Many of them had dream-like qualities. Following the fifth stimulation of a point on the posterior surface of the left superior temporal gyrus, one patient noted, "People's voices talking." After the sixth stimulation, "Now I hear them . . . A little like in a dream" (Penfield and Perot, 1963; Case 2, p. 614). Another patient said, "I keep having dreams . . . I keep seeing things—I keep dreaming of things" (Case 22, p. 635). A third patient commented, "A dream is starting. There are a lot of people." The patient then said that she did not know whether they were speaking. Asked where they were, she said, "In the living room. I think one of them is my mother" (Case 25, p. 638).

Frequently, details were felt to be inaccessible, as they often are when reporting a dream. One patient stimulated on the superior surface of the right temporal lobe stated, "It sounded like a voice saying words, but it was so faint I couldn't get it." Repeated stimulation for 15 seconds produced the comment that it sounded like a voice saying "Jimmy, Jimmy, Jimmy." She stated that that was her husband's name and that was what she called him (Case 8, p. 623). Another patient said, "Oh, it was like an attack, there was someone smoking tobacco, but I do not know who it was" (Case 23, p. 637). A 19-year-old man said, "I hear someone talking . . . I think it was about a restaurant or something" (Case 13, p. 627). Still another patient said, "Yes . . . It was said and I know what was said, but I cannot put it into words" (Case 14, p. 629).

Often a patient would remark that the evoked experience was accompanied by a sense of familiarity, as if the experience had occurred before. But patients never lost awareness of the operating room and the immediate reality. One patient said, "I feel as though I am going into an attack." When asked why, he said, "That music, from the stage hit 'Guys & Dolls.' " He said it was like when "I was listening to it." When asked whether he seemed to be there or was remembering it, he said, "I seemed to be there" (Case 37, p. 653). Another patient said, "Yes, Doctor, yes, Doctor! Now I hear people laughing—my friends in

South Africa." He also said he could recognize the people. "Yes, they are two cousins, Bessie and Ann Wheliaw." He then indicated that they were laughing but he did not know why (Case 38, p. 654).

Experiences that seemed familiar were often intermixed with other, unfamiliar or even unrealistic, fantastic situations. One patient said, "Yes I hear the same familiar woman calling. The same lady [the same lady experienced when the same site had been stimulated a moment before]. That was not in the neighborhood. It seemed to be at the lumber yard . . . I have never been around any lumber yard" (Case 36, p. 651). Another patient, a 12-year-old boy, had epileptic attacks that were usually preceded by an experience of a robber moving toward him. After stimulation of a point in the posterior portion of the right temporal lobe, the patient said, "Oh, gee, gosh, robbers are coming at me with guns!" (Case 3, p. 616). Stimulation at another point elicited the experience of overhearing a telephone conversation between his mother and his aunt. "My mother was telling my aunt over the telephone to come up and visit us tonight." Asked how he knew that the women were speaking via telephone, the boy stated that he could tell from the way that his aunt's voice sounded that they must be talking on the telephone. In this case, the patient apparently had the unrealistic experience of hearing both sides of a telephone conversation simultaneously.

On some occasions when evoked experiences seemed to relate directly to previous events in the patient's life, it was difficult to know whether what was elicited by stimulation was a specific past episode or a generic memory, i.e., a typical, average experience about something that had happened many times before. One patient said, "I am seeing a picture of a dog and cat . . . the dog is chasing the cat." She then said that they were in the driveway at her home and that she remembered seeing them do this before (Case 18, p. 632). Another patient said, "I just heard one of my children speaking." She explained that it was her older one, Frank, but that she could not understand what was being said. Ten days later, she remembered that she had heard her son during the surgical procedure. When asked if it was a memory, she said, "Oh no, it seemed more real than that." She knew she was in the operating room, but she felt as if she were looking into the yard at her son. She said, "Of course, I have heard Frankie like that many, many times, thousands of times" (Case 33, p. 646).

Patients sometimes reported a similar experience from stimulation at widely distant stimulation points. Thus: "Everybody is yelling at me." From a different point. "There they go, yelling at me, stop them!" (Case 15, p. 630). Conversely, although there was often consistency in the effects of repeated stimulation at the same point, patients sometimes reported different experiences. Thus: "Un homme se *battre*" (a man fighting). After stimulation of the same point 10 minutes later, the patient said, "Yes, a man." He then explained that he saw a man and a dog walking (Case 34, p. 646).

Interpretation of the Penfield Studies

Acceptance of these fascinating observations as evidence for localization of whole memories in the temporal lobe presents a number of difficulties. First of all, the mental experiences elicited by stimulation may not be memories at all. The reported experiences often have a dream-like rather than a memory-like quality. Elements of fantasy rather than memory sometimes appeared, as in hearing both halves of a telephone conversation. Even though many of the experiences apparently refer to familiar past events, they also sometimes included unfamiliar elements, such as a lumberyard. Furthermore, those experiences that *seemed* familiar may have been generic reconstructions of multiple, similar events rather than the evocation of a single actual event. Other critical discussions of these data (Neisser, 1967; Loftus and Loftus, 1980) have made many of these same points. The mental content elicited by stimulation is difficult to distinguish from dreams, fabricated reconstructions, and fantasies.

Quite apart from the issue of what the mental experiences actually were, there are also problems with locating the contents of the evoked experience to the vicinity of the stimulating electrode. On occasion, stimulation at different sites produced the same experience; conversely, repeated stimulation at the same site sometimes produced different experiences. Moreover, even sizable removals of the temporal lobe that included the sites of stimulation failed to destroy memory for the experiences that had been elicited (Penfield, 1958; Baldwin, 1960).

Recent Findings

Two more recent studies of human temporal lobe stimulation (Halgren, Walter, Cherlow, and Crandall, 1978; Gloor, Olivier, Quesney, Andermann, and Horowitz, 1982) shed considerable light on these issues. The use of chronically implanted electrodes in similar anatomical sites across patients permitted a systematic exploration of the effects of stimulation according to a standard protocol of stimulus parameters. Quantitative studies could therefore be conducted of the various mental phenomena evoked by temporal lobe stimulation.

In the 1978 study (Halgren et al., 1978), stimulation of the medial temporal region (in the hippocampus, amygdala, or hippocampal gyrus) in 36 patients elicited mental phenomena on 267 of 3,495 occasions (7.6%), a frequency quite close to that found in the Penfield studies. Moreover, as in Penfield's cases, the elicited mental phenomena were hallucinated images or scenes, emotions, visceral sensations, or unformed sensations. What were termed "memory-like hallucinations" were observed in six patients after a total of 35 different stimulations and at a total of 21 different electrode sites.

All types of mental phenomena were more likely when stimulation evoked after-discharges: Mental phenomena were evoked by 69% of stimulations that produced bilateral after-discharges and 36% of the stimulations that produced a unilateral after-discharge. But only 7.9% of stimuli evoking no after-discharge elicited mental phenomena. Mental experiences were therefore much more likely when the electrical stimulus was sufficiently strong to produce widespread electrographic effects. In total, 50% of the mental experiences that were elicited by stimulation occurred in the presence of after-discharges. This figure, calculated from Table 3 of the article by Halgren and his colleagues, is in close agreement with the findings of another study that presented comparable data (Gloor et al., 1982).

Repeated stimulation at the same site often elicited apparently unrelated memories, even a different category of mental phenomena. Furthermore, no systematic relationship was found between anatomical sites and the category of mental experience elicited, although there was a general tendency for anterior rather than posterior sites to be effective. The elicited mental phenomenon depended more strongly on which patient was being stimulated than on the location of the stimulation site, and the data even suggested that the category of elicited mental phenomena could be related to the personality of the patient.

The anatomical basis of these phenomena has been greatly clarified by a study of 35 epileptic patients (Gloor et al., 1982), who were stimulated both in temporal neocortex, as in Penfield's studies, and in the medial temporal region (hippocampus, amygdala, and hippocampal gyrus), as in the study by Halgren and his colleagues. This study also obtained and examined some experiential phenomena that occurred during spontaneous seizures. Eighty-eight experiential responses were elicited by stimulation, and most of them occurred after stimulation of limbic structures rather than neocortex. Of six responses (7%) obtained following stimulation of temporal neocortex or white matter, five were elementary visual hallucinations considered to be due to spread of stimulation to optic radiation fibers. A bona fide experiential response (a simple déjà vu illusion, not a complex visual hallucination) was observed on only one occasion following neocortical stimulation (Figure 21).

An additional important finding was that in 51% of the 88 cases, afterdischarges occurred in conjunction with the experiential responses; these were either confined to limbic structures alone, or they occurred in both limbic and neocortical structures. Thus limbic structures were almost always involved in the evocation of experiential responses. Indeed, if a more stringent criterion is applied, the elicitation of a complex visual hallucination rather than any experiential response, then temporal neocortical discharges never proved effective by themselves. That is, unless limbic structures were activated, either directly by stimulation, indirectly by spread of after-discharges following stimulation of temporal neocortex, or directly as the result of a spontaneous seizure, no complex experiential responses were observed. Limbic structures may possess such a capacity to evoke experiential phenomena because they have afferent and efferent connections to widespread areas of neocortex, including temporal neocortex. These findings suggest that the anatomical basis of Penfield's observations should be reinterpreted: Experiential responses elicited by temporal neocortical stimulation depend on activation of the closely associated limbic structures.

The specific experience elicited by stimulation may arise from the evocation of specific images—auditory or visual—that patients then ex-

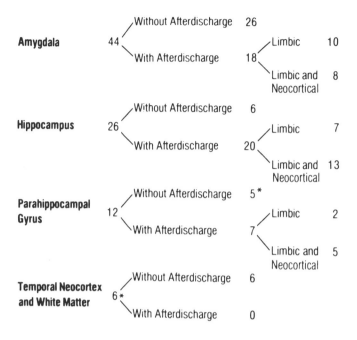

Amygdala 44
- Without Afterdischarge 26
- With Afterdischarge 18
  - Limbic 10
  - Limbic and Neocortical 8

Hippocampus 26
- Without Afterdischarge 6
- With Afterdischarge 20
  - Limbic 7
  - Limbic and Neocortical 13

Parahippocampal Gyrus 12
- Without Afterdischarge 5*
- With Afterdischarge 7
  - Limbic 2
  - Limbic and Neocortical 5

Temporal Neocortex and White Matter 6*
- Without Afterdischarge 6
- With Afterdischarge 0

* Elementary visual hallucinations (except for 1 instance in each group)

Figure 21. Temporal lobe structures from which experiential responses were elicited by electrical stimulation with and without after-discharge. Eighty-eight experiential responses were obtained from 35 patients. Medial temporal lobe structures were involved, often together with neocortical structures, in 82 of these 88 responses. Experiential phenomena appear to require the participation of limbic structures. (From Gloor et al., 1982).

perience differently, depending on their personalities, expectations, and other factors (Ferguson, Rayport, Gardner, Kass, Weiner, and Reiser, 1979; Horowitz, Adams, and Rutkin, 1968). In one detailed study of a single patient, which included a continuing interview during surgery, the content of the elicited experience could sometimes be related directly to the thoughts of the patient at the moment of stimulation (Mahl, Rothenberg, Delgado, and Hamlin, 1964).

Taken together, these later studies cast considerable doubt on the hypothesis that mental phenomena elicited through stimulation of the temporal lobe reflect the focal activation of localized neural events related to memory storage. There are a number of important facts: a lesion under the stimulating electrode does not erase the elicited experience; about half of all experiential responses occur in the presence of after-discharges, which implies involvement of brain regions well beyond the site of stimulation; limbic areas invariably participate in the production of complex experiences; finally, stimulation effects and pre-existing personality or cognitive state are connected. These considerations all point to the idea that multiple areas of neocortex, activated through limbic structures, participate in representing the memories and thoughts that give rise to evoked mental experiences.

7

Searching for Engrams:
Simple Learning

The aim of current experimental work on the problem of memory localization is straightforward and easy to summarize. The goal is to locate areas of the nervous system that store information. Implicit in this undertaking is the realization that many such locations may exist, and that any particular area might store only a particular aspect of information. However, contemporary studies put this issue in the background in order to confront a simpler and more immediate question: Can a place in the nervous system that stores any aspect of memory be identified?

Even this modest goal proves formidable. First, some knowledge of the anatomy of the neural pathways engaged during a particular kind of learning must be obtained, in order to know where to look for learning-related changes. Next, prospective storage sites must be distinguished from sites essential to the performance of a learned behavior that do not actually store the engram. Examples of such sites are those that change during learning, but only in a transient manner. These sites could be involved in functions—such as attention or arousal—that are essential to the learning process, particularly in its early stages, but do not persist for as long as memory can persist. Finally, sites that change because they store what the learning paradigm intentionally teaches an animal, and what the experimenter intends to study, must be distinguished from sites that change because they store other information that is acquired coincidentally.

The candidate sites for memory storage sometimes have been narrowed down to only a few possibilities, and in some instances sites for memory storage have been tentatively identified through several lines of converging evidence. Among the many learning tasks that have been studied, this chapter focuses on three types of learning for which continuous study has led to significant, cumulative knowledge. These are habituation, classical conditioning, and imprinting.

Habituation: The Acoustic Startle Reflex

"Habituation" refers to the gradual waning of response that occurs after repeated stimulation. Habituation is a phylogenetically primitive example of behavioral plasticity and has been described in remarkable detail in the invertebrate *Aplysia* at the cellular/synaptic level (Kandel, 1976). Studies of habituation in both invertebrates and vertebrates (Thompson and Spencer, 1966; Groves, Wilson, and Miller, 1976; Davis, Gendelman, Tischler, and Gendelman, 1982) show that the search for sites of neural plasticity is most fruitful in situations where the neural circuitry subserving the behavior of interest can first be mapped.

In mammals, the acoustic startle reflex [studied initially by Forbes and Sherrington (1914) and later by Prosser and Hunter (1936)] habituates to repeated auditory stimuli. A rat presented with a 110 dB, 90 msec tone burst exhibits a short-latency (8 msec) startle that can be electromyographically measured in the hindleg (Davis et al, 1982a). This reflex exhibits marked habituation if 60 tone bursts occur at 30-second intervals. The neural pathways responsible for this reflex—or at least its shortest-latency component—starts at the auditory nerve and then is presumed to involve the ventral cochlear nucleus (VCN), the dorsal and ventral nuclei of the lateral lemniscus (DLL and VLL), the ventral portion of the nucleus reticularis pontis caudalis (RPC), and finally the spinal cord via the reticulospinal pathway (Figure 22). Some uncertainty remains as to which of these projections are crossed and which are uncrossed.

Further information may modify this description. Since lesions of DLL

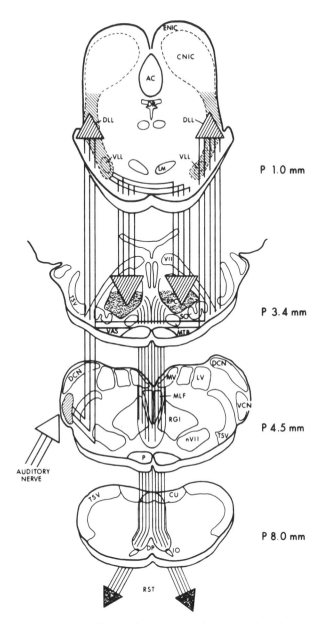

Figure 22. The proposed neural circuit mediating a short-latency (8 msec) acoustic startle response in the rat. Arrows indicate synapses at points along the circuit. VCN, ventral cochlear nucleus; DLL, dorsal nucleus of the lateral lemniscus; VLL, ventral nucleus of the lateral lemniscus; RPC, nucleus reticularis pontis caudalis. Habituation of the reflex appears to depend on changes in synapses formed by projections from VCN, VLL, or both. CNIC, central nucleus of the inferior colliculus; DCN, dorsal cochlear nucleus; LM, medial lemniscus; MLF, medial longitudinal fasciculus; RGI, nucleus reticularis gigantocellularis; SO, superior olive; VAS, ventral acoustic stria. (From Davis et al., 1982a.)

produce only transient effects on startle, DLL probably does not form part of the essential reflex pathway. Furthermore, the VLL link in the pathway may include a more medial paralemniscal zone (Davis et al., 1982a; Tischler and Davis, 1983). Finally, the lesion that proved critical in identifying the RPC could have damaged fibers of passage connecting the VLL region to the spinal cord. If so, RPC is not a critical part of the reflex pathway, and a direct pathway must exist from the VLL region to the spinal cord.

Direct stimulation of the cochlear nucleus yields habituation, but stimulation of RPC does not (Davis, Parsi, Gendelman, Tischler, and Kehne, 1982). This implies that the plastic synapses responsible for habituation are located early in the reflex pathway. Presumably, the sites of plasticity for habituation are either the synapses formed by the projection from the ventral cochlear nucleus to the VLL region, or the synapses formed by projections leaving the VLL region, or both. Since the reflex in question can exhibit sensitization to repeated stimulation (i.e., an increase in response amplitude), and since sensitization can be elicited directly by stimulation of RPC, the other synapses positioned later in the circuit must also be plastic. Of course, the synapses that sensitize must have different plastic properties than the more rostral ones that habituate. These results suggest that even though habituation and sensitization ordinarily interact to determine response strength (Groves and Thompson, 1970), they depend on separate neural loci.

Findings from the invertebrate cases support this analysis of habituation in vertebrates. Behavioral change arises from modifications in already existing circuitry, specifically in the same circuitry specialized to perform the behavior that is modified. This simple type of learning apparently requires no additional brain regions, no additional circuitry, and no additional neurons and synapses beyond those already required to perform the reflex. The neural changes responsible for habituation are *intrinsic* to the reflex pathway; and they occur as reductions in synaptic efficacy at one or more sites along the pathway. Diminished synaptic efficacy has been shown by rather direct evidence to underlie habituation in *Aplysia* (Kandel, 1976), and the same mechanism was proposed even earlier to underlie habituation in vertebrates (Thompson and Spencer, 1966).

Habituation: The Vestibulo-Ocular Reflex

The vestibulo-ocular reflex, which serves to maintain a stable retinal image during head movements, furnishes another relatively simple example of behavioral plasticity. This reflex operates even in the dark; it involves primary vestibular neurons, vestibular nuclei, and oculomotor nuclei. However, the reflex responds to visual input and can adjust within a few days to prisms that reverse the visual field (Jones, 1977). Following removal of the flocculus of the cerebellum (Ito, Shiida, Yagi, Yamamoto, 1974), or lesions of the inferior olive, which remove the climbing fibers input to Purkinje cells of the flocculus (Ito and Miyashita, 1975), this reflex loses the ability to adapt. Disagreement exists concerning whether the flocculus is the locus of the reflex modifications (Ito, 1982), or whether the flocculus furnishes information needed for adaptation to occur (Miles and Lisberger, 1981). These two hypotheses could be tested by removing the flocculus after adaptation has occurred. If the information is stored *in* the flocculus, adaptation should disappear upon its removal. Conversely, if the flocculus simply provides information needed for adaptation, its removal should not significantly alter an already established adaptive state.

The hypothesis that plasticity occurs in the flocculus extends suggestions originally made by Marr (1969) and Albus (1971) concerning cerebellar plasticity. Because the neuroanatomy of the reflex pathway and of the cerebellum is well understood, thorough study of plasticity in the vestibulo-ocular reflex should prove fruitful.

Classical Conditioning

The type of learning most frequently studied, in terms of the localization of memory, has been classical conditioning. Because classical conditioning is associative, it is potentially relevant to more complex forms of learning. Classical conditioning also has the advantage of involving stimuli (the conditioned and unconditioned stimuli) that the experimenter can rigorously define and manipulate. Unlike instrumental learning, where behavior is elicited under poorly specified stimulus conditions, classical conditioning involves neural events occurring in a known temporal sequence, which can be analyzed in relation to external events that are under experimental control.

Invertebrates have furnished particularly useful model systems in the cellular analysis of associative learning (Davis and Gillette, 1978; Hoyle, 1979; Alkon, 1984; Chang and Gelperin, 1980; Quinn and Greenspan, 1984; Hawkins and Kandel, 1984). The current number of available invertebrate systems appears adequate for testing the general applicability of newly discovered neural mechanisms, but not so small as to risk missing major mechanisms that invertebrates use during learning.

Classical conditioning in vertebrates has not been studied in so standardized a manner as in invertebrates. More than 10 different systems are now under active study and each laboratory has its favorite species and conditioning paradigm. Rather than try to summarize results from these essentially independent approaches, two cases will be examined in detail to show how cumulative information concerning the loci of memory storage can arise from systematic studies using fixed experimental conditions. These two cases are heart-rate conditioning, with emphasis on the pigeon, and the conditioned nictitating membrane/eyeblink response in the rabbit. Fuller treatments of the neural analysis of classical conditioning appear in several volumes and review articles (Thompson, Berger, and Madden, 1983; Tsukahara, 1981; Woody, 1982; Alkon and Farley, 1984; Thompson, 1986).

One general point should be kept in mind while examining these two specific examples of classical conditioning. An animal subjected to a classical conditioning procedure that involves an aversive unconditioned stimulus (US) will exhibit conditioning in many response systems. The conditioning is *not* limited to the particular response that happens to be of interest, such as limb flexion, eyeblink, pupillary dilation, or heart rate change. The fact that multiple autonomic responses and nonspecific somatic responses are conditioned rapidly (in 5 to 10 trials) reflects what might be called a general arousal response (Weinberger, 1982). The conditioning of specific skeletal responses requires significantly longer training (50 to hundreds of trials), and can develop even as the general arousal response diminishes (Powell, Lipkin, and Milligan, 1974; Schneiderman, 1972). Any particular conditioning experiment therefore represents a complex process that involves many conditioned responses and many neural loci. Even the spinal cord can show plastic modification in a conditioning paradigm (Patterson, 1980). To deal with this complexity, some investigators have attempted to identify the minimal, essential neural circuit required to maintain one particular conditioned response.

Heart-rate Conditioning

In the pigeon, a 6-second period of full-field illumination presented monocularly (CS) is paired with a 0.5 second footshock (US) that immediately follows the CS. The intertrial interval ranges from 2.5 to 5.0 minutes. Compared with either a sequence of CS-alone trials or a sequence of unpaired CS and US presentations, a sequence of paired CS-US trials produces rapid and lasting conditioning of cardiac acceleration in response to the light. The CR develops within 10 trials and reaches maximum within about 40 trials. After training, the CR emerges on each trial during the 6-second CS presentation, reaching a value of about 20 beats/minute above the pre-CS baseline by approximately the fifth second.

D. Cohen (1980; 1984; 1985) and his associates have identified certain neural pathways that support the CR. The visual CS is processed in parallel by three separate visual pathways, which converge on two cortical visual areas (Figure 23). The first pathway leads from the retina to the principal optic nucleus, the avian homologue of the lateral geniculate, and then to the visual Wulst. The second pathway is from the retina to optic tectum, then to nucleus rotundus, and then to the ectostriatum. The third pathway, less well understood, is believed to involve the retina, tectum, thalamus, and cortex near the ectostriatum. Combined lesions of the principal optic nucleus, nucleus rotundus, and the pretectum, or combined lesions of the visual Wulst and ectostriatum, prevented acquisition of the CR.

Development of a CR following repeated CS-US pairings requires that CS and US inputs converge at one or more places in the nervous system. In the case of heart-rate conditioning, the CS and US have ample opportunity to interact early in the visual pathways. In the principal optic nucleus, all the neurons proved responsive to the CS before training, and 88% were responsive to the US. The nuclei in at least two of these visual pathways, the principal optic nucleus and the nucleus rotundus, showed training-induced changes in their response to the CS. Efforts to isolate the US input have proven partly successful. Locus coeruleus lesions eliminated from the principal optic nucleus one type of single-unit response to the US (D. Cohen, 1984). Because these responses appeared to be the same ones that were plastic during conditioning, locus coeru-

CONDITIONED STIMULUS PATH

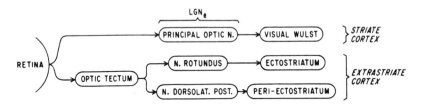

INTRATELENCEPHALIC PATH

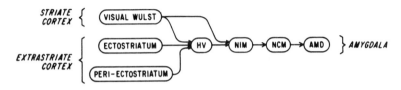

DESCENDING (CONDITIONED RESPONSE) PATH

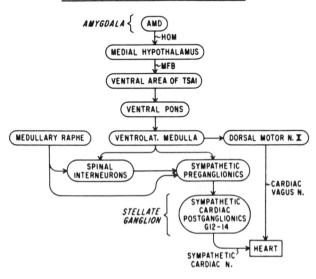

leus lesions would be expected to abolish the plasticity of these responses in the principal optic nucleus. However, the question of whether the locus coeruleus contributes US information important for neural plasticity at a particular neural site is quite different from whether the locus coeruleus is important for the conditioning of whole behavior, as revealed by the behavioral response under study. In the rabbit, locus coeruleus lesions had no effect on the acquisition of the conditioned nictitating membrane response (McCormick and Thompson, 1982). Preliminary data suggest that the same holds true for the pigeon: Locus coeruleus lesions appear not to interfere with whole animal conditioning of the heart-rate response (D.H. Cohen, personal communication). Hence there must exist US inputs to the pathways processing the conditioned stimulus other than from the locus coeruleus.

In the pigeon, a tentative pathway for processing the CS has been proposed from the visual cortical areas to reach the posterior-mediale archistriatum, the avian homologue of the amygdala. It is proposed that from there, the essential pathway projects to the medial hypothalamus via the tractus occipitomesencephalicus, pars hypothalami, and then via the ventral brain stem to the dorsal motor nucleus of the vagus (for the

---

Figure 23. Schematic diagram of pathways for visually conditioned heart rate change in the pigeon. The upper panel summarizes the visual pathways that transmit conditioned stimulus information (whole-field illumination). Each of the three ascending pathways (one to the thalamus and two to the tectum) is capable of transmitting effective conditioned stimulus information, but interruption of all three in combination prevents acquisition of the conditioned response. The brackets indicate equivalent mammalian structures. The middle panel describes schematically the route by which the telencephalic targets of the conditioned stimulus pathway ultimately access the portion of the avian amygdalar homologue that is considered the start of the descending pathway mediating expression of the conditioned response. The lower panel illustrates this descending (conditioned response) pathway. Abbreviations: AMD, Nucleus archistriatum mediale, pars dorsalis; HOM, Tractus occipitomesencephalicus, pars hypothalami; HV, Hyperstriatum ventrale; MFB, Medial forebrain bundle; NCM, Neostriatum caudale, pars mediale; NIM, Neostriatum intermedium, pars mediale; VENTROLAT. MEDULLA, Ventrolateral medulla. (From Cohen, 1985.)

cells of origin of vagal cardiac fibers) and to the last three cervical segments of the spinal cord (for the cells of origin of the right sympathetic cardiac nerve).

Even large lesions of the caudal brain stem did not affect the CR (Durkovic and Cohen, 1969). Lesions of the amygdala, its hypothalamic projection (Cohen, 1975), or its terminal field in the hypothalamus (Cohen and MacDonald, 1976) did prevent, or greatly retard, CR acquisition. Similar results for heart-rate conditioning have been obtained in the mammal following lesions of the amygdala central nucleus or medial hypothalamus (Kapp, Gallagher, Applegate, and Frysinger, 1982; Smith, Astley, DeVit, Stein, and Walsh, 1980). The rabbit, unlike the pigeon, exhibits primarily a vagal response (conditioned cardiac deceleration) to tone-shock presentations, and the rabbit has a direct projection from amygdala central nucleus to structures where vagal efferents to the heart arise: the dorsal motor nucleus of the vagus and the nucleus ambiguus (Schwaber, Kapp, Higgin, and Rapp, 1982).

Although amygdala lesions are known to cause changes in emotionality and reduction in fear (Blanchard and Blanchard, 1972), they do not affect unconditioned reflex responsiveness, as measured by flinch thresholds to shock (Russo, Kapp, Holmquist, and Musty, 1976). More to the point, the unconditioned heart-rate response to shock remains largely unaffected by central nucleus lesions that prevent CR acquisition (Kapp, Frysinger, Gallagher, and Haselton, 1979). Thus, in the pigeon, lesions in the sensory pathway for the CS as early as the principal optic nucleus, and as late in the essential circuitry as the amygdala and hypothalamus, can block the CR without affecting the unconditioned response. The critical sites that change during conditioning and that store the acquired information about the meaning of the conditioned stimulus presumably form some subset of the sites between these points.

At some point along the critical pathway, nearer the motoneurons that organize the response under study, lesions would have to affect not only the conditioned response but also the ability to perform the unconditioned response. The regions that exhibit training-induced changes essential for conditioning do not extend far enough downstream to include these sites. If plasticity were to occur in pathways essential for the unconditioned reflex, learning paradigms would not only lead to a CR, but would also change the unconditioned reflex itself. For this reason the

94

motor end of the unconditioned reflex pathway is a highly unlikely location for training-induced plastic modifications.

Even with the final motor path of the reflex pathway excluded from consideration, there exist multiple possible sites of convergence of CS and US information and multiple possible sites where plastic change could occur. For heart-rate conditioning, the precise location of these sites remains unknown. It is also possible that the essential plastic changes are limited to a small part of the essential circuitry and then passed along unmodified through other parts. Finding that a lesion abolishes the CR could imply that essential training-induced modifications existed in the damaged structure, or that the essential modifications occurred at site(s) upstream from the lesion. Whether the sites of modification are multiple or few is a fundamental question whose resolution would almost certainly illuminate the more general question of how all classical conditioning occurs in the brain.

Conditioning of the Nictitating Membrane/Eyeblink Response

The nictitating membrane/eyeblink response in the rabbit is conditioned by pairing a 350 msec tone CS with a 100 msec corneal airpuff (US). The CS is presented alone for 250 msec and terminates with the US. The intertrial interval is 30 or 60 seconds, with 120 trials given each day. CS-alone trials are scheduled every few trials in order to assess the progress of conditioning. The conditioned response (CR) consists of an extension of the nictitating membrane and an eyeblink. The CR develops substantially during a single session, and after 150–200 trials it achieves an amplitude nearly equal to that of the unconditioned response. The eyeblink initially occurs together with the airpuff US and then moves forward temporally during training until it occurs before the US. The eyeblink CR thereby functions adaptively as preparation for the airpuff.

Proceeding from previous findings that decorticate rabbits can learn the CR (Oakley and Russell, 1972; Moore, Yeo, Oakley, and Russell, 1980), Thompson and his colleagues have sought to identify the essential circuitry responsible for maintaining the CR (McCormick, Clark, Lavond, and Thompson, 1982; McCormick and Thompson, 1984; Thompson, 1986). Lesions of the cerebellum ipsilateral to the trained eye both abolished the CR and prevented its reacquisition by the same eye (Figure

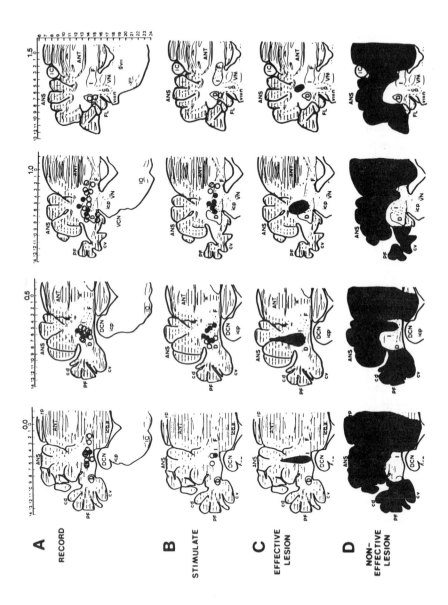

24). Bilateral lesions proved equally disruptive and abolished the CR from either eye. Several large lesions restricted to cerebellar cortex did not eliminate the CR. Lesions of the lateral dentate nucleus or the fastigial nuclei likewise did not eliminate the CR. The effective lesions either damaged two deep nuclei, the medial dentate and interpositus nuclei of the cerebellum, which receive projections from the Purkinje cells of cerebellar cortex, or damaged the superior cerebellar peduncle, the main efferent pathway of the deep nuclei. Pretraining lesions prevented acquisition of the CR. None of the effective lesions disturbed the unconditioned response, that is, the eyeblink in reponse to the airpuff, and none affected the animal's ability to learn via the contralateral eye. The smallest lesion that has produced this disruptive effect involved one cubic millimeter of tissue in the lateral interpositus nucleus (Lavond, Hembree, and Thompson, 1985; Figure 25).

The fact that the unconditioned response remained intact after these lesions shows that the lesions did not interfere with motor pathways necessary for performance of the eyeblink or for sensory processing of the

Figure 24. Essential involvement of deep cerebellar nuclei in the classically conditioned eyelid response. *A.* Sites where unit recordings did (filled circles) or did not (open circles) respond in relation to the amplitude and time course of the learned response. The large numbers above each section represent millimeters anterior to lambda. The small numbers above each section represent millimeters lateral to midline. The small numbers to the side represent millimeters below bone at lambda. *B.* Sites where stimulation did (filled circles) or did not (open circles) elicit eyeblink responses. *C.* A lesion of the dentate and interpositus nuclei that abolished the learned eyeblink response to a tone without affecting the unconditioned eyeblink response to an airpuff. *D.* Composite of three lesions that were not effective in abolishing the learned response. Abbreviations: Ans, ansiform lobule (crus I and crus II); Ant, anterior lobule; Fl, flocculus; D, dentate nucleus; DCN, dorsal cochlear nucleus; F, fastigial nucleus; I, interpositus nucleus; IC, inferior colliculus; IO, inferior olive; lob a, lobulus A (nodulus); PF, paraflocculus; VN, vestibular nuclei; CD, dorsal crus; CV, ventral crus; G VII, genu of the facial nerve; ICP, inferior cerebellar penduncle; VII, facial nucleus; VCN, ventral cochlear nucleus. (From McCormick and Thompson, 1984.)

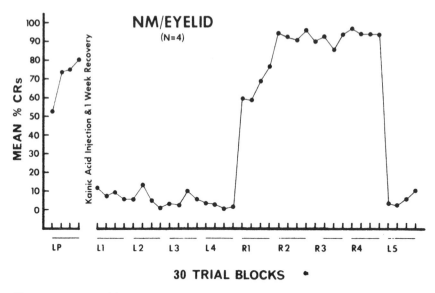

Figure 25. Loss of the nictitating membrane (NM), conditioned eyelid response in the rabbit following a 1 cubic millimeter lesion of the left dorsolateral part of the interpositus nucleus of the cerebellum. Performance of the left eye was good on the last day of paired CS-US training (LP) before the lesion. L1-4, 4 days of training on the left eye after the lesion show that the CR was abolished and not relearned. R1-4, 4 days of training on the right eye after the lesion show initial savings (R1) and further learning. L5, final day of training on the left eye without improvement. Each data point shows the average score for 30 trials. (From Lavond, Hembree, and Thompson, 1985.)

airpuff US. Earlier studies eliminated the primary auditory relay nuclei as possible sites of plasticity (Kettner and Thompson, 1982). The cerebellum may therefore be involved in some aspect of processing the CS, and the interpositus nucleus of the cerebellum may constitute at least one site where the CS and the US are associated. Some of the lesion results have been replicated using a light CS and a periorbital shock US (Yeo, Hardiman, Glickstein, and Russell, 1982). In addition, larger cerebellar lesions abolished a classically conditioned hindlimb flexion reflex using tone and shock (Donegan, Lowry, and Thompson, 1983). It therefore appears likely that the neural sites identified in these studies may be essential for classical conditioning of any skeletal musculature, at least for those involving an aversive US. However, these sites are probably *not* involved in autonomic conditioning, since cerebellar lesions that abolished classically conditioned skeletal musculature responses had no effect on the classically conditioned heart-rate response.

Recordings from the dentate/interpositus nuclei identified cells that respond both to the CS and US during learning and that alter their firing in parallel with behavioral learning. Such cells would be expected to exist there if the dentate/interpositus nuclei are places where the CS and US are associated. Some cells increased their discharge frequency in a way that modeled both the amplitude and the time course of the behavioral CR. After training the peak unit activity in these cells preceded the behavioral CR by 45–55 msec. Stimulation of dentate/interpositus nuclei in both trained and untrained animals elicited eyeblinks.

Subsequent studies suggested how CS and US information might arrive at the cerebellum. Rostral-medial inferior olive lesions result in a deficit that could not be distinguished from behavioral extinction (McCormick, Steinmetz, and Thompson, 1985). Moreover, behavioral conditioning develops when the tone CS is paired, not with the usual airpuff US, but with direct electrical stimulation of the dorsal accessory nucleus of the inferior olive (Mauk, Steinmetz, and Thompson, 1986). This result suggests that the reinforcing or teaching US input reaches the cerebellum through the climbing fibers, which originate in the inferior olive. In another study stimulation of the mossy fibers at their cells of origin in the dorsolateral pontine nucleus and the lateral reticular nucleus served as an effective CS when airpuff was used as US (Steinmetz, Lavond, and Thompson, 1985). Thus the mossy fiber input to cerebellum could serve as one source of CS input. These results suggest that CS and US information could be associated and stored in both cerebellar cortex and in the interpositus nuclei, since convergence of mossy fibers and climbing fibers occurs in both places.

Work by Yeo and his colleagues (Yeo, Hardiman, and Glickstein, 1984) suggested that areas of cerebellar cortex, which project to the interpositus nucleus, are essential for classical conditioning of the nictitating membrane response. They reported that lesions limited to the hemispheral part of lobule VI (HVI), a rostral and relatively inaccessible part of the cerebellum, abolished the conditioned reflex and prevented relearning. The training paradigm used in this series of studies differed in several ways from that used by Thompson and his colleagues, and fur-

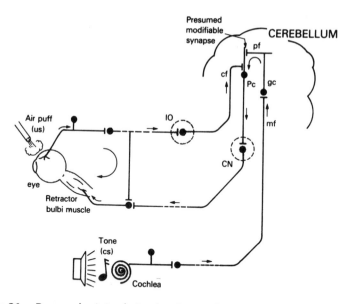

Figure 26. Proposed minimal circuitry for conditioning of the rabbit nictitating membrane reflex. An airpuff to the eye (US) is signaled to cerebellar Purkinje cells (PC) via the climbing fibers (cf), which originate in the inferior olive (IO). The tone (CS) is also signaled to the Purkinje cells through mossy fibers (mf), the cerebellar granule cells (gc), and the parallel fibers (pf). Modification at the putative plastic synapse (pf to Purkinje cell) would depend on properly timed activity in cf and pf. The Purkinje cells project to the cerebellar deep nuclei (CN: dentate and interpositus nuclei) and then on to the motor neurons mediating the eyelid response. (From Gellman and Miles, 1985.)

ther work will be needed to determine when area HVI of the cerebellum is essential to classical conditioning and whether these effects are permanent.

The cerebellar deep nuclei, afferent connections to cerebellum via mossy and climbing fibers, and efferent connections through the superior cerebellar peduncle appear to form part of the essential circuitry for performance of the CR (Figure 26). However, identification of neural sites essential for performing the CR by no means proves that the critical neural modifications actually occur there, though that certainly is a possibility. Other possibilities are that the neural modifications occur in regions afferent to the cerebellum (for example, the inferior olive and/or pontine nuclei), which send projections to the deep cerebellar nuclei via the middle cerebellar peduncle (McCormick and Thompson, 1984) or

100

that the deep nuclei and the Purkinje cells of the cerebellum are just two of several sites within a CS-related pathway where neural modifications take place. The contralateral red nucleus, generally considered to be efferent to the cerebellum, is unlikely to be the critical locus of plastic change, because the neural changes correlated to the CR already exist in the cerebellum. However, the red nucleus does send a projection back to the interpositus nucleus, so that the red nucleus could be one of several locations, including the cerebellum, where modifications occur. All these alternatives are amenable to experimental test.

It could turn out that plastic change occurs during classical conditioning at only one or two critical sites in the nervous system, or there could be many such sites. Whichever hypothesis proves correct, the evidence demonstrates that classical conditioning of skeletal musculature in vertebrates requires specific and relatively limited neural circuitry. Structures other than the cerebellar nuclei, such as auditory neocortex and hippocampus, do exhibit correlated neural activity during CR acquisition (Berger and Thompson, 1978; Disterhoft, Shipley, and Kraus, 1982). Nonetheless, removal of these structures does not affect acquisition (Solomon and Moore, 1975; Oakley and Russell, 1972). The correlated activity present in hippocampus and auditory cortex during conditioning must mean that these structures are involved during learning, but not in a way that is essential to expression of the CR itself. One possibility is that these structures are involved in processing and remembering aspects of the learning event that are not expressed in the CR. For example, these structures might help animals remember the room in which conditioning occurs.

The point is that many brain regions normally participate during classical conditioning and also exhibit long-lasting modifications as a result of the conditioning procedure, but only some of these regions are essential to the acquisition and maintenance of a specific CR such as the nictitating membrane/eyeblink response. A still smaller number of regions may be necessary to maintain the response after its acquisition. For example, morphine abolished a freshly learned CR, presumably as a function of its effects on conditioned fear (Mauk, Warren, and Thompson, 1982). But morphine had no effect on an overtrained CR, which presumably had become sufficiently autonomous not to depend on conditioned fear.

Even though any particular CS and US pair does result in a specific conditioned response, the same CS can be potentially paired with many different USs, and the same US can be potentially paired with many different CSs. Therefore many potential points of convergence must exist. If many sites of plastic change exist even for a single CS and US, perhaps the information that is encoded at each point reflects a particular aspect of what has been learned. In the case of heart-rate conditioning to a light CS in the pigeon, the neural modifications observed early in the visual pathway might be identical even if the US were an airpuff to the face rather than a shock to the foot. These early neural changes could represent the fact that the CS has attained some degree of significance, although they might not represent any information about which motor responses would be adaptive in that particular circumstance (Weinberger, Diamond, and McKenna, 1984).

At least some neural changes appear to occur early in sensory pathways during conditioning. During the conditioning of rabbits to perform a wheel-turning response to a tone CS in order to avoid shock (Gabriel, Miller, and Saltwich, 1976), and also during pupillary conditioning of cats to a tone CS/shock US (Ryugo and Weinberger, 1978), altered discharge frequency in response to the CS appeared in multiple-unit recordings in the magnocellular part of the medial geniculate nucleus. This area is a nonlemniscal component of the ascending thalamo-cortical auditory pathway, not a part of the classic thalamo-cortical projection. It projects directly to a number of subcortical areas, including the central nucleus of the amygdala (LeDoux, Sakaguchi, and Reis, 1984). In rats given tone-shock pairs the conditioned heart-rate response to tone was highly attenuated following lesions of the entire medial geniculate nucleus. The unconditioned emotional responses to shock were not affected (Le Doux, Sakaguhi, and Reis, 1984). To determine the importance of the magnocellular portion of the medial geniculate to classical conditioning, lesions should be placed in this region separately. How critical these changes in sensory pathways are to the formation of the behavioral CR remains unclear. Training-induced changes beyond the sensory pathways are of course found as well, and they are probably significant in determining the specific response that will be made to the CS. For heart-rate conditioning, the neural modifications determining the motor response could occur in the amygdala, hypothalamus, and/or brain stem.

102

The conditioning of nictitating membrane and other skeletal musculature, particularly in the overtrained animal, probably provides the best opportunity for finding the essential neural pathways needed to maintain a specific CR. Unlike autonomic conditioning, which occurs rapidly and extends to many response systems besides the system being traced, the overtrained conditioned eyeblink response is relatively circumscribed and can be stable after signs of autonomic conditioning have diminished. In studying the problem of where memory is stored, a useful simplification can be achieved by aiming to identify the minimal essential circuitry needed to maintain a particular CR, and temporarily ignoring other types of learning that occur at the same time. Following the same strategy, other processes can also be excluded, which may be necessary to support initial acquisition. Within the minimal circuitry needed for maintenance of a CR, one can expect to find the essential neural modifications underlying long-term behavioral change.

Another way to explore the location of plastic modifications is furnished by reduced preparations, where one or more elements of classical conditioning (CS, US, and UCR) are defined not as externally observable behavioral events such as tones, shocks, and muscle movements, but as a neurophysiological event within the nervous system (Tsukahara, Oda, and Notsu, 1981). This approach can assist in determining how classical conditioning occurs and can simplify cellular/neurophysiological studies. However, this approach risks the error of concentrating on pathways and synaptic junctions that are not essential to learning, and perhaps not actually used when the whole animal learns. It seems best to begin with real behavior and natural stimuli, moving toward increasingly reduced preparations only to the extent that pathways and nuclei in the nervous system can be tied to the original CS, US, and UCR.

For classical conditioning in vertebrates, a general outline of the organization of critical neural pathways appears almost within reach. The need now is for a concrete concept concerning the interaction of neural pathways carrying CS and US information that could guide experimental work, a credible framework within which to fit the accumulating data. A specific mechanism for classical conditioning has recently been described in the invertebrate *Aplysia* (Walters and Byrne, 1983; Hawkins, Abrams, Carew, and Kandel, 1983). In the *Aplysia* a CS-specific pathway is contacted by a second pathway carrying US information. The CS pathway can be potentiated if the US pathway is stimulated just after activation of the CS pathway. The potentiated CS pathway then makes direct contact with the motoneurons mediating the behavioral response. This principle might also be used by vertebrates, as suggested by D. Cohen (1984), although in vertebrates the route from the sensory-specific, CS pathways to the motoneurons must be polysynaptic and less direct than in *Aplysia*. Alternatively, other mechanisms may exist. For example, additional mechanisms would seem to be required to explain how in vertebrates classical conditioning can involve the emergence of a new conditioned response, not just the amplification through US presentation of a response that was already weakly elicited by the CS. In vertebrates, it should soon be possible to identify the separate sources of critical CS and US information and their site(s) of convergence at one or more places critical for storing information (see Figure 26). Knowledge of this scheme could lead to more detailed study of the cellular events underlying conditioning and could provide the single greatest clue to the description of the neural organization of the conditioned response.

Imprinting

Filial imprinting in the domestic chick has provided a focus for studies of memory localization during the past two decades (Horn, 1981; Bateson, 1984; Horn, 1985). Chicks develop an attachment toward any visually conspicuous object exposed to them soon after hatching, and later exhibit a preference toward such objects in comparison with other novel objects. Quantitative studies were done 16–24 hours after hatching in which chicks were exposed to an imprinting stimulus for about 2 hours. While exposed to the imprinting stimulus (either a rotating, illuminated box or a rotating, stuffed bird), each chick remained inside a running wheel that turned as the click moved. The number of revolutions made by the wheel as the chick tried to approach the imprinting stimulus gave a measure of the intensity of approach activity. One or two days later, chicks were placed in the wheel for 2-minute test periods during presentation of either the imprinted or the alternate stimulus. The number of wheel rotations in response to each stimulus provided the measure of preference. Normal chicks exhibited more than three times the approach activity to the imprinted stimulus as compared to the unfamiliar stimulus.

Biochemical studies of a small area of the anterior forebrain roof identified the intermediate zone of the medial hyperstriatum ventrali (IMHV) as metabolically active during imprinting. Increased incorporation of uracil into macromolecules furnished the best-studied index of biochemical activity. Certain nonspecific influences could be ruled out. For example, the magnitude of the biochemical change correlated with the measure of preference at retest, but not with measures of behavior such as the amount of locomotor activity during imprinting. In one particularly useful control test, chicks received various amounts of training on the first day. Determinations of uracil incorporation were then made on the second day, while chicks received a fixed amount of additional training. The extent of incorporation was greatest for chicks that had been undertrained on the first day, presumably because they could accomplish the most learning on the second day. Because all groups approached the imprinting stimulus with equal vigor on the second day, these results could not be attributed to differences in activity. A second control test used split-brain chicks that were prepared with section of the supra-optic commissure and then trained with one eye covered. No transfer of learning occurred when chicks were tested via the untrained eye. These split-brain chicks exhibited increased uracil incorporation only in the hemisphere receiving input from the eye open during training.

A series of lesion studies were next done, based on the finding just described that a small area of the chick forebrain is linked to imprinting. Bilateral lesions of the IMHV either before or within 3 hours following training abolished the imprinted response permanently (McCabe, Horn, and Bateson, 1981; McCabe, Cipolla-Neto, Horn, and Bateson, 1982). This effect proved to be specific, in the sense that the lesions produced no effect on several other measures of visual capacity: the time required to peck a moving bead, the accuracy and quality of pecking at an array of seeds, and the ability to learn a visual pattern discrimination to obtain heat reinforcement. Chicks could even learn to discriminate between the stimuli employed in the imprinting experiments. These results suggest that the IMHV is a storage site for the information acquired during imprinting but that it is not needed for certain other kinds of learning.

Two recent findings have complicated the idea that the IMHV is a storage site. First, a bilateral lesion of IMHV effectively abolishes preference for the imprinted stimulus when the lesion is made 3 hours after imprinting, but not when it is delayed 26 hours after imprinting. Second, left and right IMHV do not equivalently participate in imprinting (Horn, McCabe, and Cipolla-Neto, 1983; Cipolla-Neto, Horn, and McCabe, 1982). Asymmetric effects were found if sequential, unilateral lesions were placed in IMHV three hours and 26 hours after imprinting was complete. If the left lesion was made 3 hours after training, the imprinted response survived both this lesion as well as a right lesion made 26 hours after training. However, if the right lesion was made 3 hours after training, the imprinted response survived the first lesion but was then lost following an additional, left lesion 26 hours after training. If the first lesion was made before training, the imprinted response was lost after the delayed second lesion, regardless of the order in which the two lesions were made.

These rather surprising results suggested that the left IMHV is a storage site for learning during imprinting, while the right IMHV is needed only to establish memory in another, as yet unidentified, area. Furthermore, the work of the right IMHV requires at least 3 hours (Horn, McCabe, and Cipolla-Neto, 1983). An additional finding consistent with this idea is that exposure to an imprinting stimulus for 2 or 3 hours, but not 20 minutes, produced measurable morphological changes in left IMHV. The overall length of the postsynaptic density of dendritic spine synapses increased by 17.2% (Horn, 1985). No changes were observed in the right IMHV. While these results are unambiguous in their support for the idea that the left and right sides of the brain are differently involved in imprinting, it is not yet entirely clear how the two sides participate. Perhaps each IMHV is involved in storing information someplace else, but with different time courses. Detailed studies of the time course of all the lesion effects will help sort out the possibilities. Split-brain chicks with unilateral lesions could also provide information concerning the separate role that each hemisphere plays in the storage of memory at different times after learning.

The present uncertainty about the specific role that the left and right IMHV plays in imprinting should not obscure a more general lesson about memory and the brain that can be learned from this interesting series of experiments. Whereas the IMHV, and particularly the left IMHV, is required to acquire and maintain the imprinting response, the IMHV is not necessary for forming other kinds of associations, even associations between motor responses and the imprinting stimulus itself (Horn, 1985). The function of IMHV is probably not so narrow as to be concerned only with imprinting because this structure shows signs of increased metabolic activity during one-trial, inhibitory avoidance learning (Kossut and Rose, 1984). Nevertheless, the function of IMHV in memory is limited to only some kinds of learning and memory.

One possibility is that it is required to form central representations of the external world, which can then be used in a flexible way to direct behavior. At the same time, it is not needed to form simple associations, which depend on incremental changes in specific behaviors. Horn (1985) describes this idea in the following way:

> When an animal learns to associate a stimulus with a reward two things may happen. A habit is established and need consist of little more than the strengthening of connections between receptors activated by the stimulus and neurons controlling the response which the animal emits. In the normal course of events it is likely that, in addition, the animal recognizes the stimulus which it associates with the response . . . (p. 124).

By this view imprinting depends on an acquired representation whereby the imprinted stimulus can be recognized as familiar. Other kinds of acquired behavior involving the imprinted stimulus can proceed without recognition of familiarity, by virtue of the stimulus having formed associations with specific responses. The same dissociation, or a similar one, is reflected in the distinction between habit and memory, which emerges from studies of memory in nonhuman primates (Mishkin, Malamut, and Bachevalier, 1984); and in the distinction between declarative and procedural knowledge, which emerges from studies of human amnesic patients (N. Cohen, 1984; Squire, 1986). These ideas are developed more fully in Chapter 11.

Imprinting may prove to be a special type of learning, one that occurs naturally during a sensitive period in early life, and requires no special rewards. An animal exposed to an object early in life simply develops a preference for that object. In these respects, imprinting exhibits striking similarities to other kinds of early learning. In many bird species, for example, song development depends on experience, a phenomenon ex-

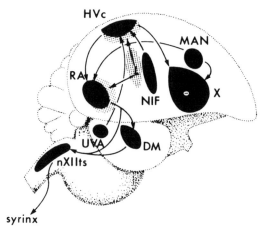

Figure 27. Schematic diagram of the vocal control system in songbirds, parts of which show seasonal fluctuations in size corresponding to fluctuations in singing. Arrows indicate anterograde connections between nuclei. Neural signals for song originate in NIF (nucleus interfacialis) and end at the vocal organ, the syrinx, via HVc (nucleus hyperstriatum ventrale, pars caudale), RA (nucleus robustus archistriatalis), DM (dorsomedial nucleus of nucleus intercollicularis), and nX11ts (nucleus hypoglossus, pars tracheosyringealis), in that order. Other nuclei (MAN = magnocellular nucleus of the anterior neostriatum, X = area X, and UVA = nucleus uva) are inactive during vocalization. Hatched areas indicate known projection zones of the telencephalic auditory area (Field L). (From Konishi, 1984.)

tensively studied by ethologists (Marler, 1984) and more recently by neuroscientists (Nottebohm, 1980; Konishi, 1985). Exploration of the neural basis of learning in these natural situations, which have great significance for the species, seems a very useful strategy. In these cases, plasticity is likely to occur in specialized processing systems, specifically in the neural circuitry involved in song production (Figure 27). Furthermore, it may prove easier to obtain information about the neural basis of so essential a behavior as song learning in birds than to obtain information about more arbitrary types of learning, because the brain presumably has dedicated considerable resources to insuring its success. Finally, the mechanisms that the nervous system uses to accomplish these biologically significant types of learning may well be general ones, which are also used in accomplishing other types of learning.

8

Searching for Engrams:
Complex Learning

Everyone would probably agree that the search for engrams is easiest when relatively simple learning tasks can be used, especially when both the stimuli causing the behavioral change and the response demonstrating the change can be brought under rigorous experimental control. Nevertheless, great interest also exists in the neurobiology of complex forms of learning. Although this work has necessarily proceeded slowly, a considerable amount has been learned. This chapter focuses first on brightness discrimination learning, then on examples of more complex learning, especially visual object learning. The latter, it is argued, provides the best evidence yet available for the idea that some kinds of information are stored in neocortex.

Brightness Discrimination

Lashley's (1929) cortical lesion studies were among the first to examine carefully the brightness discrimination task, and work with this task continued most notably in the laboratories of Meyer and Meyer (1977) and of Robert Thompson (1969; 1976). The learning of a discrimination habit based on the ability to distinguish black from white cards depends critically on posterior neocortex in both rat and monkey (Lashley, 1929; Kluver, 1942). The posterior neocortex relevant to brightness discrimination performance includes striate cortex together with much of the immediately adjacent circumstriate cortex (Pasik and Pasik, 1982; Meyer and Meyer, 1977). Removal of posterior neocortex abolishes the discrimination habit. It can be relearned, but then the discrimination depends upon the ability to distinguish differences in total luminous flux rather than differences in brightness (flux per unit area). It turns out that the ability to discriminate on the basis of brightness, rather than on the basis of total flux, does depend on the neocortex. However, the capacity for flux discrimination is independent of neocortex.

The distinction between brightness and flux is crucial for understanding the experimental work in this area. Having learned a black-white card discrimination, for example, approach the black card (but not the white card) to obtain reward or escape mild footshock, rats could relearn it following a posterior cortical lesion. However, they required more trials to relearn than were necessary for original acquisition of the task (Bauer and Cooper, 1964). In another laboratory, relearning a black-white card discrimination after posterior cortex removal has been reported to require exactly the same number of trials as were required for original learning (Meyer and Meyer, 1977). In contrast, rats who learned to distinguish lightness from darkness, instead of white from black cards, were only partially disrupted by a posterior cortical lesion, and required *fewer* trials to relearn the task than were required originally. Apparently, light versus dark discrimination tasks encourage the development of a discrimination based on flux cues, which survive the posterior cortical lesion, whereas white and black cards encourage the use of brightness cues. In support of this idea, rats who learned to distinguish light from dark while wearing translucent plastic cups over their eyes, in order to force dependence on flux cues, retained fully the light-dark habit following posterior cortex removal (Bauer and Cooper, 1964). Translucent occluders presumably required the rats to make judgments based on the total luminous flux coming from one direction of gaze, and prevented them from making brightness judgments.

The common interpretation of these results is that in normal rats the posterior neocortex stores essential aspects of the brightness discrimination habit, while subcortical structures are responsible for discrimination based on luminous flux. Although this conclusion seems approximately correct, in the case of the brightness discrimination habit the question remains whether subcortical structures might participate along with neocortex. Because anterior neocortical lesions do not affect retention of brightness discrimination habits (Thompson, 1960), any areas participating in brightness discrimination learning other than posterior neocortex must be subcortical.

One point of view has been that, so far as brightness discrimination habits are concerned, memory storage is largely if not entirely subcortical, and cortical lesions cause only a retrieval deficit. This idea derives in part from the report that amphetamine facilitates recovery of a previously learned brightness discrimination habit following posterior cortical lesions, even though the same dose has no effect on initial learning of the discrimination in operated animals (Braun, Meyer, and Meyer, 1966). However, this effect is minimal and has been difficult to replicate (Jonason, Lauber, Robbins, Meyer, and Meyer, 1970).

The idea that the neocortex does not store brightness discrimination habits also came from a study of reversal training (LeVere and Morlock, 1973). This study was founded on the idea that, if the brightness discrimination habit were forgotten completely after posterior cortical lesions, rats should be able to reverse the original discrimination in about the same number of trials as were required to learn originally. (Reversal learning entails learning a second discrimination, but with the originally "correct" stimulus made "incorrect" and vice versa). However, if the original habit had not been completely forgotten, then information about the original habit that remained after the lesion would have to be unlearned before the reversal could be acquired. As a result reversal learning would be slower than original learning.

The results were that rats were significantly retarded in acquiring the reversal task compared to the original task, suggesting that a considerable amount of information about the habit survived the posterior cortical lesion. On the face of it, this result would suggest that brightness discrimination habits are stored subcortically to a significant extent. However, the task used in this study was a discrimination between light and no light, not a discrimination between black and white cards; and the light-dark discrimination is known to survive posterior lesions quite well (Bauer and Cooper, 1964). Therefore, in the study under discussion the original task probably did not depend fully on neocortex in the first place. It survived the lesion and interfered with reversal learning. The question thus remains whether reversal learning after posterior lesions would be retarded at all if original learning involved black and white cards. In summary, the evidence for exclusively subcortical memory storage of brightness discrimination habits is far from compelling.

An alternative interpretation of all the data is that the brightness discrimination habit is stored in both posterior cortex and in subcortical structures. One type of evidence supporting this conclusion was based on studies of animals with surgical section of the corpus callosum, the so-called split-brain preparation. Complete transfer of brightness discrimination tasks from the trained to the untrained eye has been reported in studies with split-brain rats, cats, and monkeys (Black and Myers, 1968; Meikle and Sechzer, 1960; Trevarthen, 1962). However, distinct limits on such transfer have also been reported (Butler, 1968; Peck, Crewther, and Hamilton, 1979). Most significant, however, is the fact that unlike the consistent failure to find any transfer for visual pattern discrimination tasks, *some* transfer of brightness discrimination tasks appears possible. One large study of monkeys reported 24% transfer of the brightness discrimination task (Peck, Crewther, and Hamilton, 1979). A study of albino rats, which compared brightness discrimination and pattern discrimination, showed 54% transfer of the brightness task but only 19% of the pattern task (Sheridan, 1965). In cats and rats for whom section of corpus callosum was supplemented by deeper sections that included the posterior commissure and the commissure of the superior colliculus, no transfer of brightness discrimination was found (Hoffman, Sheridan, and Levinson, 1981; Meikle, 1964).

These studies together suggest that a large part of the brightness discrimination task, that is, the part that fails to transfer, is stored cortically, but the remainder is stored subcortically. Simply stated, the brightness discrimination habit depends on subcortical structures more than the pattern discrimination habit. This interpretation also gains support from the finding that lesions of nucleus posterior thalami (now called anterior pretectal nucleus [Scalia, 1972]) proved more debilitating to the brightness habit than to the pattern discrimination habit (Thompson and Rich, 1963).

A series of lesion studies in the rat (Thompson, 1969, 1976, 1978)

112

have addressed the question of which particular subcortical areas participate in storage of the brightness discrimination habit. More than 600 rats learned to discriminate black from white cards, with eight trials given daily at intervals of 60 seconds. After rats had achieved a learning criterion of no more than one error on two consecutive days, they were subjected to lesions in one of 50 different brain structures. Two to three weeks after surgery, animals were retrained to criterion. This study therefore explored virtually the entire brain from cortex through the mesencephalon.

Posterior neocortex, posterior diencephalon, and ventral mesencephalon proved to be the only brain regions where lesions consistently and severely disrupted retention of brightness discrimination. Because the lesions tended to be large, it was difficult to identify them with specific nuclei or tracts. The posterior diencephalic lesion sites included the lateral geniculate, nucleus posterior thalami (i.e., anterior pretectal nucleus), nucleus parafascicularis, the subthalamic nucleus, and the zona incerta. Ventral mesencephalic sites were the red nucleus, substantia nigra, the lateral half of the cerebral peduncle at the level of the substantia nigra, the ventral tegmental area, and the interpeduncular nucleus. Lesions in other brain areas, including superior colliculus, caudate-putamen, and dorsal midbrain, produced no effect on retention of brightness discrimination. The results were virtually identical if the brightness discrimination habit was motivated by thirst rather than by foot shock (Thompson and Spiliotis, 1981).

In interpreting these results, a difficulty arises from the fact that in most cases the effective lesions that abolished brightness discrimination did not prevent relearning. This was so even for rats with combined lesions of the striate cortex and nucleus posterior thalami (anterior pretectal nucleus) (Thompson and Rich, 1963). Moreover, when relearning did occur, it was unclear whether performance still relied on brightness cues to any extent or whether performance now depended on luminous flux cues. Which of the identified brain regions are *essential* for retention of the brightness discrimination habit in the rat therefore remains uncertain.

Pasik and his colleagues (Pasik and Pasik, 1982) attempted to identify which structures in the monkey must be damaged to abolish permanently the ability to learn or maintain brightness discriminations. In some cases, these studies involved flux-equated stimuli in order to assure that animals were discriminating on the basis of brightness alone. Ablations of circumstriate cortex, superior colliculus, or pulvinar in addition to striate cortex proved sufficient to abolish brightness discrimination habits permanently. This demonstrates that in addition to the geniculo-striate pathway, the visual pathway involving retina-colliculus-pulvinar-circumstriate cortex can support brightness discrimination. Many of the neural changes constituting acquired information about brightness probably occur in these two systems. In addition, the results in rats suggest that ventral mesencephalic structures, located caudal to the thalamus and colliculus, may also be involved.

Like all recent work on the problem of memory localization, these findings emphasize that the sites of memory storage are specific brain regions that belong to specialized brain systems. A "mass action" effect, i.e., one based on the quantity of tissue removed, cannot explain the findings for the brightness discrimination habit. For example, dorsal or lateral mesencephalic lesions did not impair performance even though the size of these lesions far exceeded the effective diencephalic lesions. Retention of visual habits, like retention of the conditioned reflex, depends on a fairly limited amount of brain tissue. The still popular belief that memory for complex habits is distributed throughout the entire brain should be lain to rest once and for all.

Arguments for Cortical Memory Storage

Although simpler forms of behavioral plasticity such as habituation and classical conditioning depend on neural changes in parts of the brain that are phylogenetically old, more complex kinds of learning, such as the brightness discrimination habit just discussed, probably depend on neocortex. The evidence remains indirect, but the conclusion seems almost inescapable that in some cases the neocortex itself must be a a storage site for memory. In addition to the data just reviewed for brightness discrimination habits, a variety of other evidence is relevant to this idea. The evidence includes split-brain experiments, the demonstrated plasticity of individual neurons in neocortex, and studies of inferotemporal cortex and visual memory. These three lines of evidence will be discussed next.

114

Split-Brain Studies

One type of evidence implicating the neocortex as a storage site for complex information comes from studying how the cerebral commissures integrate information. Cats and monkeys with section of optic chiasm and the major forebrain commissures (corpus callosum and anterior commissure) can learn a visual pattern discrimination with one eye and then behave naively with the other eye (Myers, 1955; Sperry, 1961). Hence, the experience can be recorded in one cerebral hemisphere while remaining inaccessible to the other. The fact that the forebrain commissures connect areas of neocortex in each hemisphere makes it reasonable to suppose that the acquired information resides in neocortex. If pattern discrimination habits were stored subcortically to a significant degree, such habits should survive commissurotomy. Certain elemental features of tasks do survive. For example, simple discriminations such as discriminations based on luminous flux or flicker frequency that are acquired through one eye of a split-brain animal are available to the untrained hemisphere (Peck, Crewther, and Hamilton, 1979). Furthermore, split-brain monkeys trained with only one hand on tactile discrimination problems, and then tested for the first time with the untrained hand, showed transfer of the gross reaching movements acquired during training (Glickstein and Sperry, 1960). Transfer of the gross arm movements usually occurred without transfer of fine finger movements or transfer of the acquired tactile discrimination itself.

Sperry (1959) made an attempt to isolate the record of experience within a particular area of neocortex of one hemisphere. Previous observations had demonstrated that split-brain cats who had learned tactile discriminations using one forepaw had to relearn completely using the other forepaw. In split-brain cats prepared with large lesions of right neocortex, and sparing only frontal cortex (including the somatic sensory and motor areas), the spared cortical remnant in the right hemisphere proved capable of supporting retention of preoperatively acquired tactile discriminations. New tactile discriminations could also be learned. The point is that this cortical island supported performance by the left paw, suggesting that memory for the acquired habits was localized in the island. Findings from three cats who sustained lesions of the left frontal sensorimotor area without disturbing discrimination performance ruled

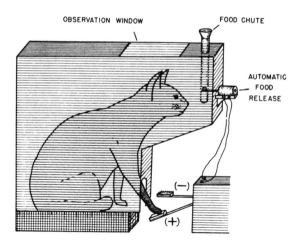

Figure 28. *Top.* Apparatus used by Roger Sperry in his classic cortical island experiments. Cats learned a series of tactile discriminations. The right-left position of the correct pedal was shifted randomly from trial to trial. *Bottom.* Cats were prepared with section of the corpus callosum and hippocampal commissure. Previously acquired tactile discriminations could be performed by the left forepaw and new ones could be learned, even following removal from the right hemisphere of all neocortex except the frontal area shown here. The extent of the removal is shown for four individual animals. Removal of the same area from the left hemisphere abolished performance by the right forepaw. (From Sperry, 1959.)

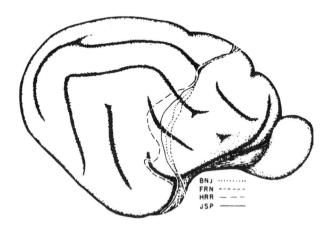

out the participation of the intact left hemisphere. Importantly, one of these three cats received a lesion of left frontal cortex roughly of the same size as the cortical remnant on the right side. Thirty days after surgery, this cat had no difficulty performing with its left paw four previously acquired tactile discriminations (Figure 28).

In one cat, the dependence of performance on the cortical remnant was further demonstrated by the loss of discriminative ability when the cortical remnant itself was damaged. These data do not entirely rule out the possibility that subcortical areas participate in the storage of tactile discrimination habits. Yet this possibility appears unlikely, because these habits can be confined to one hemisphere by section of the corpus callosum and can be completely abolished by cortical damage. Although more extensive cortical tissue may be required to store visual information than to store tactile habits (Sperry, 1961; Nakamura and Mishkin, 1980; Nakamura and Mishkin, 1982), small cortical regions are sufficient in the case of tactile information.

> . . . it would seem safe to infer that the cat is able to perceive, to some extent at least, with only a small island of cortex, and that widespread cortical integration is not essential for perceptual learning and memory (Sperry, 1958, p. 421).

Plasticity of Cortical Neurons

The fact that cortical neurons can be altered by experience (Rosenzweig, 1979; Greenough, 1984a) provides additional support for the hypothesis that the neocortex itself participates in memory storage. A study of learning in normal kittens (Spinelli and Jensen, 1979) provides an interesting example of plasticity in cortical neurons that depends neither upon deprivation, nor upon special rearing conditions, nor upon prolonged special treatment. In this study, kittens learned to raise the forearm to avoid a mild shock that was signaled by the presentation of horizontal or vertical lines. After about 10 weeks of training (8 minutes per day), the area of sensorimotor cortex within which cells responded to forearm shock had become two to six times larger on the side opposite the trained forelimb than on the side opposite the untrained forearm. Furthermore, three-quarters of the cells within trained sensorimotor cortex responded after training to tactile and visual stimuli similar to those used as the conditioned stimulus, whereas only 30% of the cells on the untrained side did so. Finally, in visual association areas, where cells of normal, untrained cats respond to all stimulus orientations with equal probability, cells in the trained kittens responded prominently to stimulus orientations congruent with those used during training.

These changes arose from less than 30 total minutes of exposure to the visual stimulus and less than 30 total minutes of electric shock. Because many of these changes apparently appeared in a control animal who received unpaired presentations of visual stimuli and shock, the extent to to which these changes reflect associative learning processes remains unclear. Nevertheless, it seems clear that experience can influence the physiology of cortex directly and radically. Experience can also change the morphology of cortical neurons. For example, 20–30 hours of maze training given one hour each day had measurable effects on dendritic morphology (Chang and Greenough, 1982).

Inferotemporal Cortex: Visual Processing and Visual Memory Storage

Perhaps the strongest support for the identification of the neocortex as a site of memory storage comes from combined anatomical, physiological, and behavioral information about the visual system. The striate cortex (V1) comprises the first in a sequence of cortical visual areas which includes many extra-striate cortical areas (V2, V3, V3a, V4, MT, PO, FST) and which extends into lateral temporal cortex (area TEO and TE). These extra-striate visual areas allow for numerous representations of the visual field (Allman, 1977; Merzenich and Kaas, 1980) and probably for the analysis of particular stimulus features (Cowey, 1981). Additional information concerning the cortico-cortical connections of the visual system and a discussion of nomenclature can be found in an early review (Gross, 1973). For a more recent discussion, see Ungerleider and Desimone (1986).

The final cortical visual area in the sequence described above is inferotemporal cortex (area TE), which receives projections from many regions of extra-striate cortex, as well as area TEO in temporal cortex (Figure 29). Area TE processes visual information received from the

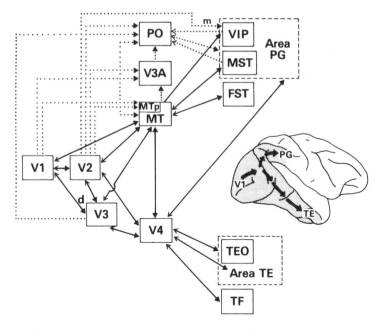

Figure 29. Summary of cortical visual areas and some of their connections. There are two major routes from striate cortex (V1): One follows a ventral route into the temporal lobe via area V4, and the other follows a dorsal route into the parietal lobe via MT. Heavy arrowheads indicate "forward" projections, and light arrowheads indicate "backward" projections. "Intermediate" projections are indicated by two heavy arrowheads. 'd' indicates that the projection is limited to the dorsal portion of the area, 'm' that it is limited to the medial portion. Other potential pathways into the parietal lobe include those carrying input from the peripheral visual field (dotted lines). (From Ungerleider and Desimone, 1986.)

geniculo-striate system still further. The neurons in TE resemble other neurons of the visual system in that they respond only to visual stimuli; they are also sensitive to multiple stimulus parameters (e.g., shape, size, wavelength, orientation, and direction of movement). However, unlike other neurons, neurons in TE have large, often bilateral receptive fields, and their receptive fields always include the fovea (Gross, Roche-Miranda, and Bender, 1972). Moreover, the response of area TE neurons to specific stimuli proceeds largely independently of the location of a visual stimulus within the receptive field, which suggests that they might accomplish stimulus equivalence across retinal locus. In addition, neurons in TE sometimes possess highly specific and complex trigger features. For example, neurons that respond more efficiently to three-dimensional stimuli than two-dimensional ones have been found, while other neurons prove to be so specific in their trigger features that it is difficult to know when an optimal stimulus has been found. Some neurons appear to fire best in response to a silhouette of a hand, to a bottle brush, or to a particular kind of curvature. Other neurons appear selective for faces of a particular orientation. Neurons do not respond selectively to particular faces, but rather to many (but not all) faces, suggesting that the recognition of individual faces is done by collections of neurons working together in an ensemble. Studies of single neurons in area TE of awake, behaving monkeys have shown that, if an adequate stimulus is to elicit neuronal activity, active looking on the part of the animal must occur (Gross, Bender, and Gerstein, 1979). Area TE might therefore be seen as the cortex's highest-level visual processing region, the final stage in the hierarchy of visual information processing that begins in the retina (Ungerleider and Mishkin, 1982).

Excision of area TE in the monkey produces a severe deficit in learning, specific to the visual modality. Discriminations between two-dimensional shapes and patterns learned prior to surgery are lost following TE removal, as are discriminations involving separate visual dimensions, such as color, size, and brightness. These discriminations can be relearned, but such learning requires more training than a normal monkey requires to learn them for the first time (Mishkin, 1966; Pribram, 1967). After surgery, monkeys with TE lesions attempting visual discriminations for the first time learn more slowly than normal monkeys do. The impairment must be one of central visual processing. A pattern discrimination deficit can be demonstrated in TE monkeys even if differential visual fixation is the only required response, and monkeys need not reach or otherwise perform arm movements to localize stimuli in the visual world (Bagshaw, Mackworth, and Pribram, 1970). Moreover, the deficit occurs despite normal visual acuity, normal visual perimetry, and normal detection thresholds for gratings, food-morsels, discs, colors, and angles.

In understanding this impairment of visual function, it is useful to contrast the effects of TE lesions with those following lesions of area

TEO, an adjacent and more posterior visual area in the temporal lobe. In general, TEO lesions produce a more severe impairment in pattern discrimination tasks than TE lesions. On the other hand, TE lesions more severely impair performance on concurrent object discrimination tasks, where several discriminations must be learned at the same time. Compared to TEO lesions, TE lesions also produce greater disruption of retention when irrelevant material is introduced between test sessions.

These results have suggested that whereas the effects of TEO lesions are primarily perceptual or attentional, the effects of TE lesions are more associative and mnemonic. It has been known for many years that experience can permanently affect the properties of visual cortical neurons located earlier in the sequence of visual analysis than area TE (Wiesel, 1982). That is, visual experience can alter the same neural pathways that engage in visual analysis. Inferotemporal cortex is a high-level visual processing area, and it also may be a locus of plasticity. This view has been developed in some detail by Mishkin (1982).

> . . . the synthesis of these several physical properties [of a visual object] into a unique configuration representing the unique object may normally entail the funneling of the outputs from the prestriate-posterior temporal region into area TE. It is this postulated convergence or integration of visual inputs in area TE that makes it particularly well suited to serve not only as the highest-order area for the perception of visual stimuli but also as the storehouse for their central representations (p. 87).

The best support to date for the hypothesis that area TE is involved in memory storage comes from recent evidence that area TE is critical for visual recognition, as well as for visual discrimination. Monkeys with TE lesions show no particular impairment in learning to discriminate among highly distinctive three-dimensional objects, presumably because such objects have redundant features that can be adequately processed by the more posterior, visual areas left intact. Yet, monkeys with TE lesions show severe impairment when the same objects are presented just once in a test of visual familiarity. This test, delayed nonmatching to sample using trial-unique stimuli, involves presenting a single object and then presenting it again 10 seconds later together with a new object. The monkey is rewarded for choosing the new object. This pair of objects is then discarded, and the same steps are repeated with a new pair. Within

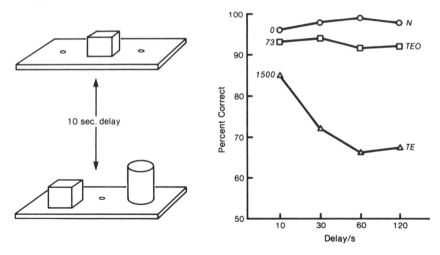

Figure 30. Recognition performance on the delayed nonmatching to sample test. *Left.* In the test, a monkey sees an object and then 10 seconds later must choose the novel, unfamiliar object. Different objects are used on every trial. *Right.* Performance by groups with bilateral lesions of posterior temporal cortex (TEO) or anterior temporal cortex (TE) and a group of unoperated controls (N). Numbers to the left of the curves show the average number of trials needed to relearn the basic task after surgery, which involved remembering a single object for 10 seconds. The first point on the curve is the average final score in this condition. Animals were subsequently tested in the same task, with the delay gradually increased from 10 seconds to 120 seconds. (Adapted from Mishkin, 1982.)

100 to 200 trials, normal monkeys can learn the principle and repeatedly choose the unfamiliar of two objects (the object not presented a few seconds earlier). However, monkeys given TE lesions after first learning this task could not relearn it, although after 1,500 trials they did manage an 85% correct performance rate. At this stage, increasing the interval between the sample trial and the choice trial in steps, from 10 seconds to 2 minutes, markedly deteriorated performance. This deficit seems to reflect a failure to recognize the familiar object on each new choice trial. By contrast, neither normal monkeys nor monkeys with TEO lesions had difficulty in visual recognition, even after long delays (Figure 30).

TE lesions in monkeys therefore impair not only the ability to discriminate among many classes of stimuli, but they also impair the ability to retain the experience of a visual object. TE lesions appear to damage neural tissue that would ordinarily be used for both the analysis of the visual features of objects and for the representation of visual objects in memory. This idea explains the two key findings obtained after TE lesions: the loss or serious impairment of previously acquired visual information and the inability to acquire new visual information.

The preceding discussion has emphasized the role of inferotemporal cortex in visual memory storage. Analogous arguments implicate other areas of neocortex, such as the inferior parietal lobe, in storing information about the location of stimuli; and somatosensory cortex (SII), in storing tactile pattern information (Ungerleider and Mishkin, 1982; Mishkin, 1979). It should not be assumed, however, that memory for any category of function so broad as these is located exclusively in any one area of neocortex, nor should subcortical areas be neglected as sites of plasticity that contribute to total behavioral performance.

Where Is Memory Stored?

The foregoing discussion can be summarized by stating that memory is both distributed and localized. Memory is distributed in that no single memory center exists, and many parts of the nervous system participate in the representation of a single event. Memory is localized in that the representation of a single event involves a limited number of brain systems and pathways, and each part of the brain contributes differently to the representation. The brain is a highly differentiated and specialized organ. Those areas of the brain within which memory is equivalently represented probably contain no more than a thousand neurons. Each of these "equivalence sets" of neurons must represent only a narrow "microfeature" of information. In the case of visual object memory, perhaps in the case of memory for any complex event, the neocortex is a likely storehouse of representations. The most likely site of storage is the set of particular cortical processing systems that are engaged during the perception, processing, and analysis of the material being learned. The next chapter explores this same idea from the perspective of psychological data.

9

Memory Is Determined by
Information Processing

Previous chapters suggested that memory is not an undifferentiated representation of whole events, but is instead parceled according to the different information-processing systems that participate in the analysis of events. Chapter 8 suggested that those same regions of cortex involved in high-level perceptual analysis and identification may also be involved in representing identified percepts in memory. This chapter focuses on this link between memory and processing, as a way of beginning a discussion of the structural, psychological organization of memory. How should memory be classified? When are we speaking about memory itself and when are we speaking about the information processing structures that give rise to memory? For example, distinctions have been made among many types of memory (e.g., verbal memory, nonverbal memory, spatial memory, musical memory, numerical memory). Do these distinctions arise from differences among the information processing capacities of the brain, or do they refer to differences in how memory itself is formed and stored?

The brain not only processes information within different modalities (for example, sights and sounds) but also processes different kinds of information within each modality (for example, faces, written words, color, orientation, and movement). Does each of these kinds of information processing result in a different kind of memory? Alternatively, perhaps these cases are not relevant to the problem of memory, but instead to distinctions between the types of information-processing structures that cause memory to be realized. By the latter view, memory could always depend on the same neural mechanisms and principles of organization, even though it can arise out of very different kinds of processing.

The Link between Processing and Storage: Which Cells Are Plastic?

The idea that processing and storage functions are closely linked raises an interesting problem. If significant aspects of memory are localized in the processing structures of neocortex, how can cortical processing systems change without altering the nature of perception itself? That is, how can extensive synaptic change occur in cortex, as is required for memory storage, while the cortex has an opposite need to preserve its information-processing functions? The scant data relevant to this question suggest that only a *portion* of the cortical cells within a population is plastic.

In one experiment, neurons within the inferotemporal region (area TE) were recorded while monkeys performed a delayed matching-to-sample task. The delays ranged from 6 to 32 seconds (Fuster and Jervey, 1981). In one experiment a red or green sample stimulus was shown to monkeys, and after the delay period the monkeys had the opportunity to select the sample stimulus from an array of two or four stimuli. After training, but not before, some area TE cells exhibited activity during the delay that was related to the sample stimulus. Thus, some units fired differentially during the delay, such that the firing depended on which stimulus had been presented as the sample. However, many units did not. In fact, 42 of 110 units in the inferior temporal convexity (38%) fired during the delay *independently* of the nature of the sample. These data are consistent with the hypothesis that some units continue to respond to fixed stimulus features or to task variables regardless of the training regimen, whereas others can participate in ensembles that represent information and retain it over time.

Cells recorded during avoidance conditioning in cats (Ramos, Schwartz,

125

and John, 1976) suggest a similar conclusion. Twenty-nine percent of the 56 cells studied proved to be plastic, responding differentially according to how a neutral stimulus was interpreted. The interpretation given the neutral stimulus was also expressed in the behavior of the animal as determined by the training history. The other 71% of the cells proved stable, exhibiting the same pattern of activity no matter how the neutral stimulus was interpreted. Unfortunately, no biochemical, morphological, or physiological markers yet exist to demonstrate directly and independently that only *some* cells change their activity in a long-lasting manner. The data cited above could be interpreted as evidence that neuronal behavior is probabilistic, and that every cell that can be recorded from has the potential to be plastic. However, it is not clear how this alternative could be correct, if the nervous system is to guarantee the stability of its basic perceptual processes.

The neural plasticity that underlies long-term memory storage probably occurs preferentially in the higher reaches of modality-specific pathways and in polymodal areas as opposed to early-stage, cortical processing areas. To take one example, in the case of vision, inferotemporal cortex (area TE) seems a more suitable site for memory storage than striate cortex. Indeed, neurobehavioral data identify a gradient of increasingly mnemonic, associative functions as one moves in a rostral direction through the temporal lobe (through areas TEO and area TE) and a gradient of increasingly visual-perceptual functions in the opposite direction (Iwai and Mishkin, 1968).

The Link between Processing and Storage: Considerations from Cognitive Science

Some well-known demonstrations in experimental psychology show how, at least for a short time after acquisition, information storage is tied to the particular processing systems used to analyze the incoming information. One hundred milliseconds after the visual presentation of a letter, a visual flash can erase the memory of which letter was presented (Kahneman, 1968). Since stimuli in other, nonvisual modalities do not interfere effectively with memory for a visually presented letter, memory for the letter appears to reside in a highly visual store, at least at an early stage after input. Similarly, when a string of words is heard, presentation of another word by the same voice and from the same location impairs recall of the last word in the string (Crowder and Morton, 1969). Visual events, or even words spoken by a different voice or from a different location, do not have the same effect. In addition, a pause before presentation of the interfering word sharply reduces the interference. These results indicate that newly acquired information, perhaps for as long as a second or two, is stored in a form that preserves the modality and many of the physical characteristics of the original stimulus.

Neisser (1967) adopted the term icon to describe the image or memory of a visual stimulus that outlasts its presentation and that corresponds closely to the sensory experience that gave rise to it. Efforts to measure the duration of iconic memory by backward masking and by other techniques suggest an upper limit of about 1 second (Sperling, 1960). The term echoic memory was applied analogously to the short-lasting trace of an auditory event, one that temporarily preserves the acoustic features of recently presented sounds. In this sense, representation is initially tied closely to the processing systems used to analyze information.

Information can be acquired through five separate sensory modalities. The facts of cross-modality generalization demonstrate that considerable opportunity must exist for interaction to occur among memories formed by the different modalities. Having once palpated an object, a person can then recognize it visually in an array of several objects. Having heard a familiar voice, one can then select the face that goes with that voice. These facts of everyday experience carry implications for the ways in which information is represented in the brain. According to one view, information is represented in codes that maintain a tie to particular modalities. Thus, the dual-code theory (Paivio, 1971) holds that information is represented primarily as visual images and verbal memories. Cross-modality generalization occurs in this case by operating across these separate representations. An alternative theory argues that subjects, in addition to coding by modality, represent the meaning of an event in an abstract, propositional code (Anderson, 1976; Kintsch, 1974; Norman and Rummelhart, 1975).

A body of evidence has accumulated in favor of this second view that, after some time has passed, information can be represented in an abstract code that is not tied to modality. In one experiment, subjects studied

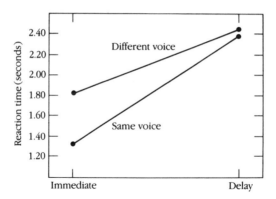

Figure 31. Subjects studied sentences constructed in either the active or passive voice and then judged whether new sentences had the same or a different meaning. In the delayed (2-minute) condition, the construction of the sentence did not affect processing time, suggesting that information quickly comes to be represented in an abstract, propositional code, independent of its original grammatical structure. (From Anderson, 1980.)

sentences, then either immediately or 2 minutes later judged whether other sentences had the same meaning or a different meaning (Anderson, 1980). These other sentences were sometimes written in the same voice (active or passive) and sometimes were written in the opposite voice. At the immediate test, subjects made their judgments more rapidly when the study and test sentences used the same voice than they did when the sentences were in opposite voices. However, after a 2-minute delay, the voice in which the sentence was written did not affect decision time. Apparently, once some time had passed after studying the sentences, subjects remembered primarily abstract information about their meaning. The meaning of the sentences could be accessed with equal ease by active or passive grammatical constructions (Figure 31).

The same point follows from a study of the speed with which subjects can process pictures of objects and the written names of the same objects (Potter and Faulconer, 1975). Although subjects require more time to name drawings of objects than to read aloud the words that name the objects, they categorize drawings more rapidly than words. That is, drawings lead to more rapid judgments as to whether what is presented does or does not belong to a particular category. Subjects can therefore access conceptual information about objects, such as their category membership, directly from pictures without having to name the object, even implicitly. This implies that category information is not tied to a verbal system, but instead can be accessed nonverbally. Drawings appear to access an abstract, nonverbal representation of the idea of an object, which conveys information about category membership.

Such results, however, do not demonstrate that *no* information at all about the physical characteristics of stimuli or the modality of presentation is retained in memory. In a series of studies, Kolers (1979) tested the ability of college students to read text that was inverted, mirror-reversed, or otherwise transformed. Subjects were later asked to read the same or a different text, presented either in the same manner as before or in a different transformation. The finding was that subjects could read familiar text more rapidly than unfamiliar text. Moreover, performance was best when the text reappeared in precisely the same format as before, including the same type font that had been initially seen. Any changes in the physical characteristics of the text reduced the practice effect. This influence of the physical features of printed text could sometimes be detected as long as a year after the original practice sessions.

The idea is that information concerning stimuli and events is tied in part to the particular modality in which information is initially processed. In other words, the processing systems that analyze information also participate in and influence the representation of that information. In addition, information is also represented abstractly, and removed from the sensory systems that gave rise to it. These representations are also probably tied to particular processing systems. Some processing systems, rather than analyzing the physical characteristics of incoming stimuli, deal with more abstract aspects of stimuli, For example, the capacity for language depends on the ability to comprehend the meaning of words rather than the ability to perceive just their physical characteristics. This capacity is related to specific areas of the left cerebral hemisphere. Aphasic patients, who have language disturbances as a result of injury to these brain areas, also have memory impairment that is selectively verbal (Cermak and Moreines, 1976; Cermak and Tarlow, 1978; DeRenzi and Nichelli, 1975). A similar result follows from the finding that a major effect of electrical stimulation of the cortical language areas, but not other brain areas, is word-finding difficulties (Ojemann, 1983). The same areas of the brain that process language may also store information about object names.

This same link between memory and processing is also suggested by the deficits of higher function (for example, agnosia, apraxia, and aphasia) that are associated with damage to specific cortical areas in humans. As an example, agnosia can appear as a deficit in the ability to recognize the meaning or significance of one particular class of information within a given modality. The class may consist of faces (prosopagnosia), music (amusia), or spoken language (pure word deafness).

The deficit in ability is not always so specific as these labels imply, but nonetheless, certain types of information can be affected far more than others. The deficit includes both the inability to recognize or to appreciate the meaning of familiar material (for example, faces, music, or words) as well as the inability to learn the meaning of new material in the same category. The deficit in prosopagnosia therefore prevents the patient from identifying by sight not only his family and friends, who are familiar to him, but also the hospital staff, who are new. In these examples, the affected area of cortex appears to be involved both with previously acquired information in a specific domain and also with the acquisition of new information in the same domain.

The human brain includes many differentiated and specialized processing systems, which deal with tasks as seemingly disparate as language comprehension, the recognition of faces, and the computation of spatial relationships. The distinctiveness of these individual tasks has led some to hypothesize that the brain's functional organization must be modular (Fodor, 1983; Gardner, 1983), and that only limited opportunity exists for interaction among modules. This idea is easily exaggerated. Neither the number nor the types of the hypothesized modules have been well specified (see Chapter 5), nor has there been discussion of the complex and multiple interactions that must occur among modules. Nonetheless, it should be obvious that the answers to questions about the numbers and kinds of modules and psychological faculties will have considerable impact on how we understand the nature of memory. As one example, the tremendous capacity that humans have for recognizing human faces (Galton, 1883) may depend upon the operation of a species-specific, specialized brain mechanism evolved for analyzing faces (Yin, 1970) rather than upon any ability that depends simply on memory capacity.

Extraordinary Processing and Extraordinary Memory

Certain acquired capacities likewise make the point that many feats that appear to require enormous memory capacity depend more upon processing skill than upon memory *per se*. In one famous series of experiments, chess players of differing ability levels examined a chess board displaying authentic game positions involving up to 26 of the 32 possible chess pieces (Chase and Simon, 1973; deGroot, 1965). Players viewed the board for only 5 seconds and then on a second, empty board, reproduced the arrangement of pieces from memory as best they could. The principal finding was that experts rated as master or grandmaster could replace about 16 pieces correctly, whereas less skilled class A players correctly replaced about 8 pieces, and beginners correctly replaced about 4. When quiet board positions were used, namely those where no exchanges were in progress at that moment of the game, then experts recalled more than 20 pieces correctly. In a second phase of the experiment, random positions on the board were constructed using the same chess pieces. Under these conditions the difference between ability levels disappeared completely: All players replaced only three or four pieces correctly (Figure 32).

Thus, the ability exhibited by expert chess players represents a chess-specific skill that depends in large part on previous encounters with multiple patterns of chess pieces during years of playing actual chess games. This ability allows chess players to construct perceptual groupings of pieces and to remember these groupings. Such perceptual grouping is called "chunking." The data on chunking by master chess players demonstrate that the number of chunks that the players retain in memory has the same order of magnitude as the number that normal subjects retain in the course of memory experiments involving words or other material: 7 plus or minus 2 chunks (Miller, 1956). Memory performance for these tasks therefore appears to depend not so much on a general memory ability so much as on highly developed skills for encoding and organizing a particular kind of information.

Another example of extraordinary memory performance also demonstrates this point. During 230 hours of practice spread over 20 months, a college student learned to increase his memory span for digits from 7 to 79 digits (Ericsson, Chase, and Faloon, 1980). After this practice, the

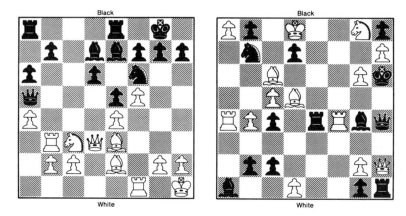

Figure 32. A chess-specific memory skill. *Left.* board position after white's twenty-first move in Game 10 of the 1985 World Chess Championship in Moscow between A. Karpov (white) and G. Kasparov (black). *Right.* a random arrangement of the same 28 pieces. After briefly viewing the board from a real game, master players can reconstruct the board from memory much better than weaker players. With a randomly arranged board, experts and beginners perform the same. (See Chase and Simon, 1973.)

student could reproduce correctly a string of 70 to 80 random digits read to him at a rate of one digit per second (Figure 33). He accomplished this feat by developing elaborate and effortful strategies for encoding and chunking. Specifically, he systematically recoded each group of three and four digits as an age, date, or as a running time for a track event, and then he structured these groups into hierarchical arrangements of subgroups and supergroups. All of this ability proved specific to memorizing digits. Late in the study, the student was tested for his ability to repeat letters of the alphabet. His memory span for letters was six.

The discussion above implies that questions concerning memory do not easily separate from questions concerning the modules, faculties, or processing systems that give rise to memory. This concept receives strong support from neurobiological studies of animals with relatively simple nervous systems. The results of such studies emphasize that behavioral plasticity occurs as changes in existing neural circuitry—circuitry that is already specialized for processing the type of information that is to be stored (Kandel, 1976). Extensive work with invertebrates has demon-

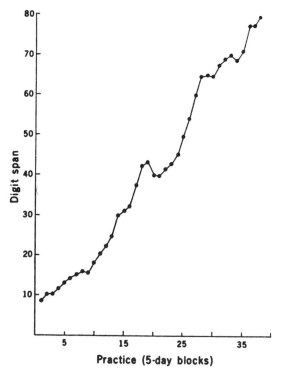

Figure 33. Acquisition of a memory skill. During 20 months involving about 230 hours of practice (1 hour a day, 3 to 5 days a week), a college student increased his digit span from 7 to 79 digits. Random digits were read to him at the rate of 1 per second. If a sequence was recalled correctly, 1 digit was added to the next sequence. (From Ericsson, Chase, and Faloon, 1980.)

strated that certain elemental forms of learning conform to this hypothesis. The same principle has been illustrated as well in the case of habituation of spinal reflexes in vertebrates (Thompson and Spencer, 1966). Current understanding of how complex learning takes place in higher vertebrates, including humans, encourages the view that this principle is a general one.

10

Short-term and Long-term Memory Processes

The previous chapter considered the differences that exist among the multiple information-processing systems of the brain. Many questions about memory acuity and memory capacity can be usefully recast in terms of how information is received and analyzed rather than in terms of how information is retained. The question that arises next is whether categories or distinctions can be identified *within* the domain of memory itself that are useful for understanding the organization of memory in the brain. For example, what useful divisions within the temporal dimension can be made? Is the time interval between learning and subsequent recall marked by any significant stages? This chapter analyzes the traditional distinction between "primary," "working," or "short-term" memory on the one hand and "long-term" memory on the other.

Neurology textbooks often divide memory into three stages: immediate, short-term (or recent), and long-term (or remote). "Immediate" memory has a time course measured in seconds, "short-term" memory has a time course measured in minutes, and "long-term" memory has a time course of days or years. However, these terms refer not so much to underlying mechanisms of memory as to areas of memory to be explored in a thorough mental status examination. A typical exam includes requests to : "Repeat these digits"; "Recall the objects that I named for you a few minutes ago''; ''Tell me where you spent your last vacation.'' Such areas of inquiry can yield useful information concerning a patient's memory functions, but the terms should not be taken as labels for separate neural mechanisms. The terms are simply descriptions of performance, not the names of processes used by the nervous system to accomplish learning and memory.

Information about biologically meaningful stages of memory comes from three separate traditions: cognitive psychology, neuropsychology, and neurobiology. These traditions have given rise to two different ways of thinking about memory stages. This chapter begins with the concept of memory stages as it developed in the psychological and neuropsychological literatures. The neurobiological tradition is then discussed, and a basis for reconciling the different views is proposed.

One of the most widely accepted and productive ideas concerning memory is the hypothesis that two forms of memory storage exist: short-term memory (STM) and long-term memory (LTM) (James, 1890; Waugh and Norman, 1965; Glanzer and Cunitz, 1966; Atkinson and Schiffrin, 1968). ''Short-term memory'' refers to a system that retains information only temporarily in a special status while it becomes incorporated, or transfers, into a more stable, potentially permanent long-term store. This concept of STM is similar to what neurologists call immediate memory. However, even within the psychological tradition, STM has been viewed in different ways.

Primary Memory

One meaning of STM appears in the original proposal by William James (1890), under the name ''primary memory.'' Primary memory refers to the information that forms the focus of current attention and that occupies the stream of thought. This information need not be brought back to mind in order to be used, because, says James:

> it was never lost; its date was never cut off in consciousness from that of the immediately present moment. In fact, it comes to us as belonging to the rearward portion of the present space of time, and not to the genuine past (p. 646).

Figure 34. William James (1842–1910), American psychologist. (From Roback and Kiernan, 1969.)

Primary memory is contrasted with "secondary memory," which James described as:

> . . . the knowledge of a former state of mind after it has already once dropped from consciousness; or rather it is the knowledge of an event, or fact, of which we have not been thinking, with the additional consciousness that we have thought or experienced it before (p. 648).

Compared to the term "short-term memory," the term "primary memory" places less emphasis on time (that is, on the duration of memory storage), and more emphasis on the roles of attention, conscious processing, and memory capacity (Miller, 1956). If a subject keeps to-be-remembered information in mind, then the content of primary memory can endure longer than it usually does, as when one holds a telephone number in mind while walking across a room to record the number.

136

Working Memory

The term "working memory" (Baddeley and Hitch, 1974) provides another meaning of the STM concept. "Working memory" describes a workspace or memory buffer in which to maintain information while it is being processed. When subjects were required to remember a string of six digits at the same time that they performed other learning or reasoning tasks, their performance was disrupted less than might have expected under the view that STM is a single common resource with a limited capacity. A key aspect of the working-memory concept is that more than one component to working memory must exist. Thus, the digit-span task and at least some other aspects of working memory do not overlap at all (Baddeley and Hitch, 1974; Baddeley, 1981).

> During the performance of complex skills, many kinds of information must be represented in states of especially high accessibility to ongoing cognitive processes. This information includes products of recent perceptual analyses, plans being evolved for motor output, retrieved fragments of permanent knowledge, partial products of various processes waiting for further processing, and various kinds of "book-keeping" or process-management information (Monsell, 1984, p. 327).

Multiple Working Memories

Recent formulations of the working-memory hypothesis provide a bridge to biological considerations of memory stages and STM. Rather than regarding working memory as a central or executive temporary-storage capacity, or as a single STM capacity, one can consider working memory as a collection of temporary capacities intrinsic to information-processing subsystems (Klapp, Marshburn, and Lester, 1983). Monsell (1984) wrote

> . . . capacities for temporary storage are distributed over diverse cognitive subsystems: these are united by no more than their membership in the cognitive system as a whole. I thus see "working memory" as merely an umbrella term for an heterogenous array of such capacities. (p. 328) . . . The view of WM [working memory] most compatible with distributed processing would

137

seem to be that of distributed storage: capacities for temporary storage specific to and intrinsic to each processing module (p. 330).

According to this view, the standard digit-span test assesses neither the span of consciousness nor the capacity of a single executive resource, but rather the span of just one particular working-memory system. Digit span STM is the particular capacity that allows for the immediate recall of verbal material. The ability to control rehearsal intentionally, which is a cardinal feature of verbal STM, was once considered to apply to all of STM or primary memory. However, in the working-memory view, digit span is not a measure of all of STM. Auditory-verbal STM is the temporary storage system only for phonologically coded speech sounds. Other information-processing systems have their own, separate working-memory capacities.

The hypothesis that multiple working-memory systems exist within the brain opens the door to biological approaches to the problem of STM. The traditional concept that STM constitutes a single, phonology-based memory system for the rehearsal of verbal material is not amenable to biological study, nor has it made useful contact with studies of learning and memory in animals. In contrast, the hypothesis that auditory-verbal STM represents the temporary, working-memory capacity of just one particular, language-based processing system leaves all other working-memory capacities open to biological analysis.

The Neuropsychological Perspective

As developed in the tradition of cognitive psychology, the concept of two memory systems (STM and LTM) derived almost entirely from work with normal human subjects. A similar idea about STM and LTM has emerged from the study of neurological patients with memory impairment. The scope and severity of human amnesia can best be appreciated in the noted patient H. M. (Scoville and Milner, 1957; Corkin, 1984), whose difficulty has been described as a complete anterograde amnesia that causes him to forget the episodes of daily life as rapidly as they occur. H. M. became amnesic in 1953 as the result of a bilateral surgical excision of the medial temporal region, performed in an effort to relieve severe epilepsy. The removal was intended to include the amygdala, the parahippocampal gyrus, and the anterior two-thirds of the hippocampus (Figure 35). As a result of the surgery, H. M. became profoundly amnesic. Although the epileptic condition was markedly improved, he could accomplish little, if any, new learning; and he appeared to have lost his memory for events that had occurred during several years preceding surgery. He retains older memories, and he has a good vocabulary, normal language skills, and an IQ in the normal to bright-normal range. Yet his impairment in new learning is so pervasive and so severe that he requires constant supervisory care. He does not learn the names or faces of the persons who see him regularly. Having aged since his surgery, he does not now recognize a photograph of himself. Nevertheless, H. M., like other amnesic patients who have been carefully tested (Talland, 1965; Baddeley and Warrington, 1970), has a normal digit span. Furthermore, when material to be learned does not exceed short-term (immediate) memory capacity, H. M. and other amnesic patients can explicitly rehearse and keep material in mind for many minutes. If distraction is introduced to prevent rehearsal, or if supra-span amounts of material are presented, new information is quickly lost. When rehearsal is made difficult by using nonverbal stimuli such as tones or difficult-to-verbalize shapes, information is also lost quickly, in less than a minute (Wickelgren, 1968; Sidman, Stoddard, and Mohr, 1968). This memory deficit demonstrates a distinction between STM and LTM similar to the one developed in experimental psychology.

A few examples will serve to show how H. M.'s deficit illuminated the STM-LTM distinction. In one task, different strings of digits were presented at a rate of 1/sec (Drachman and Arbit, 1966). If an error was made, the same string was presented again until it could be repeated correctly. When the digits were repeated correctly, then a new string of digits was presented containing one digit more than the preceding string. Under these conditions, normal subjects could extend their span gradually up to 20 digits, requiring fewer than 15 trials to succeed at any list length. H. M. began with a digit span of 6, the length of his preoperative digit span but was unable to extend his span at all beyond 6—even after 25 repetitions of the same string of 7 digits (Figure 36).

In a nonverbal analogue of this same task, subjects were asked to tap an array of blocks in a particular sequence that was first demonstrated

139

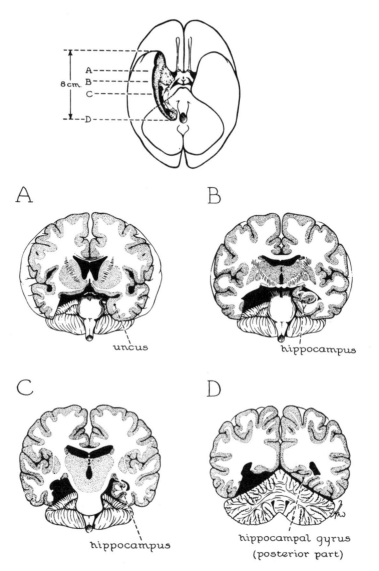

A

B

uncus

hippocampus

C

D

hippocampus

hippocampal gyrus
(posterior part)

Figure 35. Drawings in cross-section showing the estimated extent of removal in case H.M. Surgery was a bilateral, single-stage procedure, but one side is shown intact here for illustrative purposes. (From Scoville and Milner, 1957.)

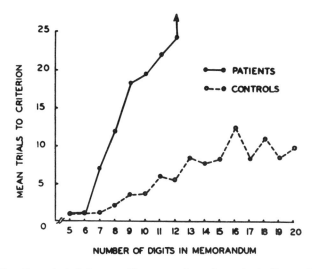

Figure 36. Extended digit span. Five amnesic patients, including patient H. M., and 20 control subjects were read a sequence of 5 digits. If the sequence was repeated back correctly, 1 digit was added to the next sequence. If not, the same sequence was given until it was repeated correctly. Amnesic patients had a normal digit span, but they required an abnormal number of trials to learn supra-span strings of digits. No amnesic patient recalled more than 12 digits within the testing limit of 25 trials. (From Drachman and Arbit, 1966.)

by the examiner (Milner, 1971). Case H. M.'s "block-tapping span" was normal, but unlike normal subjects, he could not reliably learn a sequence only one block greater than his span, even during a series of 24 trials in which the same sequence of blocks was presented 12 times. These results provide clear evidence that the medial temporal region damaged in case H. M. is not required for short-term (immediate) memory but is involved in an essential way when the task demands exceed what can be held in short-term memory.

The same distinction is illustrated in studies of the serial position curve for free recall (Milner, 1978; Baddeley and Warrington, 1970). Amnesic patients, including case H. M., listened to a list of words, which they were then asked to recall in any order. Normal subjects, under these conditions, show serial position effects; that is, they recall more words from the start and end of the list than from the middle. The greater recall of words from the beginning of the list (the primacy effect) is believed

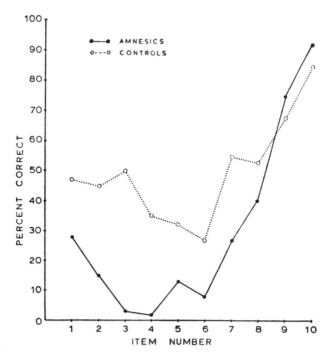

Figure 37. Serial position curves for six amnesic patients and six control subjects. Subjects were read 10-word lists and then asked to recall them in any order. The percentage of items recalled is plotted as a function of their position in the list. Amnesic patients show the normal recency effect but an impaired primacy effect. (From Baddeley and Warrington, 1970.)

to arise from the greater rehearsal given to these words and to their relative protection from interference. The tendency to remember words more easily from the end of the list (the recency effect) is attributed to the fact that these words can be recalled directly from short-term memory whereas the preceding words cannot. Amnesic patients showed a reduced or absent primacy effect, but little or no reduction in the recency effect (Figure 37). Thus, amnesia spares short-term memory.

The findings from amnesia underscore and confirm the distinction between short-term and long-term memory first emphasized by William James and developed during this century within experimental psychology. Indeed, experimental psychologists have at times concluded that the findings from case H.M. provide the best evidence of all for their distinction (Atkinson and Shiffrin, 1968; Wickelgren, 1975). The key distinction is between a capacity-limited immediate memory and a larger, longer-lasting memory. In keeping with the way that STM has been viewed recently by psychologists, the neuropsychological findings do not confine the concept of short-term memory to purely verbal tasks. Instead, the results are consistent with the hypothesis that different short-term memory capacities exist (for example, for digits or for spatial positions), and that the medial temporal region and other structures damaged in amnesia play a necessary role in memory whenever any one of these short-term capacities has been exceeded.

This same distinction between STM and LTM can be demonstrated in another mammalian species. In a radial maze, where the arms project out from a center platform like the spokes of a wheel, rats first visited eight arms in a sequence set by the experimenter. They were then tested for the ability to remember which of two arms of the maze (1 vs. 2, 4 vs. 5, and 7 vs. 8) had been visited first (Kesner and Novak, 1982). Normal rats showed a pronounced serial position curve that included both the primacy and the recency effects. Bilateral lesions of the hippocampus eliminated the primacy effect but not the recency effect. When the visits to the eight arms were separated from the choice tests by a 10-min time interval, the rats with hippocampal lesions lost the recency effect as well (Figure 38). These findings accurately reproduce the dissociation of short-term from long-term memory found in H.M. and other amnesic patients.

Some observers have favored a division of memory into three or more stages (for example, immediate, short-term, and long-term memory) rather than into just two stages, short-term and long-term. But, the literatures of experimental psychology and neuropsychology provide no compelling reason to separate "immediate" from "short-term" memory. At the global-structural, systems level of analysis, which is the relevant level for psychological and neuropsychological inquiry, there is little reason to postulate more than two stages of memory. One must, of course, allow for sensory memory, which is modality-specific and endures only a second or two after registration (Neisser, 1967; Sperling, 1960). Aside from sensory memory, however, memory can be held in short-term storage for a minute or two, depending on rehearsal; it then enters the long-term store.

The distinction between the STM and LTM stages of memory is linked

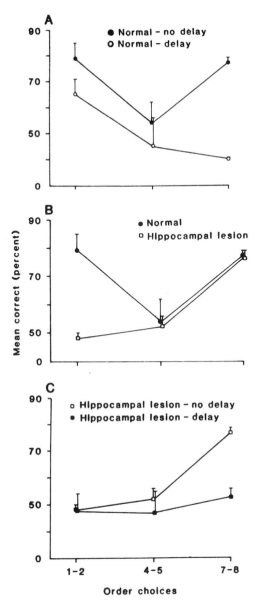

Figure 38. Serial position curves for normal rats and rats with hippocampal lesions. Rats first visited eight arms of a radial maze in a fixed sequence. Then 20 seconds (no delay) or 30 minutes (delay) later, they were given a choice test involving arms 1 vs. 2, 4 vs. 5, or 7 vs. 8 and they were rewarded for entering the arm that had been visited earlier in the sequence. A. Performance of normal animals showing both a "primacy" and "recency" effect in the no-delay condition but only a "recency" effect in the delay condition. B. Performance of normal and operated animals in the no-delay condition. C. Performance of operated animals in the no-delay and delay conditions. (From Kesner and Novak, 1982.)

directly to the supposed function of the medial temporal region and as-sociated brain structures. The medial temporal region of the brain be-comes important either when the capacity of short-term storage has been exceeded or when whatever is being held in short-term storage has been mentally put aside for a moment. This region of the brain permits lists of items to be remembered that are too long to be held in STM. It also permits even a short list of items to survive in memory even when re-hearsal of the items is interrupted by a distracting event, and even when attention is shifted to some other mental activity. Information placed in LTM continues to change for many years. Some or all of it can eventu-ally become independent of the medial temporal region. In this sense, it could be said that there exists within LTM an additional, temporal divi-sion. Memory remains dependent on the medial temporal region during a lengthy period; eventually, at least *some* memories become indepen-dent of the medial temporal region. Chapter 13 discusses this aspect of memory organization under the concept of consolidation.

The Neurobiological Perspective

How one defines memory stages depends on the level of analysis. The preceding section considered memory at the level of whole behavior and at the level of neural systems. Yet memory can also be discussed in terms of synaptic change. The formation of long-term memory depends ultimately on changes in synaptic connectivity, and these changes must depend on successive biological steps (metabolic events, synthesis of macromolecules, morphological change). Each of these biological steps can in principle be dissected and in some sense constitutes a stage in the formation of memory. Synaptic changes that begin at the time of learn-ing and are completed quickly could reasonably be described as short-term. Synaptic changes that begin later and that subserve long-lasting memory could be called long-term. This neurobiological perspective leads to concepts of STM and LTM quite different from those just discussed.

Hebb (1949) and Gerard (1949) originally proposed a dual trace hy-pothesis, according to which a short-lasting, labile trace that depends on perseverative synaptic activity gradually develops into a longer-lasting structural memory trace. Subsequently, more specific proposals concerning the sequence of cellular events that leads from temporary to permanent memory have been developed (Gibbs and Ng, 1977; Kandel and Schwartz, 1982). What are the time courses of these memory-subserving processes, and how do such proposals make contact with the psychological constructs of STM and LTM?

One way to make the neurobiological meanings of the terms STM and LTM more concrete is to determine how long short-term, labile memory is supposed to last before LTM is operative. This question can be addressed in experimental animals by assuming that short-term, labile memory should be disrupted by the disorganizing effects of a seizure on brain electrical activity. From this starting point, attempts have been made to determine the temporal characteristics of memory disruption (McGaugh and Herz, 1972). In particular, studies sought to measure the maximum length of retrograde amnesia; that is, how long before the administration of an amnestic event like electroconvulsive shock (ECS) would learning have to occur in order to protect the learning from the amnesic effects of ECS? At one time it appeared that memory might be susceptible to ECS for only a few seconds after learning. However, it later became clear that the temporal characteristics of retrograde amnesia could vary widely depending on the species, the learning task, and the strength of the disruptive manipulation.

> RA [retrograde amnesia] gradients do not provide a direct measure of the time required for the consolidation of long-term memory . . . These results need not imply that there is a maximal amnesic gradient, but may simply indicate that the disruptive effectiveness of a given treatment is limited under the particular experimental conditions used. (McGaugh and Gold, 1976, p. 550).

In short, studies of retrograde amnesia have shed no light on the time course of any putative short-term, labile neural process. Information regarding its duration must be sought elsewhere.

Another kind of evidence relevant to the neurobiological concept of STM, that is, the concept of a short-lasting neuronal/synaptic process, is the finding that inhibitors of cerebral protein synthesis block the formation of permanent memory (for review, see Davis and Squire, 1984). This result has been obtained for fish, rodents, and birds using a variety of tasks. When animals are given brief training during inhibition of cerebral protein synthesis by any of several drugs having different mecha-

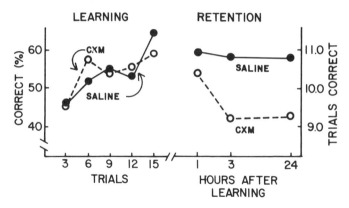

Figure 39. Following inhibition of 90–95% brain protein synthesis by cyclo-heximide (CXM), mice learn at a normal rate, but amnesia develops gradually thereafter. (From Squire and Schlapfer, 1981.)

nisms of action (e.g., puromycin, anisomycin, cycloheximide), they acquire the learning task normally but then are impaired on a later retention test (Figure 39). If inhibition of protein synthesis is established at other times, including during the retention test itself, memory is not affected.

Because changes in gene expression could give stability and durability to memory, it has seemed a reasonable and attractive hypothesis that long-term memory depends on this critical step. Moreover, it is known that certain short-term forms of synaptic plasticity do not require protein synthesis (Schwartz, Castelluci, and Kandel, 1971). Although the evidence available to date is indirect and does not prove definitively a role for protein synthesis in memory, a strong, internally consistent case can be made in vertebrates for the view that protein synthesis during or shortly after training is an essential step in the formation of memory.

Estimates of the time required for assembly of mammalian proteins (Hunt, Hunter, and Munro, 1969) indicate that at least 10 seconds are required for synthesis of a small protein (molecular weight 10,000; 100 seconds for one of molecular weight 100,000). Some additional time would be required for proteins to move from the ribosomes where they are synthesized to the membrane of the synaptic region, where they could influence synaptic action. It would therefore appear that a protein synthesis-independent phase of memory must be capable of supporting memory for at least one minute after learning, and perhaps longer, while the protein synthesis-dependent phase is being put into place. Should this protein synthesis-independent stage of memory be termed short-term memory?

If short-term memory is defined in this way, the concept differs markedly from the neuropsychological concept concerning short-term memory outlined above. Case H.M., as well as rats with hippocampal lesions, exhibited deficits in serial position tasks that could be revealed within seconds after the initial registration of information. H.M. can repeat a string of six digits, but never seven or eight. Rats with hippocampal lesions cannot recall the sequence of visits made to the arms of a maze only seconds earlier. In these examples, the time that has passed since learning is not the principal factor in determining when LTM must come into play. The amount of information being learned and retained is important. Moreover, LTM is needed as soon as capacity is exceeded or as soon as distraction is introduced, often within seconds of initial learning. Protein synthesis proceeds too slowly to provide the basis for the putative long-term memory system that is deficient in H.M. and in rats with hippocampal lesions.

Neuropsychology and Neurobiology Reconciled

The two approaches to STM and LTM described above are not incompatible. Their apparent contradiction arises because in each case a different level of analysis is used to explain memory. The neurobiological approach analyzes memory at the level of cells and synapses. In this context, "short-term" and "long-term" memory describe synaptic events, and they refer particularly to the temporal sequence of events leading to stable changes in synaptic efficacy. In contrast, experimental psychology and neuropsychology employ the terms "short-term" and "long-term" memory as systems-level concepts. Short-term memory is spared in amnesia; it is independent of the neural system damaged in amnesia. In psychology, short-term memory embodies such concepts as rehearsal, attention, and distraction. Long-term memory requires the integrity of the medial temporal region and certain associated brain structures. Damage to these areas impairs long-term memory, leaving only the capacity for short-term memory.

In the language of neuropsychology and neural systems, the concepts of STM and LTM refer to how brain systems function, not to sequential events at individual synapses. Long-term memory does depend on changes in synaptic efficacy to be sure, presumably in multiple and geographically separate storage sites. These synaptic changes must occur outside of the medial temporal region, and they undoubtedly take some time to develop fully. Moreover, these changes, which represent stored information, can subserve short-term memory on their own, without the help of the medial temporal region. In contrast, long-term memory requires the participation of the medial temporal region, which apparently operates in conjunction with the assemblies of neurons that represent stored information. The participation of this brain system permits recall after a distraction and allows large amounts of information to be organized in long-term memory.

The neuropsychological meaning of short-term and long-term memory thus differs from the neurobiological meaning implied by focusing on the sequence of synaptic changes leading to permanent memory storage. Whatever cellular events are required to establish long-lasting synaptic plasticity, these events can be initiated and can begin to unfold without the medial temporal region. If the amount of information to be stored is very large, then an intact medial temporal region is necessary if these synaptic changes are to be the basis for recall even immediately after learning. An intact medial temporal region is also required if synaptic changes are to provide a basis for recall at later times after learning. It is possible that the medial temporal region influences what eventually happens to the synaptic changes that represent memory, that is, whether they are preserved or are subsequently lost to any degree. Alternatively, the medial temporal region might not affect the fate of synaptic change itself, but only the degree to which synaptic changes can be organized into coherent, stable ensembles in order to provide an effective basis for recall.

Synaptic plasticity describes a variety of phenomena with different time courses, such as facilitation, post-tetanic potentiation, and long-term potentiation (McNaughton, 1982). Such stages of synaptic change lead ultimately to stable synaptic modifications, underlying long-term memory. However, there has been a confusing tendency to assume that stages of synaptic change must reveal themselves literally at the behavioral level. The terms "short-term" and "long-term" memory refer most usefully to behavioral categories, which depend not on stages of synaptic change but on how brain systems are organized to express synaptic changes in behavior.

11

Divisions of Long-Term Memory

The distinction between short-term and long-term memory developed in the previous chapter provides a first step in the fundamental task of classification. Divisions will now be drawn based on differences in how information is represented in long-term memory. Two distinctions are considered here: the distinction between ''declarative'' and ''procedural'' memory (that is, between memory for facts and episodes and memory for skills and other cognitive operations), and a subdivision of declarative memory into ''episodic'' and ''semantic'' memory.

Even though amnesic patients have profound and pervasive deficits in learning and memory, they can accomplish certain kinds of learning very well. First, amnesic patients show intact learning and retention of a variety of motor, perceptual, and cognitive skills, despite poor memory for the actual learning experiences. Second, amnesic patients show normal priming effects. Recent exposure to stimulus material can influence performance even when patients cannot recognize the material as familiar. These findings suggest that the amnesic condition has exposed a natural division between kinds of learning and memory. Some kinds of learning are severely impaired, while other kinds are completely intact. The question then is: Exactly what kind of learning is impaired, and what kind is intact? And, how should each category be characterized?

151

Declarative and Procedural Memory

The data from amnesia have suggested a distinction between declarative and procedural knowledge (N. Cohen, 1981; 1984; Squire, 1982a; Squire and Cohen, 1984). Declarative memory is memory that is directly accessible to conscious recollection. It can be declared. It deals with the facts and data that are acquired through learning, and it is impaired in amnesia. In contrast, procedural memory is not accessible as specific facts, data, or time-and-place events. Procedural memory is memory that is contained within learned skills or modifiable cognitive operations. It is spared in amnesia. Before examining this distinction further and inquiring about its biological foundations, it will be useful to review in more detail the experimental evidence on which the distinction rests. Accordingly, the discussion turns next to findings of spared learning and memory in amnesia.

The ability of amnesic patients to acquire and retain perceptual-motor skills has been repeatedly documented, beginning with the demonstration that the amnesic patient H.M. improved his performance during repeated daily testing on a mirror-tracing task, despite an inability to remember the prior testing sessions (Milner, 1962). Similarly, in spite of H.M.'s failure to learn the correct sequence of turns through a 10-choice tactile maze after 80 trials, he nevertheless gradually reduced the time required to complete each trial (Corkin, 1965). He also demonstrated steady learning over days of rotary pursuit and bimanual tracking tasks (Corkin, 1968). Other groups of amnesic patients exhibit a similar facility for learning perceptual-motor skills (Cermak, Lewis, Butters, and Goodglass, 1973; Brooks and Baddeley, 1976; Cohen, 1981).

This preserved capacity for learning in amnesia extends beyond perceptual-motor skills to perceptual and cognitive skills as well. Amnesic patients can learn and remember the skill of mirror reading as well as normal subjects (Cohen and Squire, 1980). They can improve at other cognitive tasks such as how to apply a numerical rule (Wood, Ebert, and Kinsbourne, 1982), how to put together a jigsaw puzzle (Brooks and Baddeley, 1976), and how to solve the Tower-of-Hanoi problem (N. Cohen, 1984). Finally, a previously acquired skill survives amnesia (Squire, Cohen, and Zouzounis, 1984). A mirror-reading skill was taught to depressed psychiatric patients just prior to a prescribed course of electroconvulsive therapy. After the course of treatment was completed, the skill was retained at normal levels despite marked retrograde amnesia for the training experience itself (Figure 40).

Another kind of learning that is preserved in amnesia is priming, i.e., the facilitation of performance by prior exposure to words or other material (Shimamura, 1986). This facilitation occurs despite impaired recall or recognition of the same material. Warrington and Weiskrantz (1968) first developed a testing technique that sometimes resulted in normal performance by amnesic patients. Instead of asking subjects to recall or recognize previously studied items, they provided the subjects with cues. For example, subjects saw fragments of recently viewed pictures or the first few letters of recently studied words. Often, subjects responded to these cues by producing the previously presented items.

The result of such a cueing procedure is determined by the instructions that are given along with the cues. Amnesic patients perform like normal subjects if, and only if, both they and normal subjects are discouraged from treating the task as a memory test (Graf, Squire, and Mandler, 1984). For example, in one test, subjects first see a list of words (e.g. MOTEL, ABSENCE) and then see a list of word fragments (e.g. MOT-, ABS-). Amnesic patients performed like normal subjects only when all subjects were instructed to complete each word fragment to form the first word that comes to mind. (Each word fragment could potentially form at least 10 different words, so that it was easy for subjects to comply with the instructions and treat the task as a sort of guessing game). However, when subjects were instructed explicitly to use the fragment as a clue for a recently presented word, then normal subjects performed better than amnesic patients (Figure 41). In both amnesic patients and control subjects, these priming effects were transient and disappeared after 2 hours. Thus, with word-completion instructions, amnesic patients tended to complete the fragments to form list words to the same degree as normal subjects. In contrast, with memory instructions, normal subjects improved beyond this level of performance, while amnesic patients remained at the same level.

Rozin (1976a) first proposed that priming effects are preserved in amnesia. He suggested a transient trace-activation process or ''hot tubes'' effect, which operates on already existing memory traces and persists beyond the span of short-term memory. He and others showed that prim-

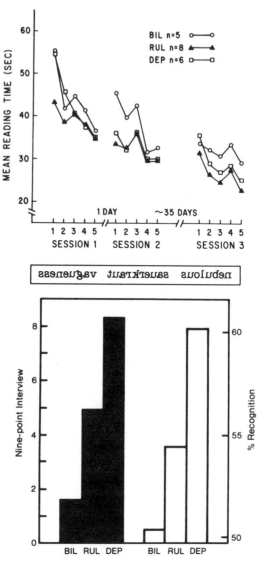

Figure 40. Acquisition and retention of a mirror-reading skill despite amnesia for the learning experience. *Top.* Patients prescribed bilateral (BIL) or right unilateral (RUL) electroconvulsive therapy (ECT) and depressed patients (DEP) not receiving ECT practiced mirror-reading during three sessions (50 trials/session). For the patients receiving ECT, one treatment intervened between the first two sessions. An average of seven treatments intervened between the second and third sessions. *Bottom.* At the beginning of the third session, subjects were tested for their recollection of the previous testing sessions (nine-point interview) and for their memory of the words they had read (recognition test, chance = 50%). (From Squire, Cohen, and Zouzounis, 1984.)

ABSENT   ABS_____

INCOME   INC_____

FILLY   FIL_____

DISCUSS   DIS_____

CHEESE   CHE_____

ELEMENT   ELE_____

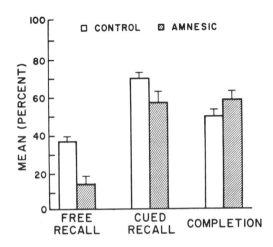

Figure 41. Intact priming in amnesia. Amnesic patients and control subjects saw common words and then were asked to recall the words (free recall) or were cued with the first three letters of the words and asked to recall them (cued recall). Amnesic patients were impaired in these two conditions but performed normally when they were given the first three letters of words and instructed simply to form the first word that came to mind (completion). The baseline guessing rate in the word completion condition was 9%. (From Graf, Squire, and Mandler, 1984.)

ing in amnesia occurs for real words but not for pseudowords (Diamond and Rozin, 1984; Cermak, Talbot, Chandler, and Wolbarst, 1985). Even though amnesic patients may not consciously recollect previously presented words, pre-existing representations of those words can be activated, and this activation can influence behavior for a period of time.

It seems reasonable that priming effects could last for a long time in the right circumstances, but this idea has not yet gained much experimental support. It is true that word completion effects can last for days or weeks in normal subjects, when the completion task has only one common solution (e.g., list words like *juice* and *assassin* are followed by *jui-* and *a--a--in*). However, it is not clear that this is precisely the same phenomenon as the one just discussed, which was intact in amnesia. For word fragments having a single solution, word completion effects were initially weaker for amnesic patients than for normal subjects, and the effects persisted in amnesic patients for only 2 hours, not for days or weeks (Squire, Shimamura, and Graf, 1987). Normal subjects probably augment their performance in this case by engaging ordinary memory strategies. Cues like *jui-* or *a--a--in* have only one common solution. When the unique solution does not readily come to mind, normal subjects probably consult their memories. Other priming tests often use cues that can be responded to in multiple ways (e.g., MOT-, ABS-), and such tests can easily be treated as a guessing game, even by normal subjects.

Whatever the explanation, the available data show that priming effects, or at least the kind of priming effects that are intact in amnesia, are rather transient following exposure to single words. Although strong evidence that such priming effects can be long-lasting has not yet appeared, there is no reason to doubt that they could be quite persistent in some circumstances. For example, priming might become very persistent in everyday situations, where subjects have frequent encounters with the same stimuli in different contexts.

The word-completion paradigm is not the only one that can reveal normal priming effects in amnesia. In a different study, subjects were asked questions that included one part of a homophone pair (e.g., "Name a musical instrument that uses a *reed*."). Subjects were later asked to spell the critical words (e.g., reed/read). Both amnesic patients and control subjects demonstrated a tendency to spell the word in conformance with the usage just heard (Jacoby and Witherspoon, 1982). Importantly, amnesic patients showed this priming effect despite the fact that they could not always remember having heard the questions.

The cues eliciting priming need not share any physical properties with the previously studied items. The cues can simply be conceptually related to the original material. Thus priming effects can be found through the technique of word association (Shimamura and Squire, 1984), and when previously heard words are cued by category names (Graf, Shimamura, and Squire, 1985; Gardner, Boller, Moreines, and Butters, 1973). For example, when common words such as *baby* and *chair* were presented to amnesic patients and control subjects, the probability was more than doubled for both groups that these particular words would later be given in answer to the question: what is the first word that comes to mind when you hear the word *cry* (or *table*)? These free-association effects disappeared in 2 hours. Moreover, when low-frequency words such as *raspberry, banker,* and *raccoon* were read to amnesic patients and control subjects, the probability was then doubled that these same words would be given when subjects were asked to produce examples of *fruits, professions,* or *animals.* These priming effects appeared in amnesic patients and control subjects to the same degree, despite the fact that the amnesic patients could recall few if any of the words that had originally been presented. Thus priming effects can occur without displaying precisely the same stimulus material that had been presented originally for study. Priming effects are not just perceptually driven; they can also be conceptually or semantically driven.

Priming effects are independent of the ability to recognize previously presented material as familiar. If priming effects were used to support familiarity judgments, then amnesic patients should be capable of making familiarity judgments, at least to some degree, whenever priming is intact. Yet in an experimental test of this question, amnesic patients exhibited intact priming effects, but then could do no better than chance at selecting which of three words had been recently seen. That is, when a recently presented word was displayed with two other words, amnesic patients could not pick it out of the group. However, given the first three letters of the word, and instructions to say the first word that comes to mind beginning with these letters, amnesic patients (like normal subjects) produced the forgotten word about three times more often than if it had not been presented (Squire, Shimamura, and Graf, 1985). Thus, amnesic patients ordinarily make no use of priming effects to judge whether an item is familiar or not.

The preservation of skill learning and priming in amnesia, in the face of impaired performance on conventional tests of recall and recognition, supports the hypothesis that a fundamental distinction exists between at least two different kinds of knowledge and the memory systems supporting them. The term *procedural* has been applied to the kind of learning and memory that is spared in amnesia, because the acquired information is embedded in procedures, or it occurs as changes in how pre-existing cognitive operations are carried out. The term *declarative* has been applied to the kind of learning and memory that is impaired in amnesia, because this kind of information is explicit: It can be brought to mind as a proposition or an image. It thus includes the facts, lists, and data of conventional memory experiments and everyday remembering. By contrast, skills and priming are expressed through the operation of a memory system (or systems) that does not allow explicit access to the contents of the knowledge base. The memory can be expressed only in performance, and it does not permit a patient's accumulating experience to be reflected either in verbal reports or in nonverbal tests asking for judgments of familiarity.

Although priming effects are spared in amnesia, some uncertainty remains as to how they should be classified. They could be considered a kind of procedural memory, to emphasize the idea that the knowledge represented is implicit and that priming effects reflect an improvement in the way that specific, already established cognitive operations are carried out (Crowder, 1985). Tulving (1983) has also discussed priming effects in this regard, while noting that many questions remain about their classification. It is also true that priming (word priming) involves the activation of pre-existing, declarative representations (representations of vocabulary words), which are presumably used whenever we attempt explicitly to learn and remember verbal material. For this reason, priming might seem to lead to a form of declarative knowledge. However, in the sense that the term is being used here, the information acquired through activation is not declarative because it is implicit, not accessible to awareness, and does not have other properties exhibited by declarative representations. For example, one striking difference between priming

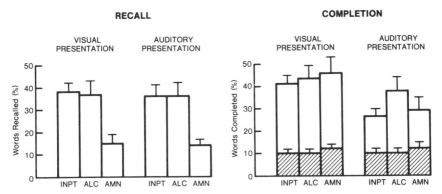

Figure 42. Diminution of priming effects across modality boundaries. Amnesic patients (AMN), alcoholic control subjects (ALC), and medical inpatients (INPT) read or heard words and then were cued visually with the first three letters of these words and asked to form the first words that came to mind. Priming was equivalent across groups and was higher when the study words and the test cues were in the same modality *(right)*. Amnesic patients were markedly impaired at recalling words, and recall was unaffected by the modality of word presentation *(left)*. (From Graf, Shimamura, and Squire, 1985.)

effects and declarative memory is that the information acquired through activation is accessed better through the same modality in which the priming stimulus was first presented, whereas a declarative representation can be accessed equally well through any modality (Figure 42) (Graf et al., 1985).

Another possibility is that priming is sufficiently different from both declarative and procedural learning to merit separate treatment altogether. Although priming effects have usually involved the activation of pre-existing knowledge representations, priming-like effects have also been demonstrated with new associations (Graf and Schacter, 1985; Schacter and Graf, 1986). For example, presentation of the word pair *window-reason* followed by *window-rea-* leads to a higher word completion score than if *rea-* appears alone, or if it appears with some word other than *window*. This effect occurs only if subjects make a meaningful connection between the two words at the time of their presentation.

Although the influence of unrelated words on word completion performance does have some of the characteristics of priming (Graf and Schacter, 1987), these effects also have characteristics of declarative knowl-

159

edge: Priming of new associations is not fully intact in amnesia. One possibility is that the process of forming a new connection, or association, between two unrelated words depends on the neural system damaged in amnesia. The subsequent priming of these association could then be independent of this neural system. In this sense, priming effects that involve newly formed associations may depend both on declarative and procedural memory.

The terms used here, declarative and procedural knowledge, first appeared in the literature of artificial intelligence (Winograd, 1975; Winston, 1977) and cognitive psychology (Anderson, 1976) before being applied to biological memory (Cohen, 1981; Squire, 1982a). Students of artificial intelligence and cognitive psychology have to some extent turned away from this distinction. Knowledge that seemed declarative at one level of analysis often seemed procedural at another (Rumelhart and Norman, 1985; but see Anderson, 1980). Also, formal accounts of knowledge representation showed that most or all information can be represented in either a declarative or a procedural way. It is easy to find cases where either declarative or procedural knowledge can be available for the same purpose. Consider a standard example from cognitive psychology. How does one answer the question, "How many windows do you have in your house?" One could have memorized the answer and then generate it by recollecting the stored information directly, from a declarative representation. Alternatively, one has available a procedure that could yield the same answer. One could implement a search process and mentally count the windows room by room.

Yet neither the utility or the correctness of this distinction can be decided on purely deductive grounds. The point is not that information can be formally represented in either a declarative or procedural manner. The point is that one wants to know how the brain itself actually stores information. One wants to find a level of analysis for describing brain function that is biologically useful. This is necessarily an empirical question, not a philosophical debate about how to classify knowledge. Experimental work suggests that the nervous system recognizes a distinction between two kinds of memory processes or systems. Specifically, memory functions in the brain do seem to be organized so as to honor a distinction between declarative and procedural knowledge (or something very similar), and making such a division has explanatory power.

It is important to note that the distinction discussed here, in the context of asking how biological systems actually work, differs slightly but significantly from the distinction originally used in the field of artificial intelligence. The version presented here emphasizes the idea that declarative memory is uniquely accessible to consciousness and is acquired through different brain mechanisms than procedural memory (N. Cohen, 1981; 1984; Squire, 1982a; Squire and Cohen, 1984). The two types of memory reflect different representations which cannot be substituted for one another.

It is sometimes supposed that the appropriate distinction is not between two different forms of memory, but between two different processes, either of which can be used to retrieve the same representation. In this view, a particular representation might be retrieved automatically, and without conscious awareness, thereby using it as procedural knowledge. Alternatively, the same representation might be used declaratively, through intentional retrieval. Stated differently, amnesic patients lack the ability to perform one type of retrieval, but they can perform another type satisfactorily. However, that is not the view presented here. Priming does not simply provide an alternative access route by which amnesic patients can reach previously presented words that are otherwise unavailable. What is obtained through priming, and available in word-completion tests, is different information than what is obtained through intentional learning and later expressed in recall.

First, priming is a short-lived phenomenon. Declarative memory can endure for a long time. Second, what is available through priming is a modality-bound representation to some extent. Declarative memory is available through all modalities. Third, the performance level achieved as a result of priming in both normal subjects and amnesic patients falls short of the level that can be achieved by normal subjects when standard cued-recall techniques are used that instruct subjects to produce a previously presented word from declarative memory. Normal subjects can reach this higher level of performance. Amnesic patients cannot. Finally, priming has never been shown to yield all of the information concerning previously presented words that is available in declarative memory (for example, when and where the learning occurred).

The present discussion thus emphasizes the kind of information that is stored rather than the strategy used to retrieve it. One might try to acquire and retrieve a declarative representation of a motor skill, but it would be difficult. Motor skills do not lend themselves to declarative representations. Similarly, one might try to learn as a skill the fact that the word *army* was once paired arbitrarily with the word *table*. But it would take many repeated trials before this unnatural pairing could become skill-like or automatic. Instead, a declarative representation can be acquired, one that works well after a single trial. The ability to accomplish this kind of memory storage depends on the neural system that is damaged in amnesia. Declarative and procedural knowledge are thus considered to differ in their biological organization: Differences exist in what kind of information is stored, how it is used, and what neural systems are required.

Procedural memory is considered to be tied to and expressible through activation of the particular processing structures engaged by learning tasks. It is acquired and retained by virtue of the plasticity inherent in these structures. That is, direct on-line changes occur that tune or otherwise increase the efficiency of these systems. These changes provide the basis for priming effects through temporary activation, and for the longer-term modifications that underlie skill acquisition. The two kinds of memory (declarative and procedural) are in this sense considered to depend on different processes and to result in different products. In many and probably most cases the same experience will lead to both kinds of products. For example, perception of the word "motel" will transiently activate the pre-existing assembly of neural elements whose conjoint activity corresponds to that perception. This process subserves priming effects. The same external event will also establish a longer-lasting declarative memory that the word "motel" was seen at a particular time and place, by establishing an interaction between the neural system damaged in amnesia and the particular neural elements that constitute the central, neocortical representation for the word and its context.

Declarative memory is viewed as more cognitive, fast, adapted for one-trial learning, and it permits storage of information as single events that happened in particular times and places. This kind of representation also affords a sense of familiarity about previous events. Such a representation is accessible to information-processing systems other than the one in which the learning occurred. It is modality-general. In contrast, procedural memory is slow, more automatic, adapted for incremental learning, and it is not always accessible to information-processing systems other than the ones that participated in its formation. Its availability can be limited by modality boundaries. It is possible that more complex learning has this same feature. Some learning can be accomplished by amnesic patients after much practice and repetition, and it can appear inflexible or "hyper-specific" (Schacter, 1985). However, further work is needed to determine whether this learning, which amnesic patients achieve as a result of repetition, is truly different (i.e., less flexible) than what one sees in normal subjects. In one study of amnesic patients, the correct responses were best recalled when precisely the same stimuli that were used during learning were presented again at retest (Glisky, Schacter, and Tulving, 1986). Additional tests will be able to show whether this effect is larger, or in some way different, than in normal subjects.

Procedural memory can be given a more concrete, biological meaning by examining three well-studied cases. The first of these is the tuning of visual cortical cells in cats by selective early experience. Restriction of an animal's early visual environment to only horizontal contours modifies individual neurons in visual cortex such that they acquire special sensitivity to horizontally oriented lines (Hirsch and Spinelli, 1970; Blakemore, 1974). But these changes do not depend upon the representation of any particular experience; nor do they necessarily imply knowledge of the "fact" that the world once consisted primarily of horizontal lines. The animal's experience has simply made the animal different. There has been a gradual modification of the neural elements involved in visual analysis. This modification changes the rules by which the animal operates, but implies nothing about memory for the specific instances that formed the learning experience. The storage of memory for those instances, and the ability to recollect them, are additional tasks for the nervous system. These tasks require additional brain mechanisms beyond the visual cortex—mechanisms that are damaged in amnesia.

A second example that makes the same point comes from studies of habituation of the gill withdrawal response in *Aplysia* (Kandel, 1976). In this case, the neural pathways responsible for executing the gill withdrawal response are themselves modified by experience. Habituation does not require a representation of having experienced several different stimulations at particular times and places. Instead, the animal simply changes as a cumulative result of many stimulations, and the animal now behaves differently because its reflex has been modified.

A third example of procedural learning is based on studies in mice of the effects of early stress on later behavior (Denenberg and Bell, 1960). Mild footshock or handling given to young mice, even as young as 1–9 days, affects avoidance learning ability in adulthood, 2 months later. The early experience has clearly changed behavior, but the early experience need not itself be remembered. The animals that had received handling when only a few days old are unlikely to be able to demonstrate behaviorally any direct memory of the event itself. For example, they should not be able to discriminate between places where they had received handling and places where they had not. They do carry the mark of early experience, in that the experience has changed behavior in a predictable and observable way. But apart from the evident influence of the early events on a few behavioral measures, there may be no independent way for the animal to demonstrate its knowledge of the early events. The animal is different because of its early experience, but it need not possess any record of the specific events that produced the behavioral change.

These examples imply that direct knowledge of a previous event requires a different kind of memory system from the one supporting procedural learning. Something extra is needed to acquire and retain the specific outcomes produced by the processing operations engaged during learning. To begin with, the particular brain structures damaged in amnesia must be intact if the outcomes are to be stored. Specifically, these structures must be able to interact with the sites of declarative memory storage. In contrast, procedural learning does not depend on the integrity of the brain structures damaged in amnesia. Procedural learning does require the integrity of particular processing structures, where the traces of experience are presumed to reside. In addition, it has also been suggested that the extra-pyramidal motor system might be required for many kinds of skill learning (Mishkin, Malamut, and Bachevalier, 1984). With the possible exception of skill learning, procedural memory does not appear to depend on any one structure or location. Indeed, procedural memory is not a single thing. It is a collection of different abilities, each dependent on its own specialized processing system. It includes motor skill learning, cognitive skill learning, perceptual learning, classical conditioning, priming, as well as simpler examples of behavioral plasticity such as habituation, sensitization, and perceptual after-effects. One therefore should not expect that a single lesion would affect all of procedural memory, in the way that a lesion of, for example, the hippocampus can affect declarative memory.

164

Classical conditioning deserves special mention in this context, because it has been extensively studied in laboratory animals (Mackintosh, 1983; Rescorla and Wagner, 1972). In rats and rabbits, simple classically conditioned responses are intact following hippocampal lesions. Animals learn stimulus-response associations incrementally, and what is learned is a disposition to behave in a certain way under particular circumstances. This kind of knowledge may therefore be the product of procedural learning. With this finding in mind, it is interesting to note that simple eyeblink conditioning was learned well by two amnesic patients, who nevertheless were unable to recognize the training apparatus (Weiskrantz and Warrington, 1979). Similarly, one can speculate that, although animals with hippocampal lesions acquire simple classical conditioning normally, they might fail a declarative memory test that asks for recognition of the place where conditioning occurred. Different kinds of simple classical conditioning must depend on their own specific neural circuitry, outside of and independent of the hippocampus. For example, the classical conditioning of the eyeblink response in mammals depends on specific cerebellar pathways (Thompson et al., 1983).

In other classical conditioning paradigms, animals are sometimes able to demonstrate their knowledge outside the original training situation, for example by demonstrating through a response system other than the conditioned one that the value of a reinforcer has changed. In this case, the animal seems to demonstrate declarative knowledge (Mackintosh, 1985). Thus classical conditioning paradigms can produce both declarative and procedural knowledge. Indeed, in contrast to the findings for simple classical conditioning, some more complex conditioning paradigms are severely impaired following hippocampal lesions. These include latent inhibition, reversal of discriminative conditioning, and conditional discrimination learning (e.g., where one stimulus identifies the occasion when a second, different stimulus predicts food) (Ross, Orr, Holland, and Berger, 1984; Thompson, 1983; Berger and Orr, 1983). Further analysis of classical conditioning with the present distinction in mind should be fruitful.

Whereas simple classical conditioning of skeletal musculature depends at least in part on neural pathways in the cerebellum, other examples of intact learning in amnesia may depend exclusively on cortex. For example, priming effects may depend on intact neocortical representations of the information being primed. Priming effects are markedly reduced in patients with dementia due to early-stage Alzheimer's disease, but not in amnesic patients with equivalently severe memory problems and not in patients with dementia due to Huntington's disease (Shimamura, Salmon, Squire, and Butters, 1987). The neural elements that actually represent declarative and procedural information may in some cases be geographically quite separate (e.g., cortex and cerebellum) or they may overlap and occupy the same general location (e.g., within neocortex). But the two types of memory should depend on different changes in synaptic connectivity, and therefore depend ultimately on different assemblies of neurons. Declarative memory additionally requires the participation of the structures damaged in amnesia.

If declarative and procedural memories are stored sufficiently far apart in the brain, or if they depend on separate connections to a significant extent, than it should be possible to obtain a double dissociation of the two kinds of memory by the lesion technique, i.e., one lesion should impair only delarative memory and another lesion should impair only procedural memory. This has been demonstrated in the case of visual object memory and visual pattern discrimination learning (Zola-Morgan, Squire, and Mishkin, 1982), and it presumably could be demonstrated in the case of classical conditioning of the eye blink, on the one hand, which depends on cerebellum, and learning during the training procedure about the place where conditioning occurs, on the other hand, which must depend on the hippocampus and related structures.

However, finding a double dissociation in one or two cases does not mean that declarative and procedural memories are *always* stored separately. It is possible that storage of declarative memory sometimes occurs in the same neocortical areas that also exhibit (and store) procedural learning. Consider the case of word priming and word memory. It is known that declarative memory can be impaired despite intact word priming. Would it be possible to find the opposite dissociation: impaired word priming in the absence of impaired declarative memory for the same words? The answer to this question should depend on the extent to which the neural elements representing a previously known word, which can be activated in a word-priming experiment, occupy the same location as (or are identical with) neural elements that can store the memory of a single presentation of the same word. Here, the term "store" means representing the identity of the word, the knowledge that it was presented, and the context in which it was presented. Although no good answers are available, it is difficult to envision declarative memory for a word being established without in part involving the neural elements that already represent that word in a person's vocabulary. If the neural elements that are activated in priming also participate in declarative memory storage, than a double dissociation would never be found. Any lesion that affected word priming would also affect the ability to remember the word that was presented.

Declarative memory may prove to be a relatively recent evolutionary innovation. This idea is based on the notion that learning evolved originally as adaptive solutions to special problems and that memories were originally encapsulated within the particular neural machinery that produced them. Rozin (1976b) proposed that a major event in the evolution of intelligence was improved access to adaptive specializations that initially served only a limited purpose.

> Adaptive specializations, by their nature as solutions to specific problems, tend to manifest themselves only in the narrow set of circumstances related to the problem that directed their evolution. The same navigationally brilliant bee may perform poorly in a simple conditioning experiment . . . (Rozin, 1976b, p. 254).
>
> I call all the specific, tightly wired, limited-access machinery in the brain the cognitive unconscious. Part of progress in evolution toward more intelligent organisms could then be seen as gaining access to or emancipating the cognitive unconscious (Rozin, 1976b, p. 256).

Such specialized capacities yield knowledge about the world that is both narrow and inaccessible to other information-processing systems. The evolution of a brain system capable of accessing such specialized knowledge and making it available across modalities and situations may have afforded a new kind of solution to the problem of learning and memory. According to this idea, each new learning problem initially had to be solved separately: Both the processing structures adapted to each problem and the products of the processing were encapsulated and not generally accessible. Among the vertebrates, another mechanism subsequently evolved and was used cooperatively by existing, specialized processing structures. This mechanism could function in all learning situations and make the product of processing, that is, memory, accessible to

167

many processing systems. It involved the development of the medial temporal region and associated structures, and it reached its greatest development in mammals, thereby affording animals the capacity for declarative memory.

A related idea is that in ontogeny declarative memory develops later than procedural memory (Nadel and Zola-Morgan, 1984; Schacter and Moscovitch, 1984; Bachevalier and Mishkin, 1984; Mandler, 1984). The late development of the declarative memory system could provide an explanation of infantile amnesia, the unavailability of memories dating from the first year or two of human life.

Other descriptions of memory processes or systems exist that are similar (and in some cases identical) to the distinction drawn here. They come from a variety of traditions, from philosophy on the one hand, and from experimental work with normal adult humans, children, amnesic patients, and experimental animals, on the other (Figure 43). These other descriptions include "knowing how" versus "knowing that" (Ryle, 1949), "memory without record" versus "memory with record" (Bruner, 1969), "taxon" versus "locale" (O'Keefe and Nadel, 1978), "habit" versus "memory" (Mishkin, Malamut, and Bachevalier, 1984), "semantic memory" versus "cognitive mediation" (Warrington and Weiskrantz, 1982), "horizontal association" versus "vertical association" (Wickelgren, 1979), "skills" versus "conscious recollection" (Moscovitch, 1982), "automatic recollection" versus "conscious recollection" (Baddeley, 1982), "integration" versus "elaboration" (Mandler, 1980), "perceptual memory" versus "autobiographical memory" (Jacoby and Dallas, 1981), "dispositional memory" versus "representational memory" (Thomas, 1984), and "implicit" versus "explicit" memory (Graf and Schacter, 1985).

The division of memory into declarative and procedural systems is a different distinction from that drawn earlier between short-term and long-term processes. The former distinction concerns the type *of information* to be remembered, whereas the concepts of short-term and long-term memory concern *capacity* and *time*. The distinction between short-term and long-term memory applies only to declarative memory. Declarative memory moves through both a short-term and a long-term stage, and requires the medial temporal region and its associated neural structures. However, procedural memory seems not to require differentiation into short-term and long-term stages. Procedural memory does not involve

168

TWO KINDS OF MEMORY

FACT MEMORY	SKILL MEMORY
DECLARATIVE	PROCEDURAL
MEMORY	HABIT
EXPLICIT	IMPLICIT
KNOWING THAT	KNOWING HOW
COGNITIVE MEDIATION	SEMANTIC
CONSCIOUS RECOLLECTION	SKILLS
ELABORATION	INTEGRATION
MEMORY WITH RECORD	MEMORY WITHOUT RECORD
AUTOBIOGRAPHICAL MEMORY	PERCEPTUAL MEMORY
REPRESENTATIONAL MEMORY	DISPOSITIONAL MEMORY
VERTICAL ASSOCIATION	HORIZONTAL ASSOCIATION
LOCALE	TAXON
EPISODIC	SEMANTIC
WORKING	REFERENCE

Figure 43. A variety of terms have been used to describe two kinds of memory. Although not all the distinctions are identical, they share the idea that memory should be subdivided into one or more processes or systems.

the ideas of capacity, rehearsal, and distraction in the same manner as declarative memory, nor does it require the integrity of the medial temporal region.

Episodic and Semantic Memory

Declarative memory can be further subdivided into "episodic" and "semantic" memory (Tulving, 1972; 1983). Episodic memory refers to memory for past events in an individual's life. This system represents information concerning temporally dated episodes that can later be recollected. Episodic memory stores the cumulated events of one's life, an individual's autobiography. Semantic memory refers to knowledge of the world. This system represents organized information such as facts, concepts, and vocabulary. The content of semantic memory is explicitly known and available for recall. Unlike episodic memory, however, semantic memory has no necessary temporal landmarks. It does not refer to particular events in a person's past. A simple illustration of this dif-

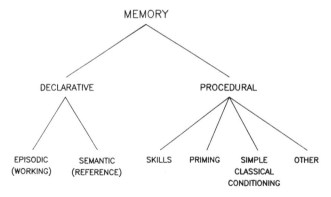

Figure 44. A tentative memory taxonomy. Declarative memory includes what can be declared or brought to mind as a proposition or an image. Procedural memory includes motor skills, cognitive skills, simple classical conditioning, as well as habituation, sensitization, various perceptual after-effects, and other instances where the facility for engaging specific cognitive operations is improved by experience.

ference is that one may recall the difference between episodic and semantic memory, or one may recall the encounter when the difference was first explained.

This distinction appears in earlier writings (Bergson, 1911; Reiff and Scheerer, 1959), but its influence on recent psychological research comes primarily from the work of Tulving (1972; 1983). The relationship between the semantic-episodic and the declarative-procedural distinction has not always been clear. Semantic and episodic memory constitute two types of declarative memory (Squire and Cohen, 1984; Tulving, 1983). Figure 44 provides a beginning at classifying kinds of learning and memory.

> The similarities and parallels between episodic and semantic systems become particularly clear when we compare them with another memory system, that concerned with the acquisition and utilization of procedures and skills. The distinction between episodic and semantic memory on the one hand and memory for procedures and skills on the other is probably as important in the taxonomy of memory systems as that between episodic and semantic memory. Let us classify episodic and semantic memory as two systems of *propositional* memory, and think of the memory for procedures and skills as *procedural memory* (cf. Winograd, 1975) (Tulving, 1983, p. 33).

If memory is defined as retention and utilization of acquired knowledge, then the knowledge of how to knit a sweater, tell a claret from a burgundy, read Cyrillic script, and thousands of other such learned ways of responding to and interacting with the environment entail memory, but this memory cannot be classified as either episodic or semantic (p. 28).

Confusion over the episodic-semantic distinction, particularly with respect to the neural organization of memory functions, has arisen in part because this distinction has sometimes been applied to the human amnesic syndrome. The proposal has been that episodic memory is affected in amnesia but that semantic memory is spared (Kinsbourne and Wood, 1975; Wood, Ebert, and Kinsbourne, 1982; Parkin, 1982). Similarly, the distinction between working and reference memory, which is similar if not identical to the episodic-semantic distinction, has been used to describe the effects of hippocampal lesions in experimental animals (Olton, Becker, and Handelmann, 1979).

These ideas do not describe amnesia accurately. The deficit associated with human amnesia, and with hippocampal lesions in rats, involves both episodic and semantic memory, and both working and reference memory. This would be expected if the episodic-semantic and working-reference distinctions represent a further subdivision of the declarative memory system that is impaired in amnesia. Amnesic patients have difficulty both in learning new facts (semantic memory) and in acquiring information about specific events (episodic memory) (Shimamura and Squire, 1987). Their retrograde amnesia likewise applies to both episodic and semantic memory (Cohen and Squire, 1981; Zola-Morgan, Cohen, and Squire, 1983; Shimamura and Squire, 1987). Semantic memory can be impaired, especially when it was acquired recently. Episodic memory can be spared, especially when it was acquired long ago. Furthermore, rats with hippocampal lesions show impairment on reference memory tasks (Morris, Garrud, Rawlins, and O'Keefe, 1982) as well as on working memory tasks.

The idea that amnesia selectively affects episodic memory seems to rest on the observation that amnesic patients do exhibit intact language functions and have available as well all the semantic information that they acquired in early life. Indeed, their IQ scores are normal. All of this intact semantic knowledge in amnesic patients stands in sharp contrast to their impaired capacity for acquiring new episodic information.

171

Yet this contrast is less compelling than it first appears to be, for it is based on comparisons from two different time periods—the remote past and the time after the onset of amnesia. What is needed instead are separate comparisons of episodic and semantic memory from both these time periods. When this is done, it is observed that amnesic patients can recall episodic memories from early life (Zola-Morgan, Cohen, and Squire, 1983). Moreover, amnesic patients exhibit a pronounced impairment in semantic knowledge about the world, when that knowledge is tied to events that occurred just before the onset of amnesia or during the years since the onset of amnesia (Cohen and Squire, 1981; Shimamura and Squire, 1987).

These arguments notwithstanding, the two contrasting views of amnesia (that both episodic and semantic memory are affected and that only episodic memory is affected) collapse into one view if certain additional assumptions are made about the relationship between episodic and semantic memory. Suppose that all of semantic memory develops out of episodic memory and that all episodic memory eventually becomes semantic memory (Cermak, 1984). Then a selective impairment in the ability to acquire episodic memory would lead to the same syndromes of anterograde and retrograde amnesia as would an impairment that affected the formation of both episodic and semantic memory. Of course, this way of defining terms changes much of what was originally meant by them and it asserts in addition that remote memory contains no episodic memory.

Holding to more traditional definitions of episodic and semantic memory leads to the conclusion that both kinds of memory depend on the integrity of the brain structures damaged in amnesia. If so, then what aspects of brain organization are relevant to this distinction? There has been almost no effort directed toward this problem, but two possibilities can be imagined. Some further subdivision of the brain regions damaged in amnesia might be discovered, some division of neural organization within these brain regions, that has particular significance for episodic and semantic memory processes. Alternatively, other brain regions might be important for either episodic or semantic memory, in cooperation with the brain regions responsible for declarative memory. This issue is not well understood at the present time.

One ambiguity that needs to be addressed in further developments of the episodic-semantic distinction is the status of laboratory experiments on memory. Having read a list of words, a subject can later recall them. Having visited one arm of a radial maze to find food, a rat later visits other arms and avoids the arm that is empty of food. Does this ability to recall the contents of a recent episode also entail remembering the episode itself as a particular event that occurred at a particular time? Or does recall in these cases involve only the semantic contents of an episode without necessarily remembering the episode itself? Do these examples involve episodic memory or semantic memory? Tulving (1983) considered this particular issue and distinguished between personal episodes and their semantic contents.

This seems a promising way to draw the episodic-semantic distinction. Subjects under posthypnotic amnesia (Evans and Thorn, 1966) and some amnesic patients (Schacter, Harbluk, and McLachlan, 1984; Shimamura and Squire, 1987) can exhibit a phenomenon termed source amnesia. They can remember recently acquired items of information, without remembering when or where they acquired the information. Importantly, source amnesia is a separate deficit, unrelated to the memory impairment itself. It does not appear in all amnesic patients, but the ones who show it do so consistently. Moreover, the patients without source amnesia can have just as severe a memory impairment as patients with source amnesia. If the term episodic memory is reserved for acts of remembering that are specifically autobiographical, then episodic memory might refer usefully to that aspect of memory functions that is lost in source amnesia and that ordinarily permits a sense of personal connection to one's past. In normal subjects recall and recognition are ordinarily accompanied by recollection of the learning episode. However, in some amnesic patients the quality of personal familiarity and connectedness to a recent episode can be lost despite successful recall and recognition of material learned in the episode. Preliminary evidence suggests that frontal lobe pathology may contribute to this phenomenon.

Additional biological evidence suggesting different neural organization for episodic and semantic memory would be of great interest. Distinctions based on psychological evidence alone are difficult to pin down satisfactorily, and it is often difficult to agree in these cases about the importance of a proposed distinction. At a sufficiently detailed level of analysis, almost any ability or process can be distinguished from others.

The question is not whether a distinction can be made at all. The question is whether a proposed distinction is trivial (for example, the difference between remembering large and small objects) or whether it provides a fundamental organizing principle for how biological systems process information. Cognitive psychology and neuroscience can clearly work together to answer these questions. Although some have regarded these two disciplines as independent or irrelevant to each other, their agendas are in fact mutually reinforcing (Kandel, 1983; Hebb, 1983; Tulving, 1984; Schacter, 1984).

12

A Neural System
with Memory Functions

The preceding chapters drew on psychological, neuropsychological, and neurobiological facts to outline a tentative scheme for how memory might be partitioned: short-term and long-term, declarative and procedural, episodic and semantic. Yet, the hope is to go beyond the simple dissociation of one component of cognition from another. The ultimate objective is to understand how functions are actually organized in the brain and how they are related to each other. Studies of impaired memory can contribute to this undertaking. The strategy of studying errors, disease, or dysfunction in order to learn about normal function is a traditional one in biology, but whether any particular strategy will be useful is an empirical question. Criticism of the lesion method is heard frequently, usually on *a priori* grounds: for example, how can the function of a complex, highly interrelated system be understood by placing a hole in the middle of it? In addition, because any lesion will exert effects at distant points as well as at the locus of injury, how can a lesion illuminate the functional significance of damaged tissue?

The answer to this criticism is that if the nervous system were highly interrelated, with little specialized function of its component parts, then the lesion method would be of little use. Any lesion would produce a global impairment, one that blurred across categories of behavior and

Figure 45. *Left.* Theodule Ribot (1839–1916), French psychologist. *Middle.* Sergei Korsakoff (1853–1900), Russian psychiatrist. *Right.* George Talland (1917–1968), American psychologist. (Left, Courtesy of Daniel Schacter; middle, from Haymaker and Schiller, 1970; right, from Poon et al., 1980.)

affected all of mental life. However, the facts are that lesions can produce strikingly specific patterns of impairment, which suggests that particular components or systems of the brain have been damaged. At the same time, the lesion technique is only one of many methods for studying how the brain accomplishes learning and memory. The problem of function is complex, and all of the techniques of psychology and neuroscience must be applied to the task.

Since the classic reports of amnesic syndromes by Ribot (1881) and Korsakoff (1887), memory disorders have been recognized as being quite circumscribed in some instances. In these instances, the study of amnesia has been useful for understanding normal memory. The disorder of amnesia is often limited to the capacity for learning and memory; it need not affect other cognitive functions such as attention, perception, or general intellectual ability. Indeed, amnesic patients may exhibit no discernible impairment of higher function except an inability to accomplish new learning and a loss of memory for some events that occurred prior to the onset of the disorder. Remote memory for distant events can also remain normal. In addition, the ability to reproduce information immediately after its presentation can remain normal, provided that the amount of

176

information presented does not exceed immediate memory capacity (see Chapter 10; for reviews, see Squire and Cohen, 1984; Mayes and Meudell, 1983).

Case N.A.

A somewhat more extended discussion of amnesia might be useful at this point, in order to illustrate how memory impairment can occur against a background of normal cognition and to illustrate the impact that memory impairment can have on the quality of life. The following account is based on our acquaintance with N.A., who was first described by the late Professor Teuber and his colleagues (Teuber, Milner, and Vaughan, 1968). We have tested N.A. and visited him frequently during the past 10 years.

N.A. was born in 1938. He grew up with his mother and stepfather, attended public schools, and then after a year of junior college joined the Air Force. In October, 1959, he was assigned to the Azores as a radar technician, and he remained there until the time of his accident in December, 1960. According to his medical charts, and his own narrative retelling, N.A. was assembling a model airplane in his barracks room. His roommate had removed a miniature fencing foil from the wall and was making thrusts behind N.A.'s chair. N.A. turned suddenly and was stabbed through the right nostril. The foil penetrated the thin cribiform plate, taking an upward course to the left into the forebrain. He lost consciousness a few minutes later. Initially, N.A. exhibited right arm and leg paresis and paralysis of the third cranial nerve. A dural tear was repaired during exploratory craniotomy, and eventually he was sent home to California. His neurological deficits recovered, except for mild paresis of upward gaze, mild diplopia, and a severe memory impairment for verbal material.

In 1979, CT (computed tomography) scans identified a small lucency in the position of the left mediodorsal thalamic nucleus (Squire and Moore, 1979). This radiographic finding means that brain injury has occurred in the identified region, but it does not mean that no other damage has occurred. CT scans will not detect neural damage if it is very patchy or diffuse, or if glial cells have proliferated into the damaged region such that the region becomes as dense to x-rays as normal tissue. N.A.'s IQ, as assessed in 1975 and again in 1981, was 124. He exhibits no aphasia or apraxia, and he scores in the superior range on many tests of language, visuo-perceptual ability, and frontal lobe function. Yet, he can recall only spottily from the 25+ years since his injury. His memory from the period prior to 1960 is very good. Like other amnesic patients we have studied, N.A. fails badly on formal tests of new learning ability (see Figure 51). He is better at remembering faces than names, consistent with the left hemispheric locus of his diencephalic lesion.

His memory impairment is best understood as a difficulty in retaining the events of each passing hour and day. Even significant events are recalled vaguely, if at all. He knows that "Watergate" signifies some political event, but cannot provide additional information. He cannot recall the significance of the phrase "Three Mile Island." The events of daily life present an even bigger problem. He loses track of his possessions, forgets what he has done, and forgets whom he has visited.

Presumably as a result of his inadequate memory, he gives the impression of living behind the times. He wears his hair in a crew-cut. He recently mentioned the name Betty Grable, as if she were a contemporary film star. He has no close friends. His socializing is limited by his difficulty in keeping a topic of conversation in mind and in carrying over the substance of social contacts from one occasion to another. He cannot cook for himself satisfactorily, because the correct sequence of steps places too great a burden on his memory. He says that watching television is difficult, because he forgets the story content during commercial breaks.

Despite his severe memory disorder, N.A. appears entirely normal on first meeting. He stands 6 feet 1 inch, at 210 pounds, has a relaxed and cheerful manner, and a good sense of humor. He is not prone to depression. Visitors at his house are invariably invited to inspect his collections and souvenirs. He tells stories about each object, apologizing occasionally for forgetting things. Only after several visits with him does one come to see his memory impairment as a clear and disabling condition. It is extraordinary how unremarkable amnesia can appear on first impression, yet how profound and devastating an effect it can nevertheless have.

Currently, N.A. is 48 years old, living alone a short distance from his mother. His house is near a group of stores, where he walks to do some of his shopping. His mother also shops for him and prepares some of his meals for him. However, he often forgets that meals are ready in the refrigerator and goes out to eat instead. His closet is full of new clothes, which he does not wear. It is as if he prefers to wear clothes that are familiar. He keeps his house arranged neatly, with everything in its proper place. His mother says that if she moves a pillow on the couch, he will straighten it. If she displaces the telephone slightly, he will move it to its original position. His obsessive concern with orderliness seems to be a compensation for inadequate memory. N.A. wants all his furniture and belongings in a fixed location, so that he can have a chance through repetition to learn where they are and to find them when he wants them. He spends his time alone or with his mother and her friends. He takes walks near his house, helps neighbors with chores, watches television, and works on hobbies at home.

He has had a number of physical complaints and symptoms: high blood pressure, gout, a chronically sore jaw, lower back pain, and dental problems. He forgets to take medication and forgets to refill prescriptions. He steadfastly refuses to keep regular notes for himself, stating that this would be a crutch that would prevent him from exercising his memory. His mother often speaks of his stubborn, single-minded ways. He will keep one thought in his head and then cannot be diverted to another topic until whatever is on his mind is answered or resolved. All of these things, his compulsion for order, his stubbornness, his personal health habits, derive from his memory problem. A narrow handicap in memory has broadly affected his life. His mother eloquently expresses this same idea: "Everything surrounding him is a memory thing. . . . You've got to have a memory to remember."

Amnesia: Damage to a Specialized Neural System

The striking selectivity of N.A.'s amnesia might seem surprising in view of the idea that memory is tied to the various information-processing systems of the brain. Given a close link between information processing and information storage, one might expect that any brain injury causing a memory disorder should cause difficulty in acquiring new information as well as the loss of all previously acquired information of the same kind. Amnesic patients, however, not only have normal *immediate* memory, which indicates that many of their information-processing systems remain intact and available for use, but they also can have normal *remote* memory, which demonstrates that many memory storage sites have been preserved.

These simple observations make an important point about the normal function of the brain regions damaged in amnesia. Amnesia appears to reflect neither direct injury to, nor loss of, those brain regions in which information is processed and stored. Instead, amnesia seems best explained by hypothesizing a neural system, which is damaged in amnesia, that ordinarily *participates* in memory storage without being itself a *site* of storage. This chapter identifies the brain structures belonging to this neural system, as they are currently understood. The following chapter considers the function of this system.

Two regions of the brain, the medial aspect of the temporal lobe and the diencephalic midline, have been linked to human amnesia for nearly a century. Clinico-neuropathological studies of Korsakoff's syndrome first identified the midline diencephalic region (Gudden, 1896). Since that time, neuropathological studies of this syndrome (Victor, Adams, and Collins, 1971; Mair, Warrington, and Weiskrantz, 1979; Brion and Mikol, 1978) have concentrated attention on two structures within the diencephalic midline, the mammillary complex and the mediodorsal thalamic nucleus. Diencephalic amnesia has also been observed in patients with third ventricle tumors (Williams and Pennybacker, 1954), patients with thalamic infarctions (Speedie and Heilman, 1982; Michel, Laurent, Blanc, Foyatier, and Portafaix, 1982; Winocur, Oxbury, Agnetti, and Davis, 1984; von Cramon, Hebel, and Schuri, 1985; Graff-Radford, Damasio, Yamada, Eslinger, and Damasio, 1985), and in cases of accidental trauma (Lehtonen, 1973; Squire and Moore, 1979).

Damage to the medial temporal lobe was first identified at the turn of the century in a patient who had had memory impairment during life (von Bechterew, 1900). Nevertheless, it was the noted surgical case H.M. who firmly established the significance of this region for normal memory functions (Scoville and Milner, 1957; Corkin, 1984). Amnesia following damage to the medial temporal region has also been found after viral encephalitis (Rose and Symonds, 1960), posterior cerebral artery occlusion (Benson, Marsden, and Meadows, 1974), and ischemic injury (Volpe and Hirst, 1983; Zola-Morgan, Squire, and Amaral, 1986).

Diencephalic Amnesia

The hypothesis that the mammillary nuclei must play an important role in the etiology of diencephalic amnesia derives largely from the fact that they are consistently damaged in Korsakoff's syndrome. A connection between mammillary nuclei and amnesia has also been made frequently in single case studies (Grunthal, 1939, Remy, 1942) as well as in several well-known multiple-case studies (Brion and Mikol, 1978; Gruner, 1956; Kahn and Crosby, 1972; Malamud and Skillicorn, 1956; Mair et al., 1979). Nevertheless, in Korsakoff's syndrome and in the available case reports, the mammillary nuclei are seldom if ever the sole locus of damage. Some uncertainty therefore persists concerning whether damage to the mammillary nuclei alone can produce amnesia in humans.

The hypothesis that the mediodorsal nucleus has an important role in diencephalic amnesia was first advanced by Victor and his colleagues. In their now classic monograph on the Wernicke-Korsakoff syndrome, they (1971) identified five cases in which the mammillary nuclei had been damaged but memory loss had not been observed. In their series of cases, all those with memory loss had lesions of both the mediodorsal thalamic nucleus and the mammillary nuclei. This suggested that damage to the mediodorsal nucleus either alone or in combination with damage to the mammillary nuclei may be necessary to produce amnesia (Table 1).

However, reports that mediodorsal nucleus lesions sometimes do *not* occur in diencephalic amnesia appear to contradict this conclusion. In one series of 11 cases of Korsakoff's syndrome, each patient was described as amnesic and also had mammillary nuclei lesions (Brion and Mikol, 1978). But the mediodorsal thalamic nucleus was reported as damaged in only 7 of the 11 cases. Since 10 of these 11 cases proved to have damage in at least one of three other thalamic nuclei that were examined, this series of cases makes no strong claim concerning the effects of lesions limited to the mammillary nuclei.

Other reports suggest that diencephalic amnesia can occur following

Table 1 Incidence of involvement of various brain regions in the Wernicke-Korsakoff syndrome[a]

Region	Number of Cases Examined	Number of Cases Involved	Percentage Involved
Hypothalamic nuclei			
Medial mammillary	47	47	100.0
	21	21	100.0
Dorsal area	32	23	71.9
	21	16	76.2
Thalamic nuclei			
Medial dorsal	43	38	88.4
	24	24	100.0
Medial pulvinar	20	17	85.0
Lateral dorsal	25	17	68.0
Other regions			
Cerebral cortex	51	29	56.9
Cerebellum	27	15	55.5
Hippocampus	22	5	36.4
Fornix	22	5	22.7

[a]From Victor, Adams, and Collins (1971). The second row of figures for some structures refer to cases in which the amnesic syndrome of Korsakoff's psychosis had been recognized during life.

damage to the thalamus, in the vicinity of the mediodorsal nucleus, without direct damage to the mammillary nuclei (for review, see Markowitsch, 1982). The cases best demonstrating this point are those that report amnesia after bilateral infarction in the territories of the tuberothalamic (polar) or paramedian arteries (Mills and Swanson, 1978; Winocur, et al, 1984; von Cramon, et al, 1985; Graff-Radford, et al, 1985). However, the variability of arterial territories among individuals makes anatomical generalizations difficult. Although the damage in these cases frequently involves the mediordorsal nucleus, other structures are also damaged and the mediodorsal nucleus is sometimes only minimally involved. One suggestion is that the critical lesion causing amnesia lies within the mammillothalamic tract and the internal medullary lamina (von Cramon, et al, 1985), a lesion that could cause degeneration within the mammillary nuclei. Thus, even with these cases there is uncertainty about the role of the mediodorsal nucleus itself. To date, the human cases simply allow no definite conclusion as to whether amnesia can arise from damage limited to either the mediodorsal thalamic nucleus or the mammillary nuclei, nor do they allow any diencephalic structures (either alone or in combination) to be identified with certainty.

Two problems occur in trying to piece together findings from the clinical literature. First, information concerning the nature and extent of brain damage comes either from indirect information (for example, radiographic data) or from identified lesions that cross anatomical boundaries. Second, quantitative information is seldom provided. Reports offering only impressions based on informal testing or observation make it difficult to judge the severity of the impairment and impossible to compare amnesia across different cases.

The recent development of an animal model of human amnesia in the monkey provides a way to address these issues (Mahut and Moss, 1984; Mishkin, Spiegler, Saunders, and Malamut, 1982; Squire and Zola-Morgan, 1983). Several behavioral tests of memory sensitive to human amnesia have been adapted for the monkey (Gaffan, 1974; Mishkin and Delacour, 1975; Zola-Morgan and Squire, 1985a); and when monkeys with selective surgical lesions are given these tests, their memory abilities can be precisely quantified. The behavioral test most widely used in this effort is delayed nonmatching to sample. This approach will eventually permit identification of the specific brain structures that must be damaged to cause amnesia.

Although studies with monkeys have begun only recently, some of the issues concerning memory and amnesia have already been clarified. One study revealed that midline thalamic lesions cause a severe memory deficit resembling human amnesia (Aggleton and Mishkin, 1983a). The lesions in this study included the anterior nucleus, the midline nuclei, the mammillothalamic tract, and the anterior portion of the mediodorsal nucleus. Because of the damage to the anterior nucleus and the mammillothalamic tract, some retrograde degeneration also occurred in the mammillary nuclei. Studies involving smaller bilateral thalamic lesions (Aggleton and Mishkin, 1983b) demonstrated that damage to the anterior portion of mediodorsal nucleus, plus adjacent midline nuclei, but without damage to anterior nucleus and without degeneration of the mammillary nuclei, produced moderate memory impairment. Mediodorsal nucleus

Table 2 Performance of monkeys with diencephalic lesions on delayed nonmatching to sample

		Delays (percent correct)				
Group[a]	N	15 second	30 second	60 second	120 second	10 minute
1. Controls	3	—	93.3	90.0	90.7	—
Anterior medial thalamus	3	—	84.6	79.6	74.3	—
Posterior medial thalamus	3	—	86.7	85.7	80.6	—
2. Controls	4	—	96.5	94.5	94.2	—
Mammillary nuclei	6	—	93.8	91.5	89.0	—
3. Controls	4	90.5	—	86.5	—	77.0
Mediodorsal thalamic nucleus	4	84.8	—	76.0	—	62.0

[a]Group 1, from Aggleton and Mishkin, 1983b; Group 2, from Aggleton and Mishkin, 1985; Group 3, from Zola-Morgan and Squire, 1985b. Scores are based on 100 trials at each delay. For 1 and 2, animals were trained preoperatively using a 10-second delay and then retrained after surgery with the same delay. They were then tested at the longer delays. For 3, animals were trained for the first time postoperatively using an 8-second delay and then tested at the longer delays.

damage therefore contributes to the severe deficit caused by the larger midline thalamic lesion. A more anterior lesion that damaged the anterior nucleus, plus fornix, adjacent midline nuclei, and (indirectly) the mammillary nuclei and mediodorsal nucleus, also led to a moderate impairment (Table 2). One animal who sustained a transection of the massa intermedia, and a loss of 60% of the cell bodies of the midline nuclei, performed normally. Accordingly, damage to the midline nuclei probably did not contribute to the memory impairment in these studies.

Monkeys with small bilateral lesions in the posterior portion of the mediodorsal nucleus, without damage to the adjacent midline nuclei, (Figure 46; Zola-Morgan and Squire, 1985b), showed more impairment than the monkeys described above with damage to the posterior medial thalamus, which involved the anterior portion of the mediodorsal nucleus. The posterior mediodorsal lesions involved, on the average, 38% of the volume of the mediodorsal nucleus. Another study that employed different behavioral tests also found greater behavioral impairment after posterior mediodorsal nucleus lesions than after anterior mediodorsal nucleus lesions (Isseroff, Rosvold, Galkin, and Goldman-Rakic, 1982).

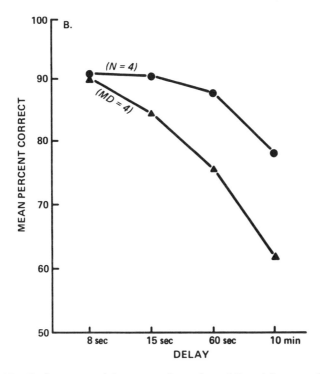

Figure 46. Performance of four control monkeys (N) and four monkeys with lesions of the mediodorsal thalamic nucleus (MD) on the delayed nonmatching to sample task. The control monkeys required a mean of 140 trials to learn the task initially with a delay of 8 seconds, and the MD group required 315 trials. The first point on the curve is the average final score during learning. Testing was then carried out at longer delays, up to 10 minutes. The extent of MD damage averaged 38%. (From Zola-Morgan and Squire, 1985b.)

These results establish firmly that mediodorsal nucleus lesions alone are sufficient to cause amnesia in monkeys. Damage in the vicinity of the anterior nucleus, together with indirect degeneration in mammillary nuclei, also contributes to memory impairment. To determine which specific thalamic lesions (besides lesions of the mediodorsal nucleus) can cause amnesia will require a series of careful behavioral studies, combined with histological verification of lesions. Amnesia is not an all-or-none phenomenon: Its severity can vary with the combination of damaged structures and with the precise location of a lesion within the critical structures. Additional studies will also be required to explore the

185

long-term effects of diencephalic lesions on memory. The available information about diencephalic amnesia in the monkey refers only to acute effects on memory during the first months after surgery; they do not answer the question of which lesions are required to support a stable memory loss persisting for years.

The mammillary nuclei lesions that are so prominent in the human clinico-pathological literature of amnesia have also been evaluated in the experimental animal. Rats with mammillary nuclei lesions are often unimpaired on behavioral tests (Woody and Ervin, 1966; Sutherland and Dyck, 1983). One preliminary report states that monkeys with mammillary nuclei lesions fail two rather difficult tests designed as analogs to the recognition tests failed by human amnesic patients (Saunders, 1983). For one task this impairment was more severe in monkeys with mammillary nuclei lesions than in monkeys with bilateral destruction of the fornix, a major pathway between the hippocampal formation and the medial mamillary nuclei. It is therefore probable that mammillary nuclei lesions can cause some degree of memory impairment. However, in another study (Aggleton and Mishkin, 1985) monkeys with lesions of the mammillary nuclei, who were studied using the same behavioral task (delayed nonmatching to sample) that had been given to monkeys with other diencephalic lesions, showed a small, negligible impairment, milder than the impairment following lesions of the mediodorsal nucleus (Aggleton and Mishkin, 1983b; Zola-Morgan and Squire, 1985b). Before any final conclusions can be reached, operated monkeys from different surgical groups must be compared across a number of behavioral tests.

Medial Temporal Amnesia

The medial temporal region was firmly linked to memory functions during the 1950s, when bilateral resections of this region were performed in a series of patients in an attempt to relieve intractable epilepsy (Scoville and Milner, 1957). The largest of these resections, which extended posteriorly along the medial surface of the temporal lobes for a distance of 8 cm and included amygdala, uncus, hippocampal gyrus, and the anterior two thirds of hippocampus, was sustained by two patients, including the famous case H.M. As the result of the surgery, H.M. developed a severe and lasting amnesia (Corkin, 1984). Two other cases (P.B. and F.C.) developed severe amnesia after equally extensive resections limited to the left temporal lobe (Penfield and Milner, 1958). These two patients were presumed to have had pre-existing pathology in the right medial temporal lobe; and for one of the two patients (P.B.), this point was later confirmed at autopsy (Penfield and Mathieson, 1974).

Hippocampal damage has traditionally been held to be the cause of the amnesia in these surgical cases. Five of six patients who sustained a less extensive resection than H.M. (extending posteriorly only so far as to involve the amygdala, uncus, and the anterior hippocampus) had a less severe amnesia. Another patient, with a resection that included only the amygdala and uncus and spared the hippocampus altogether, was not considered to be amnesic at all. Furthermore, in other cases with left or right unilateral medial temporal resections, which cause either verbal or nonverbal memory impairment respectively, the severity of the memory deficit shows a positive correlation with the extent of damage to the hippocampal region (Milner, 1974).

Aside from the view that hippocampal damage is responsible for medial temporal amnesia, there have been two other proposals concerning the critical structures within the medial temporal region. Horel (1978) suggested that the critical structure is the temporal stem, a band of white matter adjacent to and above the hippocampus. The frontal approach employed in H.M.'s surgery, Horel argued, must have damaged the temporal stem, and temporal stem damage in fact occurred in many of the subsequent studies with monkeys, where the goal was to create an animal model of H.M.'s medial temporal amnesia. However, it is now clear that the temporal stem cannot be the critical structure, so far as the amnesic syndrome is concerned, because monkeys with lesions limited to the temporal stem performed normally on memory tasks (Zola-Morgan, Squire, and Mishkin, 1982; Zola-Morgan and Squire, 1984). Moreover, monkeys with medial temporal lesions were amnesic even when the lesions spared the temporal stem altogether (Moss, Mahut, and Zola-Morgan, 1981; Mahut, Zola-Morgan and Moss, 1982; Zola-Morgan, Squire, and Mishkin, 1982). The temporal stem was likewise ruled out in a recent clinico-pathologic case study of a patient who became amnesic following an episode of anoxia (Cummings, Tomiyasu, Read, and Benson, 1984).

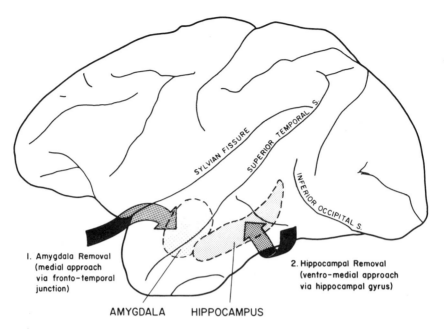

Figure 47. Lateral *(top)* and ventral *(bottom)* views of the left hemisphere of the monkey showing the two-opening approach for producing conjoint hippocampal-amygdala lesions. The same two approaches have also been used separately to produce selective lesions of hippocampus or amygdala. Areas TE and TH-TF as described by von Bonin and Bailey (1947). (From Squire and Zola-Morgan, 1983.)

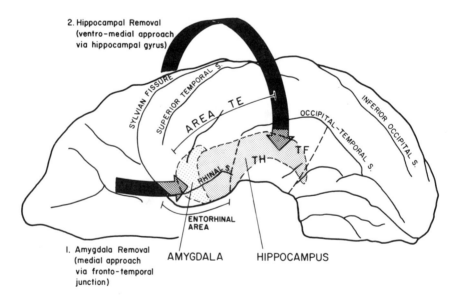

A second proposal suggested that conjoint damage to the hippocampus and amygdala is required to produce amnesia (Mishkin, 1978). Mishkin noted that all human surgical cases exhibiting amnesia included damage to both these structures. The evidence from the surgical cases is therefore equally consistent with two different possibilities: Conjoint hippocampal-amygdala damage is necessary to produce amnesia, or hippocampal damage alone is sufficient. The development of an animal model of medial temporal amnesia in the monkey has permitted significant testing of these two proposals (Figure 47).

Monkeys with bilateral medial temporal lesions that include the hippocampus and the amygdala exhibit severe memory impairment and do appear to provide a good model of human amnesia (Figure 48). But does severe amnesia require such a large lesion as this, or would a smaller removal produce the same syndrome? Behavioral studies with monkeys have tested the relative contributions to amnesia of the hippocampus and amygdala by evaluating the effects of separate hippocampal (H) lesions or combined hippocampal-amygdala (H-A) lesions on the delayed non-matching to sample task (Mishkin, 1978; Mahut, Zola-Morgan, and Moss, 1982; Squire and Zola-Morgan, 1985a). Hippocampal lesions, which included dentate gyrus, subicular cortex, most of the parahippocampal gyrus, and posterior entorhinal cortex, produced a significant impairment, but the combined H-A lesion produced an even larger deficit (Figure 49). Recent work shows that both these deficits are still present 18 months after surgery.

Further research will be needed to identify the structures that when damaged can increase the severity of the deficit associated with hippocampal lesions. The surgical approach ordinarily used during conjoint hippocampus-amygdala surgery necessarily damages entorhinal cortex, perirhinal cortex, and the parahippocampal gyrus (area TH-TF), in addition to hippocampus and amygdala. The contribution of this additional damage will need to be evaluated. One possibility is that the deficit in the large, combined lesion depends both on amygdala removal and on damage to adjacent structures typically included in amygdala surgery, especially entorhinal cortex (Murray and Mishkin, 1986).

The question arises as to why lesions limited to the hippocampal formation have been associated with a mild, almost negligible deficit in some studies (Mishkin, 1978; Murray and Mishkin, 1984) and with a

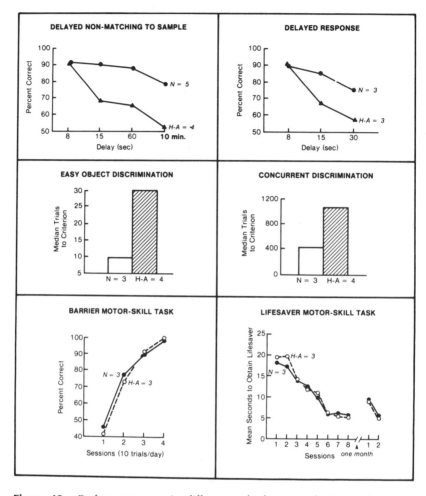

Figure 48. Performance on six different tasks by normal (N) monkeys and monkeys with bilateral medial temporal lesions (H-A) that included hippocampus, amygdala, and overlying cortex. Four of the tasks are sensitive to human amnesia. The two skill tasks are of the kind that amnesic patients can perform normally. (From Zola-Morgan and Squire, 1984; Squire and Zola-Morgan, 1985.)

moderately severe deficit in others (Zola-Morgan and Squire, 1986; Mahut, Zola-Morgan, and Moss, 1982; Figure 49). It seems likely that one important source of this difference is whether or not monkeys are given preoperative training. Monkeys received preoperative training on the delayed nonmatching-to-sample task in those studies in which the memory

190

DELAYED NONMATCHING TO SAMPLE

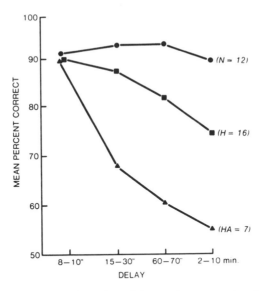

Figure 49. Combined data from three laboratories comparing the performance of normal (N) monkeys, monkeys with hippocampal (H) lesions, and monkeys with conjoint hippocampal-amygdala (H-A) lesions on the delayed nonmatching to sample task. (From Squire and Zola-Morgan, 1985; Mishkin, 1978; Mahut, Zola-Morgan, and Moss, 1982.)

deficit was mild or negligible, but training began postoperatively in the studies that found a moderately severe deficit. Could preoperative train-ing somehow facilitate postoperative performance on delayed nonmatch-ing to sample? This possibility seems unlikely at first glance, because postoperative testing requires monkeys to remember unique test objects that they have not previously encountered. However, the task requires more than remembering single objects across a delay. It also requires remembering the nonmatching principle, and it requires paying attention to the sample object and then avoiding distraction during the delay inter-val. Successful preoperative experience presumably establishes these strategies effectively, and this could facilitate performance during sub-sequent, postoperative testing. It may even be possible for a monkey to keep information about the sample in working memory throughout the delay interval, if sufficient practice has been allowed. Of course, such

191

strategies and skills would presumably be effective only when the delay interval is relatively short. In the case of a long delay, like 10 minutes, a monkey will have difficulty maintaining an effective working memory, and retrieval will have to occur from long-term memory. This idea explains why monkeys with lesions limited to the hippocampus do as poorly as they do at the long (10 minute) delay interval, and it also makes a prediction: that postoperative performance across delays this long should not be especially helped by preoperative training.

A further significant issue concerns how much memory impairment actually occurs in monkeys with selective bilateral hippocampal lesions. Although separate hippocampal lesions clearly cause memory impairment, the key question is whether this degree of impairment is clinically meaningful. Would the same lesion in a human patient produce a substantial or only a minor memory impairment? This question has been answered recently, based on autopsy information for an amnesic patient (case R.B.) who was tested extensively during a 5-year period (Zola-Morgan, Squire, and Amaral, 1986). At the age of 52, this individual had an ischemic episode as a complication of cardiac-bypass surgery, and an amnesic disorder appeared after the episode. The patient's IQ was 111, his Wechsler Memory Quotient was 91, and he had no aphasia and no neuropsychological signs of frontal lobe involvement. Indeed, no cognitive deficits other than memory impairment were ever detected. During his period of contact with our research group for 5 years after the onset of his amnesia, he frequently told the same stories and asked the same questions within a short period of time, and he was obviously forgetful, though not so severely so as some patients (for example, case H.M. and severely amnesic patients with Korsakoff's syndrome). Nevertheless, he failed paired associate learning and delayed recall tests, and on average he exhibited about the same level of impairment as our other amnesic study patients (Figure 50).

When the patient died in 1983 of congestive heart failure, detailed examination of his brain was carried out with the permission and encouragement of his family. More than 4,000 50-micron sections were cut from his brain, of which approximately 400 were stained for Nissl substance in order to reveal cell bodies. Selected sections were also stained to demonstrate myelinated fibers. This procedure allowed representative sections from the entire brain to be evaluated. Aside from two punctate,

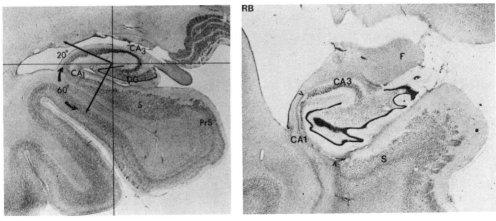

Figure 50. *Top left.* Section through the temporal lobe of a normal human brain, showing subicular cortex, PrS = presubiculum, S = subiculum, the CA subfields of the hippocampal formation, and the dentate gyrus (DG). The angle made by the two arrows subtends Sommer's sector, as defined in 1880, and identifies the region of hippocampal formation often found damaged in epileptic patients. Sommer's sector corresponds approximately to the area now known as the hippocampal CA1 subfield. *Top right.* Corresponding section from the brain of patient R.B., who developed amnesia following an ischemic episode. F = fimbria. The only significant damage was a bilateral lesion limited to the CA1 subfield, extending the full anterior-posterior length of the hippocampus. The area enclosed by the two carats identifies CA1. This region is entirely depleted of CA1 pyramidal cells. *Bottom left.* Delayed prose recall by case R.B., three other patients of similar etiology (AMN), case N.A., patients with Korsakoff's syndrome (KORS, N = 8), and two control groups. (ALC = alcoholics; CON = healthy control subjects). *Bottom right.* Delayed diagram recall for the same groups. For both tests material was presented, and retention was assessed about 10 minutes later. The data for amnesic patients are the averaged scores from three different test sessions. (N.A.'s diagram score was based on a single test. His good score on this nonverbal test is consistent with the known left unilateral locus of his injury.)

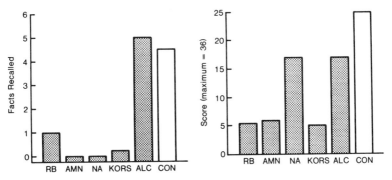

unilateral lesions, one in the globus pallidus and one in sensorimotor cortex, the only significant findings were bilateral lesions of hippocampal formation and a patchy loss of cerebellar Purkinje cells. The hippocampal lesion was limited to the pyramidal cells of area CA1 and extended the full rostral-caudal length of the hippocampal formation on both sides (Figure 50). The amygdala, the mediodorsal nucleus, the mammillary nuclei, and the structures of the basal forebrain were found to be normal on both sides. This case establishes that hippocampal lesions by themselves can result in clinically significant amnesia. Of course, one should remember that the degree of amnesia caused by hippocampal lesions in this case can be exacerbated by additional medial temporal damage. Results from monkeys underscore this point; so does patient H.M., who is more severely amnesic than patient R.B.

The neural circuitry of the hippocampal formation is rather well known. Although R.B.'s lesion was spatially limited, involving the 4.63 million pyramidal cells of each CA1 field (Brown and Cassell, 1980; Cassell, personal communication), such a lesion would be expected to disrupt the essentially unidirectional flow of information that begins in the dentate gyrus, moves through the hippocampus proper, and then ends in the subiculum and entorhinal cortex. In other words, a lesion confined to area CA1 would disrupt any computation or operation that requires the hippocampus. Indeed, the fact that the CA1 lesion resulted in amnesia shows that the hippocampus must perform some computation upon newly processed information, if that information is to be stored in an enduring and useful form. This idea is explored more fully in Chapter 13.

From Brain Lesions to Neural Systems

In developing a satisfactory neurology of memory, the identification of critical brain structures in the midline diencephalon and medial temporal region provides only an initial step. The next task is to relate these brain structures to neuroanatomy in order to delineate a neural system—a functional brain system—that consists of the identified structures. This task has not yet been accomplished, but some of the possibilities can be laid out. Lesion data will prove most useful when they can be related to neuroanatomical facts.

The detailed information now available concerning the neuroanatomy of the medial temporal lobe (for review, see Amaral, 1987) must guide any formulation attempting to delineate the functional neural system affected in amnesia. Both the hippocampus and amygdala receive information from sensory-specific cortical areas and from multimodal association areas. In particular, extensive afferent and efferent pathways from and to neocortex focus a convergence of connections on the parahippocampal gyrus (Van Hoesen, 1982). These connections can provide both the hippocampus and amygdala with access to ongoing cortical activity at memory storage sites.

One traditional view attributes amnesia to damage within a functional circuit originally described by Papez (1937) that includes most prominently the hippocampus, fornix, and mammillary bodies (Brierley, 1977; Barbizet, 1970). Although this pathway seems incapable of explaining all the neuropathological facts of memory disorders, it could form one component of a more extended neural system. Importantly, the traditional view assigns no role to the mediodorsal thalamic nucleus. Furthermore, this view is inconsistent with the relatively mild effects of fornix section on memory. The best-known, most thoroughly studied of the human cases (Sweet, Talland, and Ervin, 1959) has only a mild amnesia (a difference between IQ and Wechsler Memory Quotient of 13 points), in comparison with the amnesic cases that provide the basis for virtually all contemporary experimental study. Our own case of bilateral CA1 lesions, for example, had an IQ-MQ difference of 20 points; case N.A. (Kaushall, Zetin, and Squire, 1981) has an IQ-MQ difference of 27 points, and case H.M. has an IQ-MQ difference of 35–54 points, based on testing carried out between 1955 and 1983 (Corkin, 1984). A second, widely cited case of fornix transection and memory loss (Hassler and Reichert, 1957) involved a patient who was disoriented and febrile, and who survived only 8 days after fornix surgery. Autopsy revealed a tumor of the frontal lobe, in addition to the fornix transection performed at surgery.

Fornix section in monkeys can produce memory impairments on specially constructed tasks (Gaffan, Saunders, Gaffan, Harrison, Shields, and Owen, 1984). But direct comparisons of the effects of fornix section with the effects of hippocampal lesions, using three separate tasks sensitive to human amnesia, showed that monkeys with hippocampal lesions

195

were impaired, while monkeys with fornix section exhibited no deficit (Mahut et al., 1981; Moss, Mahut, and Zola-Morgan, 1982; Mahut, Zola-Morgan, and Moss, 1982). Other studies suggest that fornix lesions may produce a very mild memory impairment (Bachevalier, Saunders, and Mishkin, 1985) or a selective impairment, which spares some aspects of the kind of memory that is affected in amnesia while impairing other aspects (Gaffan, Gaffan, and Harrison, 1984; Gaffan, Shields, and Harrison, 1984).

The neuroanatomy of the hippocampus and fornix is consistent with the idea that fornix section could produce a less severe amnesia, or even a qualitatively different impairment, from that associated with hippocampal lesions. In the monkey, a substantial projection from the hippocampal formation is directed not only through the fornix but also caudally, via entorhinal cortex, to a number of cortical and subcortical structures (Rosene and Van Hoesen, 1977). Because the fornix is only one of two major efferent pathways from the hippocampus, damage to the fornix should not necessarily mimic the effects of hippocampal removal. More empirical work remains to be done, but the information now available suggests that the functional link usually presumed to exist between the hippocampus and the mammillary nuclei has been overstated.

One way for medial temporal and diencephalic structures to function together as a memory system was proposed by Mishkin (1982). In this model, the critical structures are presumed to be the hippocampus, the amygdala, and their diencephalic targets, the anterior nucleus of the thalamus and the mediodorsal thalamic nucleus, respectively. This neuroanatomical perspective is also compatible with the hypothesis that additional structures with strong links to these medial temporal and medial thalamic sites play a role in the same functional system. For example, the mammillary nuclei both project to the anterior nucleus and, in addition, receive substantial input from the hippocampal formation via the fornix. Likewise, ventromedial frontal cortex receives projections from both the anterior nucleus and the mediodorsal thalamic nucleus. Consistent with these facts, lesions of ventromedial but not dorsolateral prefrontal cortex in monkeys produce a recognition memory deficit (Bachevalier and Mishkin, 1986). Recent radiographic data have also suggested that damage to the ventromedial prefrontal area can occur in those patients who develop amnesia following rupture and repair of anterior communicating artery aneurysms (Damasio, Graff-Radford, Eslinger, Damasio, and Kassell, 1985).

Finally, the basal forebrain (nucleus basalis, diagonal band of Broca, and septal nuclei) projects to both the amygdala and separately to the hippocampus (via fornix). In the monkey, preliminary findings demonstrate that a conjoint lesion of all three components of the basal forebrain, but not a lesion of two out of three components, will moderately impair performance on the delayed nonmatching to sample task (Aigner, Mitchell, Aggleton, DeLong, Struble, Wenk, Price, and Mishkin, 1984). Basal forebrain pathology has also been hypothesized as a contributor to the amnesia associated with rupture of anterior communicating artery aneurysms (Damasio et al., 1985).

The available data thus suggest that nucleus basalis lesions, or even larger lesions of the basal forebrain, do not cause severe amnesia in the absence of additional damage. Nevertheless, this idea did gain some acceptance following reports that Alzheimer's disease can present with selective neuronal loss in that region (Whitehouse et al., 1982). More recent studies of the pathophysiology of Alzheimer's disease have found prominent pathology in the entorhinal cortex and in the subiculum of the hippocampal formation (Hyman et al., 1984). Such damage would effectively isolate the hippocampal formation from neocortex. If medial temporal pathology were a typical early finding in Alzheimer's disease, this could explain why memory problems are so often the first significant symptom.

No neuroanatomical proposal can be considered well grounded so long as ambiguity remains as to *which* structures are the important ones. Systematic studies of the effects of lesions will be needed to settle these uncertainties. It is essential to try to relate the behavioral findings from lesion studies to anatomy, so that identified structures and their connections can be pieced into a functional neural system. It will also be important to use standard behavioral tasks so that the deficit associated with any particular lesion can be assessed quantitatively and compared with the deficits associated with other lesions (Squire and Shimamura, 1986).

Aging and Memory

Elderly persons commonly report that their memory is not as good as it used to be. They state, for example, that they may not recall someone's name on a particular occasion, even though that person is well known to them. They may forget where they had left some familiar item, such as the house keys or a newspaper. They report that when speaking they may not be able to think of a particular word, even though the word will seem to be on the tip of the tongue. The elderly also perform more poorly than younger subjects on a wide variety of laboratory memory tests (Craik, 1977; Poon et al., 1980). Are the changes in memory that accompany normal aging caused by a malfunction of the same neural system that is damaged in amnesia? To answer this question, it is necessary to determine what neural changes occur with aging within the neural system damaged in amnesia, and to determine whether the memory problems in aging and amnesia are similar or different.

Three kinds of age-related events have been especially studied: loss of neurons, changes in neuronal size and in the dendritic processes supported by neurons, and changes in the frequency of neuropathological markers within neurons, such as neurofibrillary tangles and senile plaques. Of these, neuronal loss provides the most unambiguous indication of lost function. Unfortunately, the work of counting neurons is notoriously vulnerable to technical artifacts. The problem seems simple enough: For individuals of different ages, how many neurons exist within a particular structure or region? However, determinations of neuronal number almost always depend on extrapolations from counted samples to calculated tissue volumes. The human brain shrinks with increasing age; and during the processing of tissue for mounting and staining, additional shrinkage occurs (Haug, Barmwater, Eggers, Fischer, Kuhl, and Sass, 1983). As a result, measures of neuronal density alone provide an unreliable index of neuronal number. Unless corrections for tissue volume are included, erroneous estimates of neuronal number will always be obtained.

Inadequate attention to these factors seems to have been the basis for one of the great persisting myths of human neurobiology: that throughout adulthood we lose an enormous number of neurons from the brain each day. This widely disseminated idea derives from early measurements of neuronal density in aged brains (Brody, 1955). However, the expression of these early results as a daily estimate apparently began with Burns (1958), who cited Brody and others, saying: "These figures imply that during every day of our adult life more than one hundred thousand neurones die!" Later, while agreeing that an enormous amount of cell loss occurred, Brody suggested that the rate of cell loss was so variable that a daily estimate was inappropriate (Brody and Vijayashankar, 1977).

More recent quantitative studies, using automated equipment and corrections for total tissue volume, provide a very different picture of aging and neuronal loss (Haug, et al., 1983). Many areas of the brain, such as striate cortex and parietal cortex (area 7) do not lose an appreciable number of neurons during life. By contrast, 15–20% of the neurons in neostriatum and prefrontal cortex are lost between young adulthood and old age. No easy generalizations can be made about the brain as a whole or the neocortex in particular. Losses from prefrontal cortex may be sizable, even in terms of a daily estimate. But other areas are rather stable. Each brain region appears to have its own time course during aging. More detailed morphometric analyses have also been useful. For example, the diameters of cell bodies in neocortex decrease during aging (Haug et al., 1983; Terry, personal communication), thereby raising the possibility that aged neurons can support fewer axonal and dendritic processes than young neurons.

As suggested above, if memory failure during normal aging is to be related to the amnesic syndrome, then one must determine whether neuronal loss occurs specifically in the hippocampus and related structures. Recently, careful cell counts in the hippocampus have been carried out. In three separate studies of human brains, the conclusion was that a small, age-related loss of neurons occurs in the pyramidal cell fields: 3.6% per decade (Miller, et al., 1984), 4.7% per decade (Dam, 1979), and 5.4% per decade (Ball, 1977). Based on recent estimates that the CA1 field of human hippocampus contains 4.63 million pyramidal cells (Brown and Cassel, 1980; Cassell, personal communication), these estimates amount to fewer than 100 neurons lost per day from CA1. At the age of 80 years, only about 20–30% of hippocampal pyramidal cells would have been lost. Nevertheless, since complete loss of CA1 pyramidal cells does result in an amnesic syndrome (Zola-Morgan, Squire, and Amaral, 1986), perhaps gradual depletion of a fraction of these cells could account for a degree of forgetfulness.

An additional relevant finding is that neuropathological abnormalities are found within the hippocampus during normal aging. Tomlinson and his colleagues (Tomlinson, Blessed, and Roth, 1968; Tomlinson, 1972) examined the brains of 28 elderly persons (aged 65 to 92), who shortly before death were considered to be well preserved intellectually. They also examined 219 additional brains, representing persons aged approximately 20 to 90 years of age. These were routine consecutive autopsies, also done in individuals who were deemed to have been intellectually intact at the time of death. The elderly brains overall showed few signs of abnormality. For example, 85% of them were judged to have no evidence or only slight evidence of cerebral atrophy. All of them showed some of the neuropathogical signs usually associated with senility, for example, signs of ischemia, neurofibrillary tangles, and plaque formation. However, these were infrequent, and the neocortex was affected to only a minor degree.

The outstanding finding in the elderly brains was the presence of neurofibrillary tangles in widespread distribution in the hippocampus and parahippocampal gyrus. Many of the 28 cases exhibited these changes only in the hippocampal complex and not at all in neocortex. Examination of the 219 younger brains showed that these changes appear gradually, beginning early in life. They were not found in any of the brains sampled from the third decade of life, but plaques and tangles were found in 5–15% of the brains sampled from the fifth decade, and in about half of the brains sampled from the seventh decade. Thus, not only does the normal hippocampus lose a small percentage of its neurons each decade, but the remaining neurons develop signs of pathology. These findings increase the likelihood that some of the memory difficulties experienced by elderly persons are due to hippocampal dysfunction.

One important point to emerge from research is that normal aging involves a spectrum of cognitive change, which includes memory but is not limited to it. For example, one of the best-studied and earliest appearing cognitive changes in aging is a reduction in performance on divided attention tasks. These tasks require subjects to divide their attention between two or more competing information sources. In one often-used paradigm, six different digits are presented, three to each ear. Subjects hear three pairs of digits in succession, but each pair is presented to the two ears simultaneously. Afterwards, subjects must report the digits that they heard. Reductions in performance on such tasks can be detected at least as early as age 30 to 40 (Barr, 1980). The problem is not memory *per se,* because most persons can easily report six digits presented in sequence to one ear. The problem is in processing information presented simultaneously to the two ears. These findings and others extend the study of age-related cognitive change beyond the domain of memory. Recent accounts of aging and cognition have developed the broader notion that processing resources are reduced in aging and that changes occur in the strategies used to process and retrieve information (Burke and Light, 1981; Rabinowitz, Craik, and Ackerman, 1982).

These examples make the point that the neurobiology of human aging may affect the neural system that is damaged in amnesia, but more than this system must be involved. Indeed, one must look outside of this neural system even to explain all the memory changes in the elderly. Forgetting where the car keys were left could reflect loss of neurons from the hippocampus. But hippocampal damage cannot explain forgetting the name that goes with a familiar face. Difficulty retrieving the names of old acquaintances or the names of objects is not a problem for the amnesic patient. Amnesic patients are normal at object-naming tests, and they are quite able to retrieve from memory proper names as well as facts and vocabulary items, provided that the material was learned long before the onset of amnesia. Accordingly, these aspects of impaired memory performance in the elderly must depend on brain changes outside the medial temporal and diencephalic structures damaged in amnesia. In this context, the most likely site of age-related neural change is neocortex, where the names of persons and objects and other long-established declarative memories are presumably stored. One region of neocortex that appears to be prominently affected by normal aging is prefrontal cortex. Neural loss in this area could account directly for some of the cognitive changes that occur during aging, such as reduced performance on divided attention tasks. Indeed, neuropsychological data (see Chapter 14) have linked frontal lobe function to processes of search and the ability to switch rapidly among competing sources of information.

13

Amnesia and the Functional Organization of Memory

For historical reasons, discussions of how the brain structures that are damaged in amnesia contribute to normal memory functions have concentrated on the medial temporal region, and particularly on the hippocampal formation. The noted amnesic patient H.M., with bilateral medial temporal lesions, has furnished an exceptionally good study case and has led to a rich body of cumulative neuropsychological findings (Milner, 1972; Corkin, 1984). More recently, patient R.B. established with certainty that a bilateral lesion limited to the hippocampus proper can produce amnesia (Zola-Morgan, Squire, and Amaral, 1986). The discussion here likewise emphasizes the medial temporal region, making the tacit assumption that the ideas presented may also apply to the critical diencephalic regions, and perhaps to other related structures as well. Together with the medial temporal region, these structures constitute the larger neural system. One should not assume, however, that all parts of the larger system must contribute to memory function in exactly the same way. For example, the particular contribution to normal function of medial temporal and diencephalic structures may prove to be unique in certain respects (Squire and Cohen, 1984; Parkin, 1984).

The key to understanding the function of the damaged neural system is the selectivity of amnesia. First, general intellectual ability is intact.

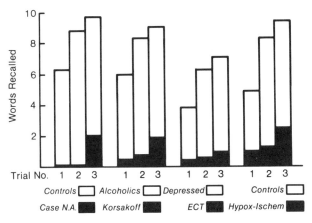

Figure 51. Paired associate learning ability by four kinds of amnesic patients and matched control subjects. Ten pairs of unrelated words (e.g., army-table) were presented, and subjects were then asked to recall the second word when given the first word of each pair. Recall was attempted after each of three successive presentations of the word pairs. Case N.A. became amnesic for verbal material in 1960 as the result of a penetrating injury from a miniature fencing foil that damaged the left dorsal thalamic region. Data are also shown for eight patients with Korsakoff's syndrome, eight patients tested 1 hour following the fourth or fifth treatments in a series of prescribed bilateral electroconvulsive therapy (ECT), and four patients who became amnesic as the result of a hypoxic-ischemic episode. Despite impaired learning ability, all patients had normal or above-normal general intellectual abilities.

Second, short-term memory is undisturbed. Amnesic patients have a normal digit span and an intact ability to maintain a limited amount of information in mind for many minutes, so long as they can rehearse and are not distracted. Indeed, they can appear strikingly normal in casual conversation. Third, they can also recall successfully a great deal of information that was learned long before the onset of amnesia. Amnesic patients encounter difficulty only when they must learn more information than they can hold in mind all at once (Figure 51), or when they are distracted from rehearsing even a small amount of information and must then retrieve it anew. They also encounter difficulty in recalling events from before the onset of amnesia, especially if those events occurred close to the time that amnesia began, as opposed to the remote past.

Because short-term memory is intact in amnesia, the neural system damaged in amnesic patients must not be required for the early stages of information analysis. Thus, percepts can be formed, attention can be deployed, and short-term memory can be established—all without the participation of this neural system. This system (at least that component of the system that includes the hippocampus and amygdala) also does not appear to be significant in the generation of the P3 evoked potential (Paller, 1986; Paller, Zola-Morgan, Squire, and Hillyard, 1986). This brain wave is a positive-going deflection from the electroencephalogram (EEG), which is elicited especially by unexpected stimuli (Hillyard and Kutas, 1983), and which occurs with a latency of about 300 msec. The P3 wave had previously been linked to memory functions. Specifically, the amplitude of the P3 wave predicts subsequent memory performance (Sanquist, Rohrbaugh, Syndulko, and Lindsley, 1980; Neville, Kutas, Chesney, and Schmidt, 1986; Fabiani, Karis, and Donchin, 1986). In view of the finding that the P3 wave does not reflect medial temporal cortex function, the processes indexed by the P3 wave would appear to be part of early-stage attentional and short-term memory processes. Events at these early stages of processing can of course influence the development of long-term memory (see Chapter 4). The medial temporal lobe has a role at a later stage of processing.

The view presented here is that the medial temporal structures damaged in amnesia play an essential role in the establishment of long-term memory and in the consolidation or elaboration of memory for a time after learning. Further, these structures are required only for establishing one kind of memory, what is here termed declarative memory. They are not required for the acquisition and retrieval of procedural memory. Moreover, within the domain of declarative memory, medial temporal structures are involved only in the establishment and consolidation of long-term memory, not short-term.

The Formation and Consolidation of Long-term Memory

The concept of consolidation appears in many discussions of how memory is organized. Consolidation refers to the idea (Muller and Pilzecker, 1900) that memory storage does not occur instantaneously but instead develops gradually after initial learning. The initial observation was that material learned during a retention interval had disruptive effects on retention related to its temporal proximity to the originally learned material. During this century the idea of consolidation was largely absorbed by interference theory (see Keppel, 1984). If similar material is learned on two different occasions, not too separated in time, the second learning episode reduces the accessibility of what was learned during the first episode. Behavioral data from studies of human learning and memory did not seem to require that the original representation itself should change with time after learning, or that new learning need ever change a pre-existing representation. Interference implies reduced access due to additional memory storage, not loss or change of the items already in storage.

In contrast, the modern biologic idea of consolidation rests on just such a notion that what is in storage can change (McGaugh and Herz, 1972; Squire, Cohen, and Nadel, 1984). The neural elements and the synaptic connectivity representing information storage are presumed to change gradually over time. The hypothesis that changes in memory continue long after learning was in fact stated many years ago by Burnham (1903):

In normal memory a process of organization is continually going on—a physical process of organization and a psychological process of repetition and association. In order that ideas may become a part of permanent memory, time must elapse for these processes of organization to be completed (p. 396).

Burnham's hypothesis states that the eventual fate of representations in long-term memory is not entirely determined at the time of learning, but rather is affected by subsequent external events (such as repetition and other acquired information) and by internal events (such as rehearsal and efforts at reconstruction). From a neurobiological perspective, this idea implies that post-learning events could influence the fate of memory by actually remodeling the neural circuitry that underlies the original representation. Indeed, the idea that consolidation is a competitive process is derived from neurobiological principles (see Chapter 3): Some aspects of memory for the original event are forgotten, while those that remain are strengthened (Squire, Cohen, and Nadel, 1984). Consolidation is thus a process that occurs within the collection of distributed sites where synaptic change representing information storage has occurred.

The neurobiological concept of consolidation is based first of all on studies of retrograde amnesia (Glickman, 1961; McGaugh and Herz, 1972). Various agents—most notably head trauma, electroconvulsive shock (ECS), or electroconvulsive therapy (ECT)—can affect past memories differentially depending on how long ago a memory was acquired (Figure 52). As the interval between learning and an amnestic event is lengthened, the severity of the resulting amnesia typically decreases. Consolidation refers to the process by which memory gradually becomes resistant to disruption by an amnestic agent. It is difficult to ascribe retrograde amnesia to interference effects, especially when a long interval is present between learning and the disruptive treatment.

Studies of retrograde amnesia in experimental animals and in patients show that the hypothesized consolidation process can continue over a long period. For example, psychiatric patients prescribed a course of electroconvulsive therapy (ECT) for depressive illness were given tests based on former one-season television programs (Squire and Slater, 1975; Squire and Fox, 1980). The treatments caused both anterograde amnesia and a temporally limited retrograde amnesia. The retrograde amnesia affected information acquired 1 to about 3 years prior to treatment (Squire, Slater, and Chace, 1975; Squire and Cohen, 1979). Information acquired prior to that time was not affected.

The finding that retrograde amnesia in humans can selectively affect the events from a period as long as a few years originally seemed to conflict with the fact that temporally-graded, retrograde memory effects in laboratory animals usually cover a much shorter time period. Animal studies, especially those where a single electroconvulsive shock is given to rats or mice, have typically found memory to be susceptible to disruption from only a few seconds up to perhaps a few minutes after learning. However, it is now clear that long gradients of retrograde amnesia can also be observed in such studies. Mice learning a 1-trial passive avoidance task and given 4 spaced ECS—to mimic the treatment that is associated with extensive retrograde amnesia in humans—exhibited graded retrograde amnesia covering 1 to 3 weeks (Squire and Spanis, 1984).

Although the combined findings from humans and laboratory animals do show that consolidation can continue for a lengthy period, consolidation has no fixed lifetime and its time course can vary widely. The passive avoidance habit in normal mice is forgotten gradually during the

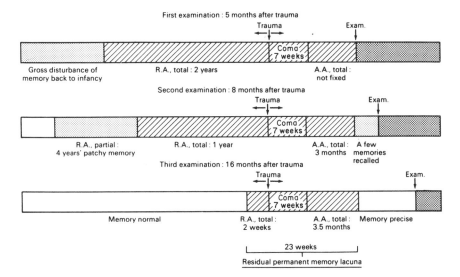

Figure 52. *Top.* Pattern of anterograde amnesia (A.A.) and retrograde amnesia (R.A.) in a case of severe head trauma, as determined by clinical interview three times after the trauma. The retrograde amnesia was temporally limited, with recent memory more affected than remote memory. *Bottom.* Temporally limited retrograde amnesia following electroconvulsive treatment, as determined by formal testing methods in mice and humans. Memory apparently changes for a long time after initial learning, such that some material becomes unavailable (forgetting), while what remains becomes more resistant to disruption (consolidation). (Top from Barbizet, 1970; bottom from Squire, 1984.)

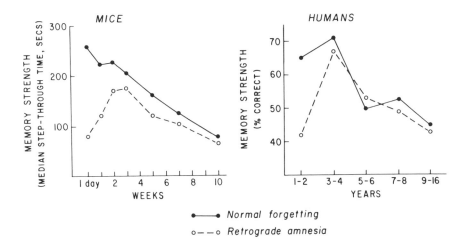

207

weeks after training and persists for at least 12 weeks. In the mice given ECS, temporally graded retrograde amnesia covered 1 to 3 weeks. Memory for one-season television programs, studied in humans, is forgotten during a period of several years and persists for more than 15 years (Figure 11). Temporally graded retrograde amnesia following ECT covered 1 to 3 years. The point is that consolidation is not an automatic process with a fixed duration. It is best regarded as a dynamic process that continues so long as information is being forgotten, and that results in the reorganization and stabilization of what remains.

What is known about the nature of retrograde amnesia outside of ECS and ECT studies? In patient H.M., retrograde amnesia has been studied by administering tests of remote memory for events that occurred at various times before or after his surgery in 1953. All the remote memory tests revealed poor memory for the events since 1953. In addition, the tests showed that he has good memory for his early life, but variable amnesia (depending on the test) for the period from 1942, when he first developed epilepsy, to 1953, the year of surgery (Marslen-Wilson and Teuber, 1975; Corkin, 1984). It is not known whether his amnesia for the time before 1953 displays a temporal gradient. The results indicate only that very remote memories are intact, and that whatever retrograde amnesia is present is temporally limited.

For some cases of head injury, good memory for premorbid events with perhaps a year or two of temporally limited retrograde amnesia has been reported (Russell and Nathan, 1946; Barbizet, 1970). Temporally limited retrograde amnesia has also been reported for cases of encephalitis (Rose and Symonds, 1960; for a review of other cases, see Parkin, 1984). It should be noted that post-encephalitic amnesia is often associated with an extensive retrograde amnesia. The variable findings reported for the post-encephalitic cases are probably due to the variable neuropathology associated with this condition.

Finally, a detailed assessment of retrograde amnesia was carried out for case R.B., who had selective hippocampal damage caused by ischemic injury in 1978 (Zola-Morgan, Squire, and Amaral, 1986). On six different tests of remote memory, sampling the period 1940-1979, R.B. performed overall as well as or better than control subjects. Thus, he had little if any retrograde amnesia. It is possible that he did have difficulty recalling events from the 1 or 2 years prior to his episode. On two tests,

he performed noticeably poorer than his control subjects on those questions that concerned the 1970s. However, these tests are too coarsely
grained and performance is too variable to detect such a deficit reliably
in a single subject.

In summary, the data from retrograde amnesia following medial temporal lobe damage suggest that at the time of learning the medial temporal region establishes a functional relationship with memory storage
sties, especially in neocortex (Squire, Cohen, and Nadel, 1984). The
hippocampal formation can exhibit long-lasting synaptic change in response to brief, high-frequency stimulation of its input pathway (long-
term potentiation, or LTP), and LTP could be one index of this relationship between hippocampus and neocortex (Teyler and DiScenna, 1986).
The medial temporal region then performs some time-limited function on
behalf of memory storage sites, which eventually allows memory storage
and retrieval to proceed without the participation of this region. One
possibility is that it could maintain the coherence of stored memory by
making contact with those distributed sites that together represent the
specific time, place, and content information that define an event. By
this view, the medial temporal region is involved in memory for only a
limited period of time after learning. A time eventually seems to come
when this system is either less involved, or entirely uninvolved, in memory storage.

The neuroanatomical facts are compatible with an interaction between
the medial temporal region and memory storage sites; and, in this regard,
the hippocampal formation has received special attention.

> If the hippocampal formation and parahippocampal gyrus perform some fun-
> damental function on the input they receive so that it is preserved in a more
> enduring form in the association cortices, then they must have widespread
> projections back to such areas. As reviewed, there is a growing body of evi-
> dence that such projections exist and that they are both extensive and wide-
> spread (Van Hoesen, 1982, p. 350).

During the lengthy process of consolidation, the critical neural system
within the medial temporal region may maintain the organization of distant memory storage sites, until such time as the coherence of these sites
increases and they can be activated as an ensemble without the participation of the medial temporal region (Figure 53). Alternatively, it is

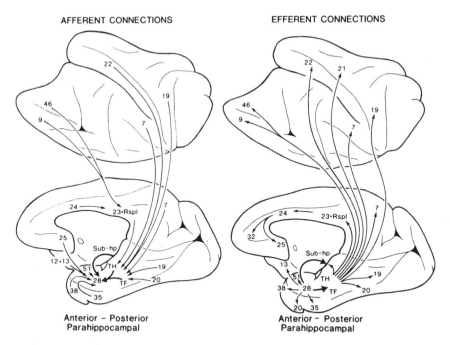

AFFERENT CONNECTIONS

EFFERENT CONNECTIONS

Anterior − Posterior
Parahippocampal

Anterior − Posterior
Parahippocampal

Figure 53. Close connection between the medial temporal region and putative memory storage loci in the rest of cortex. The diagrams summarize cortical afferent and efferent connections of the rhesus monkey parahippocampal gyrus on lateral (inverted) and medial views of the cerebral hemisphere. Projections from widespread cortical areas converge on area 28, entorhinal cortex, and most of these pathways are reciprocated by efferent projections. (From Van Hoesen, 1982.)

possible that the medial temporal region completes its work more quickly, and that changes in the organization of memory storage sites continue well beyond the time during which the medial temporal region is required. In either case, the essential idea is that the medial temporal region has a time-limited function. Memory depends on an interaction between a specialized neural system within the medial temporal region and memory storage sites in neocortex (also see Halgren, 1984; Mishkin, 1982; Squire, 1982a).

One direction of research that will be very useful in exploring these ideas about long-term memory formation and consolidation is to study retrograde amnesia following medial temporal lesions in experimental animals. Surprisingly, this problem has been worked on only infrequently (Uretsky and McCleary, 1969; Harley, 1979). The first question is whether a lesion that prevents new learning will at the same time spare retention of learning that occurred before surgery. The second question is how long before surgery must learning occur if memory is to be spared, and what is the form of the retrograde amnesia gradient? In one study bilateral entorhinal lesions in rats prevented long-term retention of a postoperatively acquired olfactory discrimination, but largely spared a similar discrimination learned just prior to surgery (Staubli, Fraser, Kessler, and Lynch, 1987). This finding suggests, in keeping with the human amnesia data, that when learning occurs before surgery, memory can survive damage to medial temporal cortex.

A second study examined in monkeys the fate of memories established 2 weeks to 8 months before surgery (Salmon, Zola-Morgan, and Squire, 1987). Monkeys learned object discriminations at five scheduled times during an 8-month period and then received bilateral lesions of hippocampus, amygdala, and overlying allocortex. After surgery, the monkeys lost all the preoperatively established memories, whereas unoperated monkeys performed at a high level. Thus, retrograde amnesia was severe in this case, and it extended at least 8 months into the preoperative period.

Further studies are needed. Possible factors influencing the nature of retrograde amnesia are the strength of original learning and how long memory for the learned material will ordinarily last (i.e., the time course of normal forgetting); the specific structures damaged; and the nature and timing of postoperative testing. Studies with experimental animals can avoid the difficulties inherent in assessing remote memory retrospectively in human subjects, and they should permit decisive tests of the idea that the medial temporal region has a time-limited role in memory.

The suggestion has sometimes been made that information might be initially contained in the medial temporal region and sometime later moved to neocortex for permanent storage. On its face, this sequence offers an alternative account of the retrograde amnesia data, that is, that medial temporal damage affects recently acquired memories more than memories acquired long ago. Yet besides being decidedly nonbiological, this hypothesis ignores the fact that short-term memory is intact in amnesic patients. Thus, memory cannot begin in the neural system damaged in amnesia; it must begin in the cortical processing areas that remain intact. Given this constraint, one would have to suppose that memory moves from neocortex to the medial temporal region and then back again; or that a long-term memory constructed in the medial temporal region moves and replaces a short-term memory already residing in neocortex. A more likely and parsimonious scenario is that short-term and long-term memory occur in the same place, that one grades into the other, and that the participation of a specialized neural system (within the medial temporal region) is needed so that the distributed sites constituting any particular instance of long-term memory can be defined, stabilized, and accessed.

An important question is whether amnesia causes actual alterations in memory storage, or whether amnesia represents a difficulty in retrieving from memory storage. In the presence of amnesia, neuronal changes representing newly formed short-memory can still occur. Do these neuronal events leave a long-lasting record to the same degree as they ordinarily would, but a record that remains inaccessible? Or are memories formed and then lost as time passes? Alternatively, are they formed incorrectly, or incompletely, in the first place? Do the neuronal changes that represent recently acquired information continue to exist after the onset of amnesia, but in an inaccessible form, or are they at some point lost from storage? This significant issue, the issue of storage versus retrieval deficits in amnesia, has received extensive debate (Miller and Springer, 1973; Miller and Marlin, 1984; Wickelgren, 1979; Squire, 1980), and direct neurobiological evidence will likely be needed before the question can be conclusively settled. Nevertheless, progress has been made by neuropsychological studies framed around these questions.

Amnesia cannot be a simple retrieval deficit. If amnesia were a retrieval deficit, patients should have difficulty recalling all past events, not only those that occurred during the few years before the onset of their syndrome and those that have occurred afterwards. However, patient H.M. and many other patients *can* access their premorbid memory. What other kind of retrieval deficit might amnesia represent? Could amnesia impair only some kinds of retrieval? That is, perhaps retrieval can succeed for very remote memories, and only the retrieval of recently established memories is affected. Such a view has been favored by some, and its proof is said to reside in the fact that, when temporally-limited retrograde amnesia occurs, it is reversible (Miller and Marlin, 1984). In

212

other words, if retrograde amnesia appears initially, and later resolves, then the once lost memories could not have been actually erased, and the problem must have been only in retrieval.

This hypothesis encounters several difficulties with the facts. Following head trauma or ECT much past memory does return. However, long-lasting, and presumably permanent, memory loss occurs for information acquired in the minutes, hours, or days immediately preceding the amnestic event (Russell and Nathan, 1946; Barbizet, 1970; Squire, Slater, and Miller, 1981). The simplest way to connect all the observations together is to hypothesize that (1) a disruptive treatment that occurs sufficiently long after learning will not affect memory; (2) a treatment that occurs at intermediate times after learning causes temporary loss of memory; and (3) a treatment that occurs soon after learning causes permanent memory loss. The assertion that retrograde amnesia is reversible overlooks the crucial fact that the recovery phenomenon is temporally graded. In particular, it overlooks the fact that a portion of retrograde amnesia, that portion affecting memory for events just prior to the precipitating incident, is permanent and not reversible. For example, long-standing (and temporally limited) retrograde amnesia occurs in certain cases of chronic amnesia like patient H.M. When retrograde amnesia is permanent, and graded temporally, there is no obvious reason to favor a retrieval view.

Another type of difficulty also arises with a retrieval view. If the neural system damaged in amnesia functioned *only* to retrieve recent memories, then retrieval should succeed once memories are no longer recent. Specifically, retrieval should succeed after memory storage becomes fully independent of the damaged system. Patient H.M. for example, who after surgery could not remember events from the previous few years, should eventually be able to do so. Yet he has remained amnesic for these premorbid events. Thus, the data do not bear out the idea that the medial temporal region serves only to retrieve memory. The general idea is that this region must perform some computation upon memory storage sites or interact with them in some way. Moreover, this interaction must begin near the time of learning. If the medial temporal region is not intact near the time of learning, memory for recent events becomes permanently unavailable, and these memories cannot be retrieved at a later time. In other words, in the absence of the medial temporal region, memory storage is either not established at all, i.e., there is a storage deficit; or it is established in such a way that retrieval can never succeed. If how memory is initially established and consolidated determines whether retrieval will succeed or not at some later time, it seems sensible to regard these determining neural events, which depend on the integrity of the medial temporal region at the time of learning, as memory *storage* events.

A more specific version of the same idea states that in amnesia information is forgotten in accord with the same biological program that occurs in normal forgetting. By this view, in amnesia the synaptic changes that initially represent information in newly formed, short-term memory do not survive completely as long-term memory. That is, as time passes these synaptic changes do not hold to their normal organization. Similarly, memory for recently occurring events is literally lost at the onset of amnesia, in the sense that the relevant synaptic changes are affected by removal of the medial temporal region. The extent of the disruption should depend on the degree to which consolidation has been completed when amnesia occurs. If consolidation is quite incomplete, the synaptic changes representing a recently established memory will not be able to achieve the final stages of coherence and organization that permit them to function as an ensemble, independently of the medial temporal region. Moreover, so long as amnesia persists, this information will be gradually lost. Whether or not an event that occurred before amnesia is remembered again after recovery from the amnesia should depend both on the recency of the event and on how long the amnesic condition lasts. The retrograde time period permanently lost should be shorter when the amnesic condition is brief than when it persists for many months.

Anterograde and retrograde amnesia can be considered to be linked deficits—joined by the fact that the neural system damaged in amnesia prevents new learning from being established and also prevents recently formed memories from becoming fully consolidated. That is, new representations cannot be established because of the unavailability of a critical neural system. This system ordinarily maintains the organization of newly acquired memories and permits their retrieval and reorganization over time. Memory for recently acquired events is affected because of the inability to maintain the coherence of recently formed, not yet consolidated, representations. Thus it is proposed that some of the neuronal changes that ordinarily subserve recently established information storage, including changes in synaptic connectivity, will be lost in amnesia by being weakened, written over, or otherwise altered.

Because the evidence remains indirect, this proposal concerning the function of the medial temporal region should be regarded as tentative. At the present time, two basic ideas should prove useful in further study of these problems: the initial organization of long-term memory, its maintenance for some period of time, and the ability to retrieve it during this period, depend on an interaction between distributed memory storage sites and the medial temporal region. When sufficient time has elapsed after learning, memory retrieval can proceed for some or all of memory, without the participation of the medial temporal region.

The Contribution of the Diencephalon

The nature of the amnesia that occurs after damage to other components of this putative neural system, including the diencephalic region, is less clear. For this reason, some uncertainty persists as to how the diencephalic structures affected in amnesia contribute to normal memory functions. Consider, for example, the phenomenon of retrograde amnesia. In the best-studied example of diencephalic amnesia, Korsakoff's syndrome, the retrograde amnesia is extensive rather than temporally limited (Figure 54). Patients with Korsakoff's syndrome exhibit a severe and extensive impairment of remote memory that affects the majority of their adult lives (Sanders and Warrington, 1971; Albert, Butters, and Levin, 1979; Cohen and Squire, 1981). The question is: What determines the extent and severity of this impairment? In some other instances of amnesia, the extent of retrograde amnesia is correlated with the severity of anterograde amnesia (e.g., in traumatic amnesia; Russell and Nathan, 1946), and retrograde amnesia has also been presumed to be correlated with anterograde amnesia in the case of medial temporal amnesia. Are anterograde and retrograde amnesia also linked in the case of Korsakoff's syndrome, or does extensive remote memory impairment constitute a separate and unrelated deficit?

One study that bears on the relationship between anterograde amnesia and remote memory impairment determined the relative abilities of patients with Korsakoff's syndrome, and patient H.M., to recognize famous faces from past decades (Marslen-Wilson and Teuber, 1975). Patient H.M. performed more poorly than the average Korsakoff patient in recognizing faces from the 1950s and 1960s (H.M. became amnesic in

FAMOUS FACES

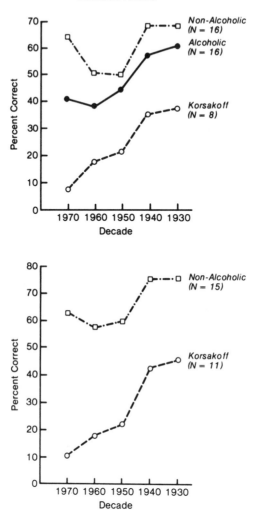

Figure 54. Extensive remote memory impairment in two different populations of patients with Korsakoff's syndrome in San Diego *(top)* and Boston *(bottom)*, as measured by the same test of famous faces. The impairment is more severe for faces that came into the news in the most recent decade or two, presumably because anterograde amnesia was either already present or was gradually developing during this period. The impairment for more remote time periods probably reflects true retrograde amnesia, i.e., loss of material that had been successfully learned before the onset of the syndrome. (Top, from Cohen and Squire, 1981; bottom, from Albert, Butters, and Levin, 1980.)

1953). Yet H.M. performed better than the average Korsakoff patient in recognizing faces from the 1930s and 1940s. Thus, H.M. had a more severe anterograde amnesia than the Korsakoff patients, but his remote memory impairment was less severe. This result shows that severe and extensive remote memory impairment does not inevitably follow from a severe anterograde amnesia. Accordingly, one possibility is that antero-grade amnesia and remote memory impairment are distinct and unrelated deficits.

A second study tested this possibility within a group of patients with Korsakoff's syndrome (Shimamura and Squire, 1986a). No correlation appeared between the overall severity of anterograde amnesia (as mea-sured by nine tests of new learning ability) and the severity of remote memory impairment (the 1940s to the 1970s). However, for the most recent decade covered by the tests (the 1970s), the severity of antero-grade amnesia did correlate significantly ($r = +.36$) with the severity of remote memory impairment. Test questions concerning the most recent decade presumably measured the anterograde amnesia already present, or developing, during that time period. Prior to the 1970s no correlation was found between remote memory performance and new learning abil-ity (1960s: $+.16$; 1950s: $+.02$; 1940s: $-.09$). Taken together, the re-sults suggest that the ability to recall remote events depends on mecha-nisms distinct from those required for new learning and for recall of recent events (also see Butters, Miliotis, Albert, and Sax, 1984). Remote memory impairment thus should depend on lesions other than, and in addition to, those that produce anterograde amnesia. More direct evi-dence would prove useful in resolving this issue. For example, it might be possible to find cases in which remote memory impairment occurs without a severe degree of anterograde amnesia (see one case by Gold-berg, Antin, Bilder, Gerstman, Hughes and Mattis, 1981).

What is known about the retrograde amnesia associated with dience-phalic amnesia in patients other than those with Korsakoff's syndrome? For such patients, the data are mixed. Some cases are reported to have no measurable retrograde amnesia (Winocur, et al, 1984; Michel, et al, 1982; Speedie and Heilman, 1982). Case N.A., who has a long-standing left dorsal thalamic lesion, exhibited normal performance on six remote memory tests and mild impairment on two others (Cohen and Squire, 1981; Zola-Morgan, Cohen, and Squire, 1983). However, N.A. has been

217

amnesic for verbal material since 1960; and now, more than 25 years later, it is difficult to interpret his mild difficulty in remembering events that occurred before 1960. N.A.'s poor performance could reflect true (albeit mild) retrograde amnesia or an indirect effect of his failing to add to or rehearse information about old events during his long period of anterograde amnesia. Still other diencephalic amnesic patients are reported to have extensive retrograde amnesia (see Parkin, 1984). These include two Korsakoff's-syndrome patients who at autopsy were reported to have diencephalic lesions restricted to the mammillary nuclei and to a small area near the medial border of the mediodorsal thalamic nucleus (Mair, Warrington, and Weiskrantz, 1979).

The available data are thus not conclusive about what type of retrograde amnesia or remote memory impairment is associated with the circumscribed diencephalic lesions that cause anterograde amnesia. One possibility is that retrograde amnesia is temporally limited and not extensive unless there is damage to structures beyond the critical diencephalic regions that have been linked to anterograde amnesia. Another possibility is that diencephalic lesions sufficient to produce anterograde amnesia also cause extensive remote memory impairment, though perhaps milder than is commonly observed in Korsakoff's syndrome. Unfortunately, many case reports still evaluate retrograde amnesia only by informal interview. Formal tests must be used, and even they are not always sensitive enough to detect remote memory impairment unless they go beyond multiple-choice methods.

Two important questions remain. First, if the same damage that causes anterograde amnesia does not necessarily cause severe, extensive remote memory impairment, which structures must be damaged to produce remote memory impairment? Second, how should a remote memory impairment be classified? Can it appropriately be termed a memory impairment, which implies a relatively specific deficit in accessing memory? Or does remote memory impairment represent only one aspect of a broader cognitive impairment that affects other mental operations as well? Clearly, before the relationship between new learning ability and remote memory capacity can be understood, more cases of amnesia must be evaluated using formal remote memory tests, and such data must be linked to neuropathology. This kind of information would also help decide whether the function of the diencephalic structures must be tightly linked to the medial temporal region and to the concepts of memory consolidation outlined above, or whether the function of the diencephalic structures in memory must, to some extent, be considered separately.

The Contribution of Damage in Other Neural Systems

Functional analysis of the memory impairment in amnesia is clearly complicated by the fact that not all amnesic patients have precisely the same lesion. Not only can amnesic patients have either diencephalic or medial temporal lesions but also, as a function of the etiology of the amnesic condition, such patients can have additional neuropathology. For example, patients with alcoholic Korsakoff's syndrome commonly have damage to brain stem, cerebellum, and neocortex in addition to the specific diencephalic lesions that have been linked to the memory deficit itself (Victor, Adams, and Collins, 1971). Similarly, patients who are amnesic as a result of encephalitis, and who have medial temporal lobe damage, often have additional damage to other brain regions such as cingulate gyrus and posterior orbital frontal cortex. These additional lesions can add to the memory impairment certain cognitive deficits with no obligatory relationship to amnesia, and these deficits can influence performance on memory tests. For this reason, as amnesia has been studied over the years the core memory disorder has been repeatedly redefined, and certain deficits once considered an integral part of the amnesic syndrome have turned out to be unrelated to it. As each dissociation is demonstrated and confirmed, what is meant by the core amnesic disorder must be revised and applied to a smaller set of deficits.

For example, some deficits that occur in amnesia are unique to Korsakoff's syndrome and do not occur in other cases of diencephalic amnesia or medial temporal amnesia. Patients with Korsakoff's syndrome exhibit a severe deficit in remembering the temporal order of learned items, a deficit too large to be explained by impaired memory for the items themselves (Squire, 1982b). Other patients, just as amnesic for previously learned items as the patients with Korsakoff's syndrome, do not exhibit such a large impairment in temporal order.

Patients with Korsakoff's syndrome likewise show no improvement of recall scores when shifted from the task of learning successive lists of items in one category (e.g., types of trees) to the task of learning items in a different category [e.g., types of foods (Cermak, Butters, and Moreines, 1974; Squire, 1982b]. This shift benefits normal subjects by eliminating the effects of cumulating interference from similar items. The beneficial effect of the shift is called "release from proactive interference"; and it occurs readily in amnesic patients other than those with Korsakoff's syndrome, including some with diencephalic amnesia (Butters, 1984; Squire, 1982b).

In patients with Korsakoff's syndrome, the severity of these two deficits—impaired temporal order judgment and failure to release from proactive interference—correlated with the severity of their impairment on tests sensitive to frontal lobe dysfunction. More to the point, these same two deficits are found in patients with surgical lesions involving the frontal lobe (Moscovitch, 1982; Milner, 1974). The location of the effective frontal lobe lesions varied from patient to patient. Hence the deficit is unlikely to be related to damage in the ventromedial portion of the frontal lobe that has been linked to the amnesic syndrome itself.

Two other deficits can also be isolated from the core disorder in amnesia. First, many amnesic patients, including case N.A. and patients with anoxic or ischemic amnesia, have intact metamemory functions (Shimamura and Squire, 1986b). That is, these patients accurately predict their performance on tests of remote memory and can also predict the level of their (impaired) performance on tests of new learning ability. By contrast, patients with Korsakoff's syndrome cannot predict their performance on memory tests. A second disorder sometimes observed in amnesia is source amnesia—the loss of memory for when and where the episode occurred. In other words, some amnesic patients, even when they are able to recall a little information from a recent learning session will nevertheless claim that they acquired the information somewhere else (Schacter, Harbluk, and McLachlan, 1984; Shimamura and Squire, 1987; see chapter 11). Source amnesia may also be related to frontal lobe pathology (Schacter, Harbluk, and McLachlan, 1984).

In principle, careful testing should be capable of revealing neuropsychological differences between any two groups of patients with different lesions. In view of the specialization of the brain, it seems inconceivable that two different structures could have identical functions. For example, even if the diencephalic and medial temporal structures damaged in amnesia do belong to a neural system that functions together in one sense, each of the contributing structures or regions could make different functional contributions to that system. It has been suggested that amnesic patients with diencephalic lesions have normal rates of forgetting, whereas those with medial temporal lesions have abnormal forgetting rates (Huppert and Piercy, 1979; Squire, 1981), but some uncertainty concerning this point persists (Freed, Corkin, and Cohen, 1984; Zola-Morgan and Squire, 1985c). Such patients may differ in other respects as well (Parkin, 1984).

The Selective Role of the Neural System Damaged in Amnesia

Medial temporal and diencephalic structures that are damaged in amnesia are required only for the formation and consolidation of declarative memory. These regions are required for the acquisition of facts and events—that is, to acquire "declarative memory"—but they are not necessary for either the acquisition and expression of skills or the phenomenon of priming. Only declarative memory requires interaction between the neural system damaged in amnesia and memory storage sites.

Some neurobehavioral studies of this neural system in experimental animals have suggested that its functional role should be defined in terms of the processing of spatial information and the storing of spatial memory. The argument for a role of this neural system in spatial functions has come especially from behavioral study of rats with hippocampal lesions and from single cell recordings in the hippocampus of freely moving rats. These observations have been developed into a comprehensive proposal about hippocampal function whose central theme is that the hippocampus forms and stores a map of an animal's spatial environment (O'Keefe and Nadel, 1978). This point of view, as well as others expressed even earlier in the animal literature (Gaffan, 1974; Hirsh, 1974) anticipated later developments in human neuropsychology, namely, the idea that the hippocampus (and the neural system to which it belongs) is involved in only one kind of learning.

However, a literally spatial hypothesis about hippocampal function does not fit well with the findings from the human cases. The human cases have a memory impairment, not an impairment restricted to spatial operations. Patients with right medial temporal resections do have difficulty remembering the spatial location of objects (Smith and Milner, 1981). But they also have difficulty in image-mediated verbal learning (Jones-Gotman and Milner, 1978) and facial recognition (Milner, 1968). Similarly, H.M.'s amnesia includes the spatial dimension but is not limited to it. He has difficulty learning mazes and finding his way around, but he also has difficulty remembering other things such as colors, sounds, and tactual impressions. Damage to the hippocampus in humans appears to cause a memory impairment that includes spatial information rather than an impairment that is exclusively spatial. One might envision a concept of space that is more abstract so that it somehow includes image-mediated learning, faces, and the variety of things that amnesic patients cannot remember. But at this level of abstraction, a spatial hypothesis becomes difficult to distinguish from a memory hypothesis.

In the case of monkeys with hippocampal lesions, the memory deficit also appears to extend beyond spatial tasks. For example, monkeys with medial temporal lesions, which include the hippocampus and amygdala, appear just as impaired on tasks that require memory for objects (delayed nonmatching to sample) as on tasks that require memory for spatial location (delayed response) (Zola-Morgan and Squire, 1985a). On the other hand, a spatial factor has been found in the impairments exhibited by monkeys with hippocampal lesions. Monkeys with hippocampal lesions were disproportionately impaired on a spatial reversal task, as compared to an object reversal task (Jones and Mishkin, 1972; Mahut, 1971), and they were impaired on a spatial alternation task, but not on a nonspatial version of the same task. Finally, preliminary study of a memory-for-spatial-location task showed that monkeys with hippocampal lesions were profoundly impaired, more so than on other kinds of memory tasks (Parkinson and Mishkin, 1982).

Perhaps there are differences between species that explain why a spatial factor emerges less prominently as one moves from rats to monkeys to man. It should be emphasized that it is difficult to separate entirely a discussion of space from discussion of memory. Thus one might speak of a neural system that maps external space, and which thereby provides a framework for storing objects and events within that space (Nadel and Willner, 1980). In any case, given the findings for amnesic patients and the similar findings in monkeys with medial temporal lesions, it seems reasonable to begin with an hypothesis of memory impairment. The data from different species may reflect differences in what animals best remember, or differences in the schemata or frameworks that are available in different species for embedding memory, rather than fundamental differences in brain organization or in the function of specific brain regions. Rats, for example, depend heavily on spatial information to learn about their environment, whereas humans have access to diverse modes of information storage.

The view developed here does rest more heavily on human neuropsychological findings and findings in other primates than on data from nonprimates. Nevertheless, it seems reasonable to suppose that the hippocampus in all mammals is involved more broadly in memory functions than is implied by a strictly spatial hypothesis. At the same time, much recent work involving different species converges on the idea that the hippocampus is not involved in all kinds of memory. The term *declarative* used here is intended to describe the kind of learning for which the hippocampus is needed. Declarative memory includes memory for spatial location but is not limited to it.

Declarative memory initially achieves its stability and coherence through the involvement of a specialized brain system that includes the medial temporal region and specific diencephalic regions. These regions interact with the cortical association areas within which the representations of acquired information presumably reside. Association areas both process and store information. They also support the specific working-memory capacities that are appropriate to each specialized area. Within these cortical areas, long-term memory can develop and persist, if these areas have the benefit of interaction with the hippocampus and the neural system to which it belongs.

14

Prefrontal Cortex

Some cortical association areas can be linked to behavior and cognition. For example, inferotemporal cortex is presumed to both process and store information about the identify of visual objects. Prefrontal cortex has been difficult to approach in functional terms, but our present understanding suggests that it deserves special consideration in a discussion of memory and brain organization. This large, heterogenous and supramodal association area lies rostral to the precentral gyrus and the premotor area (Brodmann's area 6), and receives projections from the mediodorsal nucleus of the thalamus. In the monkey, the caudal border of this area is marked by the arcuate sulcus. The lateral surface is marked prominently by the sulcus principalis, dividing it into a dorsal and ventral portion. The ventral portion of the lateral surface, usually termed the inferior convexity, extends to the lateral orbital sulcus, and it is contiguous with the ventral or orbital surface. The orbital surface ends upon meeting the flat medial wall (Figure 55).

Unlike other areas of neocortex, where combined cytoarchitectonic, anatomic, and functional criteria allow the identification of specific cortical fields, prefrontal cortex remains poorly understood. Although various regions have been specified, primarily on the basis of the distinctive and differential effects of lesions in the monkey, these regions have not

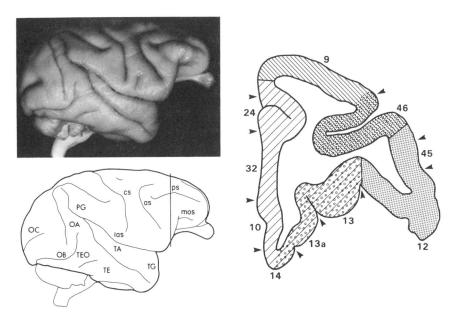

Figure 55. *Left.* Lateral view of the monkey brain. The drawing below the photograph shows cytoarchitectonic areas according to von Bonin and Bailey, 1947. The vertical line through the frontal lobe shows the level of the coronal section to the right. as, arcuate sulcus; cs, central sulcus; las, lateral sulcus; mos, medial orbital sulcus; ps, principal sulcus. *Right.* Coronal section illustrating the location of the lesions most commonly used to study frontal lobe function in the monkey. ▨ + ▧, dorsolateral convexity; ▨ sulcus principalis; ▦, inferior convexity; ▨ + ▨, ventromedial cortex; ▨, orbital cortex. The numbers refer to cytoarchitectonic areas, following nomenclature by Walker, 1940. (Courtesy D. J. Amaral.)

yet been related to definite cytoarchitectonic divisions. The best-studied regions of prefrontal cortex are the sulcus principalis, the lateral surface of the frontal lobe dorsal to the sulcus principalis (the dorsolateral convexity), the lateral surface ventral to the sulcus principalis (the inferior convexity), the peri-arcuate region, and the orbital surface.

Prefrontal cortex has been afforded the highest of functions: the capacity for insight, abstraction, and self-awareness. It has also been linked specifically to memory functions (Teuber, 1964; Fuster, 1980; Luria, 1966). The hypothesis that prefrontal cortex may subserve memory functions was based initially on behavioral studies done in the 1930s, involving monkeys with large prefrontal lesions (Jacobsen, 1935; 1936; Jacobsen and Nissen, 1937). The studies involved two tasks; delayed response, as originally devised by Hunter (1913), and delayed alternation. In the delayed-response task, the animal first watches while food is placed beneath one of two identical plaques. In this way the animal is cued to one of two locations, left or right. After a delay of a few seconds, during which the plaques are not in view, the animal is given an opportunity to choose between the same two locations and to obtain the food reward if the choice is correct.

In the delayed-alternation task, the animal likewise chooses between two locations marked by identical plaques, but now the location in which the food reward appears alternates from trial to trial, and the trials are separated by a delay of a few seconds. After the delay, the animal must select the location opposite to the one where the food was located on the previous trial. Monkeys with prefrontal lesions demonstrate profound impairment on both these tasks. One reason for supposing that these impairments might reflect deficient short-term memory was that the impairment became greater as the delay increased. In the years since Jacobsen's seminal discovery, a somewhat different description of these deficits has emerged.

The Sulcus Principalis and Dorsolateral Convexity

It is now known that the deficits in delayed-response and delayed-alternation depend specifically on damage in the depths and banks of the sulcus principalis, a region included in Jacobsen's larger lesion (Blum, 1952; Mishkin, 1957). The dorsolateral convexity of prefrontal cortex, which lies just above the sulcus principalis, is sometimes considered to belong to the same functional field as the sulcus principalis (Rosenkilde, 1979). Much of the analysis of delayed response and delayed alternation derives from studies involving these more circumscribed lesions.

The deficits in these tasks do not represent memory impairments in any general sense, because monkeys with lesions of the dorsolateral convexity can successfully perform a nonspatial version of the delayed-response test (Mishkin and Manning, 1978; they can also succeed at other tasks that require short-term memory, such as object-alternation and discrimination tasks. In the nonspatial version of the delayed-response task, delayed matching-to-sample, the monkey sees a single object (the sample) on the first trial and then must select it again after a delay, when it is presented together with a second object. On half the trials the second object serves as sample. Monkeys with dorsolateral frontal lesions can also perform delayed matching-to-sample tasks when two colors are used instead of two objects (Mishkin and Manning, 1978; Passingham, 1975). Finally, monkeys with dorsolateral frontal lesions even succeed at the trial-unique, delayed nonmatching-to-sample task with delays up to 2 minutes and when as many as 10 objects must be remembered concurrently (Bachevalier and Mishkin, 1985). These findings rule out a general memory interpretation of the lesion effects, and they focus attention on features specific to the delayed-response and delayed-alternation tasks, such as the role of spatial abilities and the specific problem of spatial memory.

Additional information about the function of these regions, especially the sulcus principalis, comes from neurophysiological studies. In a series of studies of monkeys performing the delayed-response task, single cells in the region of the sulcus principalis were found to increase their discharge activity during performance (Fuster, 1980). Most of the units sampled increased their activity during some part of the delay period. Units in parietal cortex did not respond differentially while the task was being performed. Some units remained active throughout the entire delay period; others declined in activity during the delay; still others were active during both the cue and the delay. The time of greatest activity was the transition period between presentation of the cue and the beginning of the delay. Of the units active during the delayed response task, 14% responded differentially depending on the spatial location of the cue, and 5% responded differentially depending on the direction of the response that was about to be made (Niki and Watanabe, 1976).

Neurons in the sulcus principalis zone not only respond during the cue and delay periods of the delayed-response task. Some neurons in the inferior bank of this sulcus also respond during tasks requiring visual attention, even when retention of information through a delay period is not required (Sakai, 1974). One task required the pressing of one of four levers within 1 second after presentation of a corresponding signal light. Eighty neurons were found to correlate their discharge activity to the light, lever-press sequence. The majority of these neurons altered their activity only when the lever press was made immediately after the light stimulus, and not when the light or the lever press occurred alone. This study thus shows that even in the absence of any requirement for holding information in memory on each trial, visual attention and conditioned responding can change cell firing in the sulcus principalis zone.

The sulcus principalis may combine information-processing and memory storage functions. In other studies, 2-second periods of electrical stimulation were delivered to cortex of monkeys at different points during the delayed-response task (Stamm and Rosen, 1969, 1973; Kovner and Stamm, 1972) (Figure 56). During either the cue or the early part of the delay, stimulation of the posterior two-thirds of the sulcus principalis zone disrupted performance. This effect was specific to that zone, since stimulation of either premotor cortex, the arcuate sulcus, or the anterior third of the sulcus principalis was without effect. Stimulation of posterior inferotemporal cortex had a different effect, disrupting delayed-response performance only when current was applied during cue presentation itself. In this circumstance, stimulation may have disrupted visual analysis of the cue. The results proved quite different for a visual, delayed matching-to-sample task. In this case, inferotemporal cortex stimulation impaired performance when applied during either the delay or the matching portions of the trial, whereas stimulation of sulcus principalis had little effect on performance at any point during the task.

Figure 56. Task-specific impairments in short-term or working memory caused by unilateral electrical stimulation of frontal or temporal neocortex. Horizontal lines indicate periods of stimulation. *Top.* Performance on delayed response, with a cue presentation of 2 seconds and a delay of 8 seconds. Stimulation with 2-second trains of 5.5–6.0 ma current was applied to the posterior segment of inferotemporal cortex (temporal) or to dorsolateral frontal cortex (frontal) so that the electrodes straddled the sulcus principalis. *Bottom.* Performance on delayed matching to sample, with a sample presentation of 2 seconds and a delay of 3 seconds. Vertical lines below the time scale indicate the boundaries between sample, delay, match, and intertrial interval (ITI) portions of testing. Stimulation with 2-second trains of 3.5–5.5 ma current was applied to the middle third of the temporal cortex (temporal) or to dorsolateral frontal cortex (frontal), so that the electrodes straddled the sulcus principalis. (Adapted from Stamm and Rosen, 1969, 1973; Kovner and Stamm, 1972.)

DELAYED RESPONSE

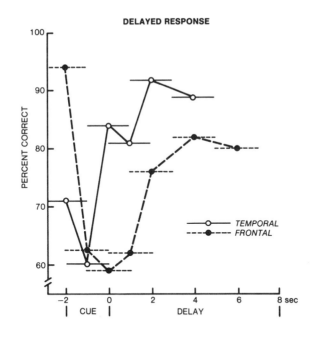

DELAYED MATCHING TO SAMPLE

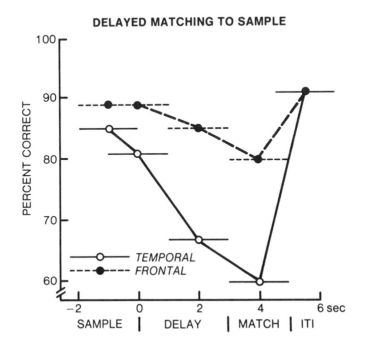

229

These results show that stimulating an area of cortex does produce a kind of memory impairment, but not for all tasks. Stimulation of inferotemporal cortex during the delay period of the delayed matching-to-sample task disrupts the short-term memory that is specific to this visual task. However, performance on the delayed-response task is not affected. In addition, some single units in inferotemporal cortex increase their activity during the sample and matching periods of the delayed matching-to-sample task; other units increase their activity during the delay (Fuster and Jervey, 1981). Thus, inferotemporal cortex is specialized to process and analyze visual information and it also subserves a working-memory capacity for the short-term retention of visual information. The sulcus principalis region of prefrontal cortex is likewise specialized for a particular type of information processing and for a correspondingly specific working-memory capacity. As a result, stimulation of this region disrupts performance when delivered during the delay period of the delayed-response task, but not during delayed matching-to-sample.

The Inferior Convexity

Another area of prefrontal cortex significantly involved in the performance of many cognitive tasks is the inferior convexity, just ventral to sulcus principalis. This region was originally studied in combination with the orbital surface (Mishkin, 1964). However, it was later shown that previously described deficits on tests of object alternation, object reversal, and go-no-go discrimination were due to the inferior convexity lesion, and that neither orbital lesions nor sulcus principalis lesions had an appreciable effect on these tasks (Iversen and Mishkin, 1970; Mishkin and Manning, 1978). The impairment following inferior convexity lesions is characterized by marked perseverative responding, apparently due to an inability of animals to overcome response tendencies that compete with the response to be learned.

Lesions to the inferior convexity thus impair both flexibility and the ability to alter responses to rapidly changing environmental demands. As a result, these lesions do impair performance on many memory tasks, but it seems inappropriate to link this area of prefrontal cortex specifically to memory functions. Damage to this region could be expected to interfere with performance especially when a test imposes on the subject a succession of potentially interfering stimuli, some of which must be ignored while others are attended to.

The Peri-arcuate Region

In the monkey, lesions of the dorsal and posterior aspects of the frontal lobe, the peri-arcuate region, selectively impair the ability to form associations between acoustic or visual stimuli and specific responses (Goldman and Rosvold, 1970; Stamm, 1973). Although early work on this impairment emphasized spatial factors, the deficit is broader and probably affects the formation of associations between any exteroceptive stimuli and any set of distinctive motor responses (Petrides, 1982). This deficit would thus be expected to interfere with many kinds of learning where overt motor responses are required, particularly when multiple associations must be formed concurrently.

Clinical Neuropsychological Studies of Frontal Lesions

The results of studies with patients are generally compatible with the findings in monkeys and bring the functions of frontal cortex into clearer focus. One limitation of the information obtained from human cases is that the lesions tend to be large and variably placed, such that a lesion usually invades two or more of the functional zones that have been identified by studies in the monkey (Figure 57). Accordingly, it usually cannot be determined which precise areas of frontal cortex are involved in behavioral deficits.

The patients available for study are not amnesic in the ordinary sense. They do not have the deficits in recall, recognition, or sense of familiarity that have come to be associated with amnesic disorders. For example, patients who have received left unilateral frontal excisions, performed in an attempt to relieve focal epilepsy, were normal at delayed recall of prose and paired associates (Milner, 1967). Similarly, patients with presumed bilateral orbito-frontal lesions resulting from leucotomy showed

231

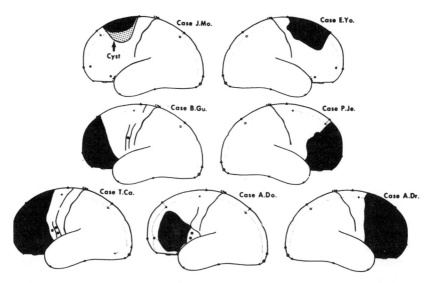

Figure 57. Diagrams, based on the surgeon's drawings at the time of operation, showing the estimated lateral extent of cortical excision in seven representative cases of unilateral frontal lobectomy carried out for relief of focal epilepsy. Dots indicate points at which electrical stimulation of the exposed cortex interfered with speech. (From Milner, 1982.)

good delayed recall of prose and nonverbal material (Stuss, Kaplan, Benson, Weir, Chiulli, and Sarazin, 1982). Patients with focal, unilateral frontal lesions likewise were normal at recalling the spatial location of an array of 16 objects, both immediately after learning and after a 24-hour delay (Smith and Milner, 1984). Finally, patients who had received left, right, or bilateral frontal injuries from missile wounds performed as well as normal subjects on memory tests for visual location and tactual position involving 15-second delays (Ghent, Mishkin, and Teuber, 1962).

Deficits do appear, however, when memory tasks go beyond the simple requirement to recall or recognize isolated events. For example, frontal patients are impaired when they must remember the order of contextually similar events, or remember only some of a group of similar, interfering events. A particularly revealing set of tests presented pairs of colors, clicks, light flashes, tones, or nonsense figures, with a 60-second, distraction-filled delay between the two stimuli of each pair. The subjects had to decide whether the second stimulus was the same as or

232

different from the first one (Milner, 1964). Patients with surgical lesions of frontal cortex performed poorly on all the tests, except those involving nonsense figures, on which they performed normally. Of all the stimuli, only the nonsense figures differed on every presentation trial. The other stimuli were available only in small sets, and they were repeated from time to time. Therefore in all tests except those involving the nonsense figures, patients had to process similar material, and ignore their memory of material encountered on previous trials so that they could focus on only the most recently presented stimulus.

A similar finding was reported for leucotomy patients, who performed well on many memory tests but were nevertheless impaired on the Brown-Peterson test, In that test, a series of consonant trigrams (JKZ, FVM) is presented, each to be remembered for several seconds in the face of distraction (Stuss et al., 1982). On every trial, subjects must discard the preceding trigram from memory and concentrate only on the new one. Patients with frontal lesions also had difficulty in spatial and nonspatial associative tasks similar to those failed by monkeys with peri-arcuate lesions. In one task patients learned to associate each of six small blue lights with six spatial locations. In another task they learned to associate each of the lights with a different hand posture (Milner, 1982; Petrides, 1985). The similarity between the associations to be made, and their susceptibility to interference, may have contributed to the impairment following frontal lesions. Indeed, frontal damage might create difficulty in any memory task that requires the learning of a large list of similar items. Patients with frontal lobe lesions were impaired in recalling from memory the names of 16 recently presented toy objects, even though (when presented with the objects) they could then remember as well as normal subjects where the object had been located in an array (Smith and Milner, 1984). Normal subjects bring organization and strategy to tasks of free recall, but frontal patients do not.

In one case, a deficit could be specifically associated with dorsolateral frontal cortex. In the Wisconsin card-sorting test, subjects see in succession a large number of cards, each of which bears one or more symbols. For example, one card displays three yellow triangles. Another displays one red star. Each card can be classified according to any of three principles (the color of the symbols, the shape of the symbols, or the number of symbols on a card). The examiner arbitrarily selects one of the sorting principles as the "correct" one, and then changes to a different "correct" principle whenever ten cards in a row are sorted properly. Patients with left or right dorsolateral lesions could not switch to a new sorting principle when the previously established and successful principle had become inappropriate (Milner, 1963). These patients would instead continue sorting according to the old, now incorrect principle. The perseverative tendencies associated with failure on this task are reminiscent of the loss of flexibility associated especially with inferior convexity lesions in monkey. Patients with orbital frontal lesions performed normally.

Patients with frontal lesions also performed poorly on a table-model, visually guided "maze-learning" task, where a hand-held stylus was used to learn a path among a 10 X 10 array of pegs (Milner, 1965). The patients were impulsive, repeated the same errors within short intervals, and had difficulty complying with test instructions. For example, instead of returning to the previous peg when an error was made, these patients would sometimes return all the way to the starting point or simply ignore the signal that an error had occurred. More severe deficits were observed following right than left lesions, especially when maze learning was guided proprioceptively rather than visually (Corkin, 1965). This asymmetry may relate to the greater contribution of the right hemisphere to spatial tasks in humans.

One good illustration of how the frontal lobes contribute to memory function comes from a study of memory for temporal order (Milner, 1971). Patients were shown a series of 184 stimuli, and were tested intermittently for their ability both to recognize the stimuli as familiar and to remember which of two stimuli had been presented more recently. Patients with unilateral temporal lobe lesions were deficient at recognition memory but had no additional difficulty with judgments of order. Patients with unilateral frontal lesions, but not temporal lobe lesions, were impaired in judging recency, though they performed normally at familiarity judgments (Figure 58). Thus, frontal lesions do not produce a straightforward, general memory impairment, but they can influence performance on memory tests.

One additional result is also instructive. The deficit in this case is also difficult to reduce to a problem in memory alone. Subjects inspected successive pages displaying up to 12 pictures of objects (or in other cases abstract designs or words). The same set of stimuli appeared on each.

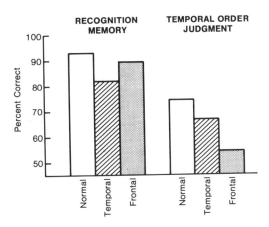

Figure 58. Performance by patients with unilateral temporal or frontal lobe lesions on a test requiring both recognition memory and a judgment as to which of two items had been presented more recently. Performance on verbal and nonverbal tests has been averaged, taking scores from left-damaged patients in the case of the verbal tests and from right-damaged patients in the case of the nonverbal tests. Patients with temporal lobe lesions were mildly impaired on the recognition memory test. Patients with frontal lobe lesions were disproportionately impaired at making judgments of relative recency. (Adapted from Milner, 1971.)

page, but they were always in a different arrangement. The task was to point to a different stimulus on each page. Thus subjects had to find on each succeeding page an item that had not yet been selected. This task requires not just the ability to identify familiar items, but also the ability to relate information to one's own actions; and to make selections among items that have been presented repeatedly. Patients with frontal cortex lesions were severely impaired (Petrides and Milner, 1982). Their difficulty in this rather complex task may be related to the problems in planning that have been well described for frontal patients (Shallice, 1982).

The Prefrontal Cortex and Memory Functions

Some have characterized the function of the frontal lobes as involving a special kind of memory. Others have tried to characterize a cognitive capacity that influences memory. For example, Luria (1973) spoke of the frontal lobes in broad terms, noting that patients with frontal injury show impulsiveness, a tendency to seize on one feature of a multidimensional scene, and difficulty in organizing their own behavior. Such patients tend to drift toward dominant response tendencies. They may verbalize a desired response but then not perform it, thereby exhibiting a disconnection between knowing and doing. Hecaen and Albert (1978) characterized the deficit in similar terms as "forgetting to remember."

It is probably not useful to argue whether prefrontal cortex is directly involved in a particular aspect of memory functions, or whether prefrontal cortex influences memory only secondarily, as a by-product of its role in information processing. Throughout this book a major theme has been that *all* cortical regions are involved in both processing and memory storage, though always within functionally specified domains. Inferotemporal cortex (area TE) for example, is considered both to process and to store visual information about objects. Area TE contains a functionally specific short-term or working memory as well as a long-term memory capacity for the same restricted domain of visual information.

Our understanding is too incomplete to be able to characterize very precisely what particular processing functions are accomplished by prefrontal cortex, and the discussion that follows is little more than descriptive. Two comprehensive treatments of the frontal lobes can be consulted that provide additional data as well as thoughtful discussion of functional questions (Fuster, 1980; Goldman-Rakic, 1987). All the modality-specific sensory areas project to prefrontal cortex (Jones and Powell, 1970). Correspondingly, prefrontal cortex must be concerned with the organization and processing of sensory information, regardless of modality. In addition, the sulcus principalis, inferior convexity, and periarcuate regions must combine their contributions to support performance in a broad spectrum of tasks. Prefrontal cortex seems to be required to organize and program voluntary behavior effectively, to suppress interfering stimuli, and to permit appropriate responses to rapidly varying environmental demands. One means by which prefrontal cortex may accomplish this task is to organize incoming information temporally. In addition, sulcus principalis and the dorsolateral convexity may be specifically involved in the organization of information according to its spatial context. This view presumes that each of the specialized functional zones in prefrontal cortex is involved in both the processing and storage of information and that each has a short-term memory or working-memory capacity for the type of information for which it is specialized to process.

Specialized short-term or working-memory capacities, which are considered to be present in prefrontal cortex as they are in each functional area of neocortex, should be distinguished from the more general capacity for long-term memory, which depends selectively on the medial temporal region and the diencephalic midline. Available data for the delayed response task illustrate this distinction. Lesions of the sulcus principalis in the monkey entirely disrupt the ability to learn the task, even at delays of a few seconds. In contrast, following lesions of the medial temporal lobe, monkeys learn delayed response normally and are then impaired only if the delay is lengthened to more than 10 seconds (Zola-Morgan and Squire, 1985a). Sulcus principalis lesions therefore disrupt both the processing and the short-term storage of the specialized spatial information required by the delayed-response task. By contrast, medial temporal lesions interfere with the ability to hold this information in memory for longer intervals, just as they affect the ability to hold other kinds of information beyond short-term memory.

This distinction between a general memory deficit, associated with medial temporal lesions, and a specialized processing deficit, associated with prefrontal lesions, also follows nicely from the findings for the delayed nonmatching-to-sample task. In the trial-unique version of this task, hundreds of objects are available, and every trial employs two new objects. Once normal animals have acquired the principle, they exhibit excellent performance at delays up to many minutes. Monkeys with lesions of the medial temporal region can perform normally at short (8-second) delays, but they are severely impaired when the delay increases from a few seconds to several minutes. Distraction interpolated during the delay makes the deficit even more severe (Zola-Morgan and Squire, 1985a). By contrast, lesions of the dorsolateral frontal convexity (Bachevalier and Mishkin, 1985) or the inferior convexity (Kowalska, Bachevalier, and Mishkin, 1984) do not affect memory performance across delays on this task. Inferior convexity lesions do produce difficulty in acquiring the task initially as the result of a marked tendency to respond perseveratively to the left or right side, but having once acquired the principle monkeys perform normally across the delays.

Monkeys with inferior convexity lesions are thus unimpaired on the trial-unique version of delayed nonmatching to sample. But monkeys with the identical lesion fail the traditional matching-to-sample task. The traditional task differs from the trial-unique version in that the same two objects are used repeatedly instead of new ones being used for every trial (Mishkin and Manning, 1978). When hundreds of objects are used, monkeys need only recognize whether an object is familiar or not. When only two objects are used, monkeys must perform a *temporal* discrimination: Which of two familiar stimuli was presented more recently? Tasks requiring a temporal discrimination depend on a specific ability that is the province of the frontal lobe.

There is a second reason why monkeys with inferior convexity lesions might fail traditional delayed matching-to-sample (with two objects used repeatedly), but succeed at trial-unique, delayed nonmatching-to-sample (with two unique objects used for each trial). Delayed matching-to-sample requires that on the choice trial monkeys act against their strong natural tendency to approach novelty. In delayed nonmatching-to-sample, the task requirements are consistent with this response tendency. Because inferior convexity lesions create a difficulty in overcoming dominant response tendencies and cognitive sets, delayed matching-to-sample could present a special problem. Testing with both trial-unique, delayed matching-to-sample and delayed nonmatching to sample (done in the traditional way with only two objects) would be needed to determine which is the determining factor for the deficit following inferior convexity lesions.

In any case, the data show that prefrontal cortex is involved in memory functions, but in a rather special sense. It (like other regions of neocortex) subserves specialized processing functions and related working-memory capacities. Prefrontal cortex is not involved in general, long-term retentive capacity. One specialized processing function of prefrontal cortex concerns the temporal and spatial organization of behavior. Delayed matching-to-sample (using two objects) cannot be mastered by monkeys with inferior convexity lesions, perhaps because they cannot remember which of two familiar objects was seen more recently. Similarly, the traditional 5-second, delayed alternation test cannot be mastered by monkeys with sulcus principalis lesions, because they cannot remember which of two familiar spatial locations was seen more recently.

Patients with frontal lesions exhibit similar deficits on memory tests to the ones demonstrated in monkeys. The patients have difficulty in placing remembered events within their proper contexts. For example, they may recognize an item as familiar but fail to remember the temporal order in which the item occurred, relative to other items. They also have difficulty in making judgments of familiarity about material that has repeatedly occurred in different contexts. For example, tests built out of a small set of frequently repeated items create difficulty when the patient must decide whether an item has been presented recently or not. Moreover, amnesic patients with signs of frontal lobe damage who try to remember two lists of items have difficulty remembering which list the items were on. The number of temporal order errors is greater than can be explained by poor recognition memory for the items themselves (Squire, 1982b). Source errors are also observed: Patients sometimes remember information, but not when or where it was acquired (Schacter, Harbluk, and McLachlan, 1984).

Frontal cortex has strong anatomical connections with the temporal lobe, and the medial temporal region itself is interconnected with frontal cortex as well as with other cortical association areas (Van Hoesen, Pandya, and Butters, 1972; Van Hoesen, Pandya, and Butters, 1975; Amaral, 1987). Frontal cortex presumably performs its computations on many kinds of information, which are analyzed concurrently for other purposes by other regions of cortex. Frontal cortex allows information to be remembered in its appropriate context, that is, in the correct temporal order and with accurate reference to other spatially and temporally coincident events. The medial temporal region then operates upon this information, allowing it to endure in the organized form it has achieved in neocortex.

Specific Events Versus Cumulative Experience

From the viewpoint of cellular neurobiology, the problem of memory is a question of how synapses change. For example, neurons in the visual cortex of cat and monkey show plasticity that depends on both the type of visual world in which the animal was reared (horizontal or vertical contours) and on the viewing conditions in that world (monocular or binocular). The final result, in terms of the neurophysiology of visual cortex, reflects the cumulation of an animal's experience. The resulting synaptic change is a sum of the moment-to-moment changes laid successively upon each other. In this way, each new moment of experience adds to, or subtracts from, whatever has just preceded. At any particular moment, the pattern of synaptic change provides a running average of what has occurred previously.

These neurobiological approaches show how experience can cumulatively affect neocortex. What about the single events that comprise the total amount of experience? How is a particular episode, such as a particular training trial or a particular event with its own context of time and place, recorded in the brain? How is a single episode accessed separately and distinctly from the cumulative record?

Synaptic analysis alone will not prove sufficient to resolve this fundamental question. Neural systems and the brain structures that belong to these systems provide the appropriate level of analysis. The computations performed by these systems do ultimately result in synaptic change. Nevertheless, the storage of individual episodes, as distinct from the cumulative record of all episodes, must be determined by brain systems that perform specific operations. Such operations cannot be reduced to single neurons or synapses.

The prefrontal cortex may be a part of the machinery by which the brain solves this problem. If prefrontal cortex is involved in organizing and establishing the context of individual events, this cortex may allow information being processed throughout cortex to be related to other spatially and temporally coincident information. In this way, the frontal lobes can construct specific time-place contexts, so that events that occur in similar locations and at similar times can be separately remembered. Whether or not they are in fact remembered depends on the interaction between frontal cortex and the medial temporal region.

240

15

Memory and Brain: A Beginning

Only a beginning has been made at understanding the complex problem of how the brain accomplishes learning and memory. Memory is presumed to depend on the cooperative participation of assemblies of neurons, which reside in cortical and subcortical brain systems, and which are specialized to process different kinds of information. Each specialized system has its own specific, short-term, working-memory capacity and also the capacity to retain in long-term memory specific features or dimensions of information. Each specialized system thereby stores the product of its own processing. Long-term memory of even a single event depends on synaptic change in a distributed ensemble of neurons, which themselves belong to many different processing systems, and the ensemble acting together constitutes memory for the whole event. Arguments by analogy from developmental neurobiology and sensory neurophysiology suggest that representations of events in memory are subject to competition and dynamic change. The strengthening of some connections within an ensemble occurs at the expense of other connections. These dynamic changes are the synaptic reflections of rehearsal, relearning, normal forgetting, and perhaps the passage of time alone; and they result in a resculpting of the neural circuitry that originally represented the stored information.

A large number of categories for information processing and memory suggest themselves, and these provide a starting place for the important problem of how to classify the kinds of learning and memory that can occur. One can begin with a distinction between the types of processing done within the left and right hemispheres, and subdivide these into the various specialized functions organized within each hemisphere, such as the capacity for understanding language and perceiving faces. Such categories reflect the different kinds of processing that the brain can accomplish. The input pathways presumably differ in each case, and the neural systems that operate on the inputs likewise differ. Study of these material-specific divisions can therefore reveal significant insights into how information processing occurs. However, no principled reason exists for supposing that these divisions reveal additional information about memory itself. Memory is the common product of diverse modes of stimulus analysis and information processing.

Certain other ways of dividing memory have proved quite useful. Thus, the available information suggests that memory can be divided into declarative and procedural knowledge systems, each with distinct modes of neural organization. Declarative memory refers to the kind of memory that is stored as events, facts, images, and propositions, which are accessible to conscious awareness as explicit knowledge. Procedural memory refers to the kind of memory that is stored as procedures, or as changes in the facility to perform specific cognitive operations. The ability to find quickly a face that is hidden in a picture is a perceptual skill, but the ability to recognize the face as familiar after it is found depends on a declarative representation in memory.

Declarative memory may be further subdivided into episodic and semantic memory, although what this subdivision may signify in terms of brain organization remains unclear. One possibility is that frontal cortex is required to represent and use episodic memory effectively. Procedural memory can be subdivided into several categories such as motor skill learning, cognitive skill learning, priming, and simple forms of classical conditioning. Another distinction, quite different from the preceding ones, is that declarative memory can be expressed in either short-term or long-term memory. This distinction is a prominent one when one considers the organization of the brain systems that accomplish learning and memory.

242

Information concerning where memory is localized is available in a few well-studied cases, where continuous study has been done over a period of many years. The favorable cases include habituation of the acoustic startle reflex and the vestibulo-ocular reflex, classical conditioning, imprinting, bird-song learning, visual discrimination learning, and visual object recognition. Identification of sites of plastic change can proceed only if something is known first about the anatomy of the neural pathways that are engaged during a particular kind of learning. Changes in these same pathways appear to store memory. The neural pathways involved in expressing the behavior of interest have been partially identified for habituation and classical conditioning, and a start has been made at locating critical sites of plastic change. In these cases, neurobiological analysis of plasticity at the cellular/synaptic level should be feasible.

The analysis of imprinting, bird-song learning, visual discrimination learning, and visual object recognition has proceeded so far primarily at the level of brain structures and brain systems. Complex learning, such as that required for the mastery of a visual discrimination problem, is almost certainly stored—at least partially—in neocortex. When the neocortex is involved in memory storage, some parts of the neocortex are more involved than others, and each part makes a different contribution. Yet, even for these difficult cases, the cortical and subcortical systems that process and store information can sometimes be related to neuroanatomical facts; and the undertaking of a cellular neurobiological analysis of complex vertebrate learning seems almost within the grasp.

The establishment of long-term memory in any of the brain systems specialized for different kinds of information processing can be influenced by, and depends on, a number of other brain systems. Certain hormones and transmitters influence the strength of learning and can modulate memory if given close to the time of learning. Some of these effects may involve the action of mechanisms that subserve attention or reinforcement. Peripherally released hormones can also modulate memory, perhaps by influencing the level of stress or arousal that follows an event. These influences could reach cortical representations of experience through any of several extrinsic, ascending brain stem pathways, each of which directly innervates wide areas of forebrain.

Memory also depends on an interaction established at the time of learning between the cortical regions that represent experience and a medial temporal/midline diencephalic brain system. This system is the one damaged in amnesia. It provides the capacity for just one kind of memory, here termed declarative memory. Procedural memory does not require this interaction. Representations of experience continue to change and to be resculpted after learning occurs. One consequence of this process is normal forgetting. A second consequence is consolidation, the reorganization and stabilization of what remains. Consolidation allows at least some representations eventually to become independent of the brain system that is damaged in amnesia. Amnesic patients therefore often retain a great deal of remote, premorbid memory, despite their impaired new learning, and despite their loss of more recent, premorbid memory.

Prefrontal cortex is involved, in part, in organizing and establishing the context of individual events. Prefrontal cortex may function together with other cortical processing areas in order to relate the information being processed to other spatially and temporally coincident information. Prefrontal cortex may thereby provide context and specificity for events, shaping them as individual spatial-temporal episodes. The neural system damaged in amnesia operates on the product of this analysis and permits individual episodes to be retained in long-term memory.

An enormous amount remains to be learned about what memory is, where it is stored, and how it is organized. Until recently, neuroscience has often asked only cellular/synaptic questions about plasticity, for example, how do synapses change? Psychology, for its part, has often restricted itself to questions concerning the organization of whole behavior, making no reference to the brain. A more coherent and broader view is now within reach, as the result of information available from intermediate levels of analysis, especially information concerning brain processes and systems. Despite the modest level of our present understanding, considerable progress has occurred in the last 10 to 20 years, and this is cause for optimism. Prior to this period data came in and out of fashion as convictions shifted about how learning and memory should be studied. Yet now, more than ever before, there is agreement about which questions are important; and some of the information that has been obtained about learning and memory should endure as building blocks of the science. Thus, although the discipline is still very young, much work on the problem of learning and memory has become truly cumulative.

The most satisfying explanations of memory will be those that refer both to whole behavior and to the brain, and that allow connections across levels of analysis: from behavior and cognition to brain systems, and ultimately to neurons and cellular events. In the coming decades, investigations of memory will benefit from the widest possible perspective, one that draws jointly on the traditions of cognitive psychology, neuropsychology, and neurobiology.

Glossary

acetylcholine (ACh).   A neurotransmitter used by the autonomic nervous system, by the neuromuscular junction, and by many neurons in the brain.

activation.   The induction of activity in an ensemble of neurons.

after-discharges.   The EEG signs of an electrically induced seizure, characterized by rhythmic synchronous firing alternating with electrical silence. Recorded from electrodes following a seizure or an electrical stimulus to the brain.

agnosia.   A neurological condition in which patients have normal acuity but nevertheless fail to recognize objects, as if percepts have lost their meaning.

Alzheimer's disease.   A progressive, degenerative disease of the central nervous system that leads to severe dementia.

aminergic.   Refers to those neurons that use an amine as neurotransmitter, e.g., a catecholamine such as norepinephrine or an indoleamine such as serotonin.

amygdala.   A group of nuclei lying within the anterior medial portion of each temporal lobe and associated with the limbic system.

aneurysm.   An abnormal dilatation of a blood vessel, especially an artery, resulting from disease of the vessel wall.

anterior communicating artery.   A short artery located in the forebrain which connects the two anterior arteries of each hemisphere.

247

anterior nucleus. A group of neurons in the thalamus directly in front of the mediodorsal nucleus.

anterograde amnesia. A loss of the ability to learn.

anterior commissure. A fiber bundle connecting structures in the anterior parts of the two hemispheres.

aphasia. A neurological condition in which the capacity for language comprehension or expression is affected, in the absence of any defect in the vocal apparatus or peripheral musculature.

apical dendrite. Dendrites, especially of pyramidal neurons, which emerge from the superficial (upper) aspect of the cell body and extend toward the outer surface of the brain.

Aplysia. The sea hare, a marine invertebrate about the size of a human fist. Its nervous system contains fewer than 2×10^4 neurons, many of them very large.

apraxia. A neurological condition in which patients fail to carry out skilled voluntary movements, in the absence of paralysis or any defect in peripheral musculature.

arcuate sulcus. A sulcus or furrow in the brain of some primates, located at the posterior border of prefrontal cortex.

backward masking. A technique in which a visual stimulus is followed rapidly by another stimulus (usually within 100 msec). The second stimulus will often interfere with (mask) perception of the first stimulus.

basal dendrite. Dendrites, especially of pyramidal neurons, which emerge from the deep (lower) aspect of the cell body and extend parallel to the brain surface and downward toward subcortical white matter.

basal forebrain. A term used to apply to structures lying at the base of the forebrain, especially the septum, nucleus basalis, and the diagonal band of Broca.

catecholamine. A class of molecules including the neurotransmitters dopamine, epinephrine, and norepinephrine.

caudate nucleus and putamen. A part of the basal ganglia, often referred to as the neostriatum. In the rat the caudate nucleus and the putamen are not histologically distinguishable.

cell body. *See* **somata.**

cerebellar peduncle. One of three bands of fibers connecting the cerebellum to the midbrain.

cerebral peduncle. A term for the portion of the cortico-spinal tract that forms a bulge at the level of the midbrain.

cholinergic. Refers to those neurons that use acetylcholine as a neurotransmitter.

248

climbing fibers. One of two excitatory inputs to the cerebellum, originating mainly in the inferior olive and entering the cerebellum through the inferior cerebellar peduncle.

consolidation. A change in the structure of memory, other than forgetting, that occurs with the passage of time after learning.

corpus callosum. The large bundle of fibers connecting the two cerebral hemispheres.

delayed alternation. A task developed to test cognitive functions in nonhuman primates. Animals must learn to alternate their choices between two identically marked locations, when a delay is interposed between each choice.

delayed matching to sample. A task developed to test memory in nonhuman primates. The animal sees a single object and then after a delay sees two objects, the recently observed one and a second one. The animal can find a reward by choosing the familiar object.

delayed nonmatching to sample. A task developed to test memory in nonhuman primates. Animals see a single object and then after a delay see two objects, the recently observed one and a second one. The animal can find a reward by choosing the second, novel object.

delayed response. A task developed to test cognitive function in nonhuman primates. One of two identically marked locations is baited with food while the animal watches. After a delay during which neither location is visible, the animal has an opportunity to find the food by selecting the baited location.

dementia. A neurological condition characterized by global loss of intellectual function and personality change.

depression (synaptic depression). A short-lasting decrease in synaptic efficacy caused by recent stimulation of a neuron and resulting in a decreased readiness of that neuron to release neurotransmitter.

dendritic spine. Dendrites of most mammalian neurons are studded with small processes, or spines, where primarily excitatory synapses are located.

diagonal band of Broca. A group of neurons in the basal forebrain composed of cholinergic neurons that project to the hippocampal formation.

diencephalic midline. The area of the diencephalon of the brain surrounding the ventricles, including the medial thalamus and hypothalamus.

dopamine (DA). A neurotransmitter used by groups of neurons located mainly in the mesencephalon, but also in the medulla, diencephalon, retina, and olfactory bulb.

ECS. *See* **electroconvulsive shock.**

ECT. *See* **electroconvulsive therapy.**

ectostriatum. A region in the forebrain of birds, ventral to the hyperstriatum.

electroconvulsive shock (ECS). Electric current delivered to the brain, usually of a rat or mouse, sufficient to produce a convulsion or seizure.

electroconvulsive therapy. A psychiatric treatment, especially for severe depression, in which electrical current passed through scalp electrodes induces a cerebral convulsion. The treatment is given after administration of a general anaesthetic and a muscle relaxant.

encephalitis. An often fatal viral disease that damages the brain bilaterally, especially the medial temporal lobe and the orbital frontal lobe.

entorhinal cortex. A region of cortex in the medial temporal lobe, anterior to the parahippocampal gyrus.

evoked response (evoked potential). A change in voltage from a recording electrode elicited (evoked) by a stimulus.

extra-pyramidal system. Structures in the brain involved in motor behavior, such as the basal ganglia and cerebellum, but excluding the pyramidal system.

facilitation (synaptic facilitation). A short-lasting increase in synaptic efficacy caused by recent stimulation of a neuron and resulting in an increased readiness of that neuron to release neurotransmitter.

flocculus. One small lobe of the cerebellum, related to the vestibular system.

forebrain. One of three major subdivisions of the vertebrate brain, comprising both the telencephalon (the cerebral hemispheres) and the diencephalon (the thalamus and hypothalamus).

fornix. A large bundle of fibers comprising a major output pathway of the hippocampal formation to subcortical structures, including the mammillary bodies and septal nuclei.

free recall. The production of material from memory without the aid of specific cues.

gamma-aminobutyric acid (GABA). A neurotransmitter believed to exert an inhibitory action on target calls.

geniculo-striate pathway. The monosynaptic neural pathway that begins with neurons in the lateral geniculate nucleus of the thalamus and ends on neurons in the striate cortex, the primary receiving area for visual information in the neocortex.

gill withdrawal reflex. A reflex studied especially in the sea hare *Aplysia*. Mechanical stimulation of the gills causes them to be withdrawn into the mantle cavity.

hippocampus. A structure located in the medial temporal lobe.

6-hydroxydopamine. A compound toxic to nerve cells, especially neurons that use a catecholamine as neurotransmitter.

hyperstriatum. A region near the roof of the avian forebrain, extending from the lateral surface of the brain to the midline.

inferior olive. A nucleus in the medulla, which forms a major source of projections to the cerebellum.

inferotemporal cortex (area TE). The anterior portion of the inferior temporal lobe, concerned with visual functions.

interpeduncular nucleus. A group of neurons in the midbrain just behind the thalamus.

ischemia. A sustained loss of blood pressure, such that an insufficient amount of blood is delivered to a region of the body or brain.

Korsakoff's syndrome. A chronic neurological condition resulting from chronic alcohol abuse, in which memory functions are prominently affected.

lateral lemniscus. A fiber tract forming part of the ascending auditory pathway. The nucleus of the lateral lemniscus is one station in that pathway.

leucotomy. A surgical procedure in which neural connections are destroyed between the frontal lobes and other brain regions, especially the thalamus.

locus coeruleus. A nucleus in the pons composed mostly of neurons that use norepinephrine as a neurotransmitter.

long-term potentiation (LTP). A change in synaptic efficacy, which can last for weeks, caused by brief, high-frequency stimulation. The capacity for LTP has been best demonstrated in the hippocampal formation, but it can probably occur at other places as well. Some authors prefer the term long-term enhancement (LTE), to emphasize the difference between this phenomenon and the shorter lasting, post-tetanic potentiation.

mammillary nuclei (mammillary bodies). Paired nuclei in the posterior hypothalamus at the base of the brain behind the pituitary gland.

mamillothalamic tract. A bundle of fibers connecting the mammillary nuclei to the anterior nucleus of the thalamus.

medial geniculate nucleus. The sensory nucleus in the thalamus that sends auditory information to the cortex. The magnocellular portion of the medial geniculate lies outside this classical auditory pathway.

medial temporal region. The inner area of the temporal lobe away from the lateral surface, including the hippocampal formation, amygdala, parahippocampal gyrus, entorhinal cortex, and perirhinal cortex.

mediodorsal nucleus. A group of neurons in the thalamus.

middle cerebellar peduncle. A band of fibers carrying connections primarily from the pons to the cerebellum.

mossy fibers (cerebellum). One of two excitatory inputs to the cerebellum.

So named because of the mossy appearance of the terminal arborizations of the axons.

mossy fibers (hippocampus). The axons of the dentate gyrus granule cells, which project to the CA3 field of hippocampus. So named because of the mossy appearance of their presynaptic terminals.

nictitating membrane. A thin membrane, present in many animals, that can close over the eye.

nigrostriatal projection. The largely dopaminergic neural pathway that originates in the substantia nigra of the mesencephalon and terminates in the neostriatum of the forebrain.

Nissl substance. Clumps of rough endoplasmic reticulum within neuronal cell bodies. When stained with a basic dye, such as thionin, the clumps appear bright blue, thereby revealing the locations of cell bodies.

norepinephrine (NE). A neurotransmitter used by the autonomic nervous system and by groups of neurons in the brainstem. Also called noradrenalin.

nucleus basalis. A nucleus in the basal forebrain composed mostly of neurons that use acetylcholine as a transmitter.

nucleus reticularis pontis caudalis. A group of neurons in the pontine reticular formation that receives projections from various regions, including higher brain centers, and that sends axons rostrally as well as caudally into the spinal cord.

nucleus rotundus. A group of neurons in the visual system of the bird.

optic tectum. The roof of the midbrain and a target of retinal projections in vertebrates. The tectum in lower vertebrates is homologous to the mammalian superior colliculus.

parahippocampal gyrus. Cortex in the medial temporal lobe ventral and lateral to the hippocampal formation.

postcentral gyrus. A gyrus or ridge of the brain in the parietal lobe concerned with sensory functions.

post-tetanic potentiation. An increase in the readiness of a neuron to release neurotransmitter that can last many minutes, caused by high-frequency stimulation of the neuron.

precentral gyrus. A gyrus or ridge of the brain in the frontal lobe concerned with motor functions.

prefrontal cortex. The cortex of the frontal lobe that lies anterior to premotor cortex.

premotor cortex. The cortex of the frontal lobe anterior to the precentral gyrus and just posterior to the arcuate sulcus.

prestriate cortex. Visual cortex located anterior to the striate cortex.

pretectal complex (pretectum). A group of nuclei anterior to the superior colliculus.

primacy effect. The tendency for the first few words on a list to be recalled better than words from the middle of the list.

priming. Facilitation of the ability to process a stimulus due to prior presentation of the stimulus.

prosopagnosia. A form of agnosia in which patients have special difficulty recognizing human faces.

protein kinase. An enzyme that catalyzes the transfer of a phosphate group from adenosine triphosphate (ATP) to a protein, thereby producing a phosphoprotein.

protein phosphorylation. A biochemical step whereby a phosphate group is added to a serine, threosine, or tyrosine residue in a protein, often changing its function.

pyramidal neuron. A relatively large cell type of the neocortex and hippocampus, whose cell bodies are roughly pyramid-shaped and which possess prominent apical and basal dendrites.

pyramidal system. The pyramidal tract and related structures. It originates in the precentral gyrus of the cerebral cortex and descends to the spinal cord and then to muscles by way of the pyramidal tract and motor neurons.

recency effect. The tendency for the last few words on a list to be recalled better than words from the middle of the list.

red nucleus. A nucleus in the midbrain receiving projections from the cerebellum.

retino-geniculate pathway. The monosynaptic neural pathway that begins with the ganglion cells of the retina and ends on neurons in the lateral geniculate nucleus of the thalamus.

retrograde amnesia. Loss of memory for information acquired prior to the event that causes amnesia.

scopolamine. A compound that blocks neurotransmission at muscarinic cholinergic synapses.

scotophobin. A 15 amino-acid peptide isolated in the early 1970s, so named because of the controversial claim that injecting it into an animal caused that animal to exhibit "fear of the dark."

septal nuclei (septum). Nuclear groups in the forebrain, which send an important projection to the hippocampus.

serotonin. A neurotransmitter used by groups of neurons in the brain, especially the raphe nuclei.

somata. Plural form of soma, the neuronal cell body. The portion of a neuron that contains the nucleus and much of the machinery for assembling cellular components for the remainder of the neuron (the axons, dendrites, and synaptic terminals).

source amnesia. Loss of memory for when and where particular information was acquired.

split-brain. A bisection of the major brain commissures connecting the two hemispheres, including the corpus callosum and sometimes the anterior commissure, hippocampal commissure, and the optic chiasm.

subiculum. A structure of the hippocampal formation lying between the entorhinal cortex and the CA1 field of the hippocampus.

submandibular ganglion. A group of parasympathetic neurons whose axons innervate the submandibular gland, a salivary gland.

sulcus principalis. A sulcus or furrow in the brain of the monkey located over each frontal lobe.

superior cerebellar peduncle. A major output pathway of the cerebellum to the red nucleus and thalamus.

superior cervical ganglion. A group of sympathetic neurons in the peripheral nervous system, whose axons innervate regions of the head and neck, including the iris.

superior colliculus. A structure in the midbrain that receives input from the retina.

suprasylvian cortex. A region of the cat neocortex.

TE. *See* **inferotemporal cortex.**

tegmentum. A major portion of the midbrain.

temporal stem. A heterogeneous band of fibers connecting temporal neocortex to subcortical structures.

TEO. A region of the temporal lobe concerned with visual processing just posterior to area TE.

trophic factor. A substance, the best known of which is nerve growth factor, which is released from a neuron and helps to maintain the integrity of the presynaptic neuron.

uncus. A bulge on the medial side of the temporal lobe, comprising portions of the amygdala and hippocampus.

unit activity. The action potentials (discharges, impulses) recorded from a single neuron.

ventral cochlear nucleus. A group of neurons located early in the primary auditory pathway.

vestibulo-ocular reflex. A rapid response of the eye to adjust to a change in head position.

WAIS. The Wechsler Adult Intelligence Scale, the best known and most widely used of the tests designed to assess general intellectual ability in adults. The WAIS consists of 11 subtests, and the overall score (the IQ or intelligence quotient) correlates highly with school performance and with scores obtained on other tests of mental ability.

Wernicke-Korsakoff syndrome. An acute neurological condition caused by chronic alcohol abuse and thiamine deficiency, consisting of ataxia, oculomotor signs, and a global confusional state. This condition sometimes progresses to Korsakoff's syndrome.

WMS. The Wechsler Memory Scale, a widely used pencil-and-paper test of memory functions, designed to be used together with the WAIS. In the normal population both tests yield a mean of 100 and a standard deviation of 15. The value of the WMS for measuring memory functions is diluted to some extent by the fact that the test measures cognitive functions rather broadly, such that a low score on the test can signify dementia rather than memory problems specifically.

References

Acheson, L., and M. L. Zigmond. Short and long term changes in tyrosine hydroxylase activity in rat brain after subtotal destruction of central noradrenergic neurons. *J. Neurosci.* 1: 493–504, 1981.

Aggleton, J. P., and M. Mishkin. Visual recognition impairment following medial thalamic lesions in monkeys. *Neuropsychologia* 21: 189–197, 1983a.

Aggleton, J. P., and M. Mishkin. Memory impairments following restricted medial thalamic lesions in monkeys. *Exp. Brain Res.* 52: 199–209, 1983b.

Aggleton, J. P., and M. Mishkin. Mammillary-body lesions and visual recognition in the monkey. *Exp. Brain Res.* 58: 190–197, 1985.

Aigner, T., S. Mitchell, J. Aggleton, M. DeLong, R. Struble, G. Wenk, D. Price, and M. Mishkin. Recognition deficit in monkeys following neurotoxic lesions of the basal forebrain. *Soc. Neurosci. Abstr.* 10: 386, 1984.

Albert, M. S., N. Butters, and J. Levin. Memory for remote events in chronic alcoholics and alcoholic Korsakoff patients. In: *Biological Effects of Alcohol,* edited by H. Begleiter. Plenum, 1980, 719–730.

Albert, M. S., N. Butters, and J. Levin. Temporal gradients in the retrograde amnesia of patients with alcoholic Korsakoff's disease. *Arch. Neurol.* 36: 211, 1979.

Albus, J. S. A theory of cerebellar function. *Math Biosci.* 10: 26–61, 1971.

Alkon, D. L. Calcium mediated reduction of ionic currents: A biophysical memory trace. *Science* 226: 1037–1045, 1984.

Alkon, D. L., and J. Farley (Eds.). *Primary Neural Substrates of Learning and Behaviorial Change.* New York: Cambridge University Press, 1984.

REFERENCES

Allman, J. M. Evolution of the visual system in the early primates. *Prog. Psychobiol. Physiol. Psychol.* 7: 1–53, 1977.

Amaral, D. G. Memory: The anatomical organization of candidate brain regions. In: *Handbook of Physiology: Higher Functions of the Nervous System,* edited by F. Plum. Bethesda, MD: American Physiological Society, 1987, in press.

Anderson, J. R. *Language, Memory, and Thought.* Hillsdale, NJ: Erlbaum, 1976.

Anderson, J. R. *Cognitive Psychology and Its Implications.* San Francisco, CA: Freeman, 1980.

Arnsten, A. F. T., and D. S. Segal. Naloxone alters locomotion and interaction with environmental stimuli. *Life Sci.* 25: 1035–1942, 1979.

Arnsten, A. F. T., D. S. Segal, H. J. Neville, S. A. Hillyard, D. S. Janowsky, L. L. Judd, and F. E. Bloom. Electrophysiological signs of selective attention in man. *Nature* 304: 725–727, 1983.

Atkinson, R. C., and R. M. Shiffrin. Human memory: A proposed system and its control processes. In: *The Psychology of Learning and Motivation: Advances in Research and Theory,* vol. 2, edited by K. W. Spence and J. T. Spence. New York: Academic Press, 1968, 89–195.

Azmitia, E. C. The serotonin-producing neurons of the midbrain median and dorsal raphe nuclei. In: *Handbook of Psychopharmacology,* vol. 9, edited by L. Iversen, S. Iversen, and S. Snyder. New York: Plenum, 1978, 223–314.

Babich, F. R., A. L. Jacobsen, S. Bubash, and A. Jacobsen. Transfer of a response to naive rats by injection of ribonucleic acid extracted from trained rats. *Science* 149: 656–657, 1965.

Bachevalier, J., and M. Mishkin. An early and a late developing system for learning and retention in infant monkeys. *Behav. Neurosci.* 98: 770–778, 1984.

Bachevalier, J., and M. Mishkin. Visual recognition impairment follows ventromedial but not dorsolateral prefrontal lesions in monkeys. *Behav. Brain Res.* 20: 249–261, 1986.

Bachevalier, J., R. Saunders, and M. Mishkin. Visual recognition in monkeys: effects of transection of fornix. *Exp. Brain Res.* 57: 547–553, 1985.

Baddeley, A. The concept of working memory: A view of its current state and probable future development. *Cognition* 10: 17–23, 1981.

Baddeley, A. Implications of neuropsychological evidence for theories of normal memory. In: *Philosophical Transactions of the Royal Society of London,* vol. 298, edited by D. E. Broadbent and L. Weiskrantz. London: The Royal Society, 1982, 59–72.

Baddeley, A. D., and Hitch, G. J. Working memory. In: *The Psychology of Learning and Motivation: Advances in Research and Theory,* vol. 8, edited by G. A. Bower. New York: Academic Press, 1974, 47–90.

Baddeley, A. D., and E. K. Warrington. Amnesia and the distinction between long- and short-term memory. *J. Verb. Learn. Verb. Behav.* 9: 176–189, 1970.

Bagshaw, M. H., N. H. Mackworth, and K. H. Pribram. The effect of inferotemporal cortex ablations on eye movements of monkeys during discrimination training. *Int. J. Neurosci.* 1: 153–158, 1970.

Bahrick, H. P. Semantic memory content in permastore: Fifty years of memory for Spanish learned in school. *J. Exp. Psychol. [Gen.]* 113: 1–47, 1984.

Bailey, C. H., and M. Chen. Morphological basis of long-term habituation and sensitization in *Aplysia*. *Science* 220: 91–93, 1983.

Baldwin, M. Electrical stimulation of the medial temporal region. In: *Electrical Studies on the Unanesthetized Brain*, edited by E. R. Ramsey and D. S. O'Doherty. New York: Hoeber, 1960, 159–176.

Ball, J. Neuronal loss, neurofibrillary tangles and granulovacuolar degeneration in the hippocampus with ageing and dementia. *Acta Neuropatho. (Berl.)* 37: 111–118, 1977.

Barbizet, J. *Human Memory and Its Pathology*. San Francisco, CA: Freeman, 1970.

Barnes, C. A. Memory deficits associated with senescence: A behavioral and neurophysiological study in the rat. *J. Comp. Physiol. Psychol.* 93: 74–104, 1979.

Barondes, S. H. Memory transfer. *Science* 176: 631–632, 1972.

Barr, R. Some remarks on the time-course of aging. In: *New Directions in Memory and Aging*, edited by L. Poon, J. Fozard, L. Cermak, D. Arenberg, and L. Thompson. Hillsdale, NJ: Erlbaum, 1980, 143–149.

Bartlett, F., and E. R. John. Equipotentiality quantified: The anatomical distribution of the engram. *Science* 181: 764–767, 1973.

Bartus, R. T., R. L. Dean, B. Beer, and A. S. Lippa. The cholinergic hypothesis of geriatric memory dysfunction. *Science* 217: 408–417, 1982.

Bateson, P. P. G. The neural basis of imprinting. In: *The Biology of Learning*, edited by P. Marler and H. Terrace. Dahlem Konferenzen, Berlin: Springer-Verlag, 1984, 325–339.

Bauer, J. H., and R. M. Cooper, Effects of posterior cortical lesions on performance of a brightness-discrimination task. *J. Comp. Physiol. Psychol.* 58: 84–92, 1964.

Beach, F. A., D. O. Hebb, C. T. Morgan, and H. W. Nissen (Eds.). *The Neuropsychology of Lashley*. New York: McGraw-Hill, 1960.

Bear, M. F., and W. Singer. Modulation of visual cortical plasticity by acetylcholine and noradrenaline. *Nature* 320: 172–176, 1986.

Beatty, W. W., N. Butters, and D. S. Janowsky. Patterns of memory failure after scopolamine treatment: Implications for cholinergic hypotheses of dementia. *Behav. Neural Biol.*, 45: 196–211, 1986.

Bennett, E. L., and M. Calvin. Failure to train planarians reliably. *Neurosci. Res. Program Bull.* 2(4): 3–12, 1964.

Benson, D. F., C. D. Marsden, and J. L. Meadows. The amnesic syndrome of posterior cerebral artery occlusion. *Acta Neurol. Scand.* 50: 133–145, 1974.

Berger, T. W., and W. B. Orr. Hippocampectomy selectively disrupts discrimination reversal learning of the rabbit nictitating membrane response. *Behav. Brain Res.* 8: 49–68, 1983.

Berger, T. W., and R. F. Thompson. Identification of pyramidal cells as the critical elements in hippocampal neuronal plasticity during learning. *Proc. Natl. Acad. Sci. USA* 75: 1472–1576, 1978.

Bergson, H. *Matter and Memory*. London: Allen and Unwin, 1911.

Black, P., and R. E. Myers. Brainstem mediation of visual perception in a higher primate. *Trans. Am. Neurol. Assoc.* 93: 191–193, 1968.

Blakemore, C. Developmental factors in the formation of feature extracting neurons. In: *The Neurosciences: Third Study Program,* edited by F. O. Schmitt and F. G. Worden. Cambridge, MA: MIT Press, 1974, 105–113.

Blakemore, C., and R. C. Van Sluyters. Reversal of the physiological effects of monocular deprivation in kittens: Further evidence for a sensitive period. *J. Physiol. (Lond.)* 237: 195–216, 1974.

Blanchard, D. C., and R. J. Blanchard. Innate and conditioned reactions to threat in rats with amygdaloid lesions. *J. Comp. Physiol. Psychol.* 81: 281–290, 1972.

Bliss, T. V. P., and T. Lomo. Long-lasting potentiation of synaptic transmission in the dentate area of the anaesthetized rabbit following stimulation of the perforant path. *J. Physiol.* 232: 331–356, 1973.

Blum, R. A. Effects of subtotal lesions of frontal granular cortex on delayed reaction in monkeys. *Arch. Neurol. Psychiatry* 67: 375–386, 1952.

Braun, J. J., P. M. Meyer, and D. R. Meyer. Sparing of a brightness habit in rats following visual decortication. *J. Comp. Physiol. Psychol.* 61: 79–82, 1966.

Brierley, J. B. Neuropathology of amnesic states. In: *Amnesia,* edited by C. W. M. Whitty and O. L. Zangwill. London: Butterworths, 1977, 199–223.

Brion, S., and J. Mikol. Atteinte du noyau lateral dorsal du thalamus et syndrome de Korsakoff alcoolique. *J. Neurol. Sci.* 38: 249–261, 1978.

Broca, P. P. ''Remarks on the seat of the faculty of articulate language, followed by an observation of aphemia'' (1861), translated by G. von Bonin. In: *Some Papers on the Cerebral Cortex.* Springfield, IL: Thomas, 1960, 49–72.

Brody, H. Organization of cerebral cortex. III. A study of aging in the human cerebral cortex. *J. Comp. Neurol.* 102: 511–556, 1955.

Brody H., and N. Vijayashankar. Anatomical changes in the nervous system. In: *The Handbook of the Biology of Aging,* edited by C. Finch and L. Hayflick. New York: Van Nostrand Reinhold, 1977, 241–261.

Brooks, D. N., and A. Baddeley. What can amnesic patients learn? *Neuropsychologia* 14: 111–122, 1976.

Brown, M. W., and M. D. Cassell. Estimates of the number of neurons in the human hippocampus. *J. Physiol.* 30: 58–59, 1980.

Brown, R., and J. Kulik. Flashbulb memories. *Cognition* 5: 73–99, 1977.

Bruner, J. S. Modalities of memory. In: *The Pathology of Memory,* edited by G. A. Talland and N. C. Waugh. New York: Academic Press, 1969, 253–259.

Bullock, T. H. Reassessment of neural connectivity and its specification. In: *Information Processing in the Nervous System,* edited by H. M. Pinsker and W. D. Willis, Jr. New York: Raven Press, 1980, 199–220.

Burke, D., and L. Light. Memory and aging: The role of retrieval processes. *Psychol. Bull.* 90: 513–546, 1981.

Burnham, W. H. Retroactive amnesia: Illustrative cases and a tentative explanation. *Am. J. Psychol.* 14: 382–396, 1903.

REFERENCES

Burns, B. D. *The Mammalian Cerebral Cortex*. London: Edward Arnold, 1958.

Butler, C. R. A memory-record for visual discrimination habits produced in both cerebral hemispheres of monkey when only one hemisphere has received direct visual information. *Brain Res.* 10: 152–167, 1968.

Butters, N. Alcoholic Korsakoff's syndrome: an update. *Semin. Neurol.* 4: 226–244, 1984.

Butters, N., and D. N. Pandya. Retention of delayed-alternation: Effect of selective lesions of sulcus principalis. *Science* 165: 1271–1273, 1969.

Butters, N., P. Miliotis, M. Albert, and D. Sax. Memory assessment: Evidence of the heterogeneity of amnesic symptoms. In: *Advances in Clinical Neuropsychology, Vol. 1.*, edited by G. Goldstein. New York: Plenum Press, 1984, 127–159.

Byrne, W. L., and 22 co-signers. Memory transfer. *Science* 153: 658–659, 1966.

Cermak, L. S. The episodic-semantic distinction in amnesia. In: *Neuropsychology of Memory*, edited by L. R. Squire and N. Butters. New York: Guilford Press, 1984, 55–62.

Cermak, L. S., N. Butters, and J. Moreines. Some analyses of the verbal encoding deficit of alcoholic Korsakoff patients. *Brain Lang.* 1: 141–150, 1974.

Cermak, L. S., R, Lewis, N. Butters, and H. Goodglass. Role of verbal mediation in performance of motor tasks by Korsakoff patients. *Percept. Mot. Skills* 37: 259–263, 1973.

Cermak, L. S., and J. Moreines. Verbal retention deficits in aphasic and amnesic patients. *Brain Lang.* 3: 16–27, 1976.

Cermak, L. S., N. Talbot, K. Chandler, and L. Wolbarst. The perceptual priming phenomenon in amnesia. *Neuropsychologia* 23: 615–622, 1985.

Cermak, L. S., and S. Tarlow. Aphasic and amnesic patients' verbal vs. non-verbal retentive abilities. *Cortex* 14: 32–40, 1978.

Chang, T. J., and A. Gelperin. Rapid taste-aversion learning by an isolated molluscan central nervous system. *Proc. Natl. Acad. Sci. USA* 77: 6204–6206, 1980.

Chang, F. F., and W. T. Greenough. Lateralized effects of monocular training on dendritic branching in adult split-brain rats. *Brain Res.* 232: 283–292, 1982.

Chang, F. F., and W. T. Greenough. Transient and enduring morphological correlates of synaptic activity and efficacy change in the rat hippocampal slice. *Brain Res.* 309: 35–46, 1984.

Changeux, J., and A. Danchin. Selective stabilisation of developing synapses as a mechanism for the specification of neuronal networks. *Nature* 264: 705–712, 1976.

Chase, W. G., and H. A. Simon. Perception in chess. *Cognitive Psychol.* 4: 55–81, 1973.

Churchland, P. S. Neurophilosophy: Toward a unified science of the mind-brain. Cambridge: MIT Press, 1986.

Cipolla-Neto, J., G. Horn, and B. J. McCabe. Hemispheric asymmetry and imprinting: the effect of sequential lesions to the hyperstriatum ventrale. *Exp. Brain Res.* 48: 22–27, 1982.

Cohen, D. H. Involvement of the avian amygdalar homologue (archistriatum posterior and mediale) in defensively conditioned heart rate change. *J. Comp. Neurol.* 160: 13–36, 1975.

Cohen, D. H. The functional neuroanatomy of a conditioned response. In: *Neural Mechanisms of Goal-Directed Behavior and Learning,* edited by R. F. Thompson, L. H. Hicks, and V. B. Shvyrkov. New York: Academic Press, 1980, 283–302.

Cohen, D. H. Identification of vertebrate neurons modified during learning: analysis of sensory pathways. In: *Primary Neural Substrates of Learning and Behavioral Change,* edited by D. L. Alkon and J. Farley. New York: Cambridge University Press, 1984, 129–154.

Cohen, D. H. Some organizational principles of a vertebrate conditioning pathway: Is memory a distributed property. In: *Memory Systems of the Brain: Animal and Human Cognitive Processes,* edited by N. Weinberger, J. McGaugh, and G. Lynch. New York: Guilford Press, 1985.

Cohen, D. H., and MacDonald, R. L. Involvement of the avian hypothalamus in defensively conditioned heart rate change. *J. Comp. Neurol.* 167: 465–480, 1976.

Cohen, N. J. Neuropsychological evidence for a distinction between procedural and declarative knowledge in human memory and amnesia. Ph.D. Thesis, University of California, San Diego, 1981.

Cohen, N. J. Preserved learning capacity in amnesia: Evidence for multiple memory systems. In: *Neuropsychology of Memory,* edited by L. R. Squire and N. Butters. New York: Guilford Press, 1984, 83–103.

Cohen, N. J., and L. R. Squire. Preserved learning and retention of pattern analyzing skill in amnesia: Dissociation of knowing how and knowing that. *Science* 210: 207–209, 1980.

Cohen, N. J. and L. R. Squire. Retrograde amnesia and remote memory impairment. *Neuropsychologia* 19: 337–356, 1981.

Cooper, L. N., F. Lieberman, and E. Oja. A theory for the acquisition and loss of neuron specificity in visual cortex. *Biol. Cybernetics* 33: 9–28, 1979.

Corkin, S. Tactually guided maze-learning in man: Effects of unilateral cortical excisions and bilateral hippocampal lesions. *Neuropsychologia* 3: 339–351, 1965.

Corkin, S. Acquisition of motor skill after bilateral medial temporal excision. *Neuropsychologia* 6: 255–265, 1968.

Corkin, S. Lasting consequences of bilateral medial temporal lobectomy: Clinical course and experimental findings in H.M. *Semin. Neurol.* 4: 249–259, 1984.

Cowan, W. M. Neuronal death as a regulative mechanism in the control of cell number in the nervous system. In: *Development and Aging in the Nervous System,* edited by M. Rockstein and M. L. Sussman. New York: Academic Press, 1973, 19–41.

REFERENCES

Cowan, W. M., J. W. Fawcett, D. D. M. O'Leary, and B. B. Stanfield. Regressive events in neurogenesis. *Science* 225: 1258–1265, 1984.

Cowan, W. M., and D. M. O'Leary. Cell death and process elimination: The role of regressive phenomena in the development of the vertebrate nervous system. In: *Medicine, Science, and Society,* edited by K. J. Isselbacher. New York: Wiley, 1984, 643–668.

Cowey, A. Why are there so many visual areas? In: *The Organization of the Cerebral Cortex,* edited by F. O. Schmitt, F. G. Worden, G. Adelman, and S. G. Dennis. Cambridge, MA: MIT Press, 1981, 395–413.

Craik, F. I. M. Age differences in human memory. In: *Handbook of the Psychology of Aging,* edited by J. E. Birren and K. W. Schaie. New York: Van Nostrand Reinhold, 1977, 384–420.

Crick, F. Memory and molecular turnover. *Nature* 312: 101, 1984.

Crowder, R. G. On access and the forms of memory. In: *Memory Systems of the Brain,* edited by N. M. Weinberger, J. L. McGaugh, and G. Lynch. New York: Guilford Press, 1985, 433–441.

Crowder, R. G., and J. Morton. Precategorical acoustic storage (PAS). *Percept. Psychophys.* 5: 365–373, 1969.

Cummings, J. L., U. Tomiyasu, S. Read, and D. F. Benson. Amnesia with hippocampal lesions after cardiopulmonary arrest. *Neurology* 34: 679–681, 1984.

Dahl, D., W. H. Bailey, and J. Winson. Effect of norepinephrine depletion of hippocampus on neuronal transmission from perforant pathway through dentate gyrus. *J. Neurophysiol.* 49: 123–133, 1983.

Dam, A. M. The density of neurons in the human hippocampus. *Neuropathol. Appl. Neurobiol.* 5: 249–264, 1979.

Damasio, A. R., N. R. Graff-Radford, P. J. Eslinger, H. Damasio, and N. Kassell. Amnesia following basal forebrain lesions. *Arch. Neurol.* 42: 263–271, 1985.

Davis, M., D. S. Gendelman, M. D. Tischler, and P. M. Gendelman. A primary acoustic startle circuit: Lesion and stimulation studies. *J. Neurosci.* 2: 791–805, 1982a.

Davis, M., T. Parsi, D. S. Gendelman, M. Tischler, and J. H. Kehne. Habituation and sensitization of startle reflexes elicited electrically from the brainstem. *Science* 218: 688–689, 1982b.

Davis, H. P. and L. R. Squire. Protein synthesis and memory: A review. *Psychol. Bull.* 96: 518–559, 1984.

Davis, W. J., and R. Gillette. Neural correlate of behavioral plasticity in command neurons of Pleurobranchaea. *Science* 199: 801–804, 1978.

Daw, N. W., T. W. Robertson, R. K. Rader, T. O. Videen, and C. J. Coscia. Substantial reduction of cortical noradrenaline by lesions of adrenergic pathways does not prevent effects of monocular deprivation. *J. Neurosci.* 4: 1354–1360, 1984.

deGroot, A. D. *Het Denken van den Schaker.* Translated as *Thought and Choice in Chess.* The Hague: Mouton & Co., 1965.

263

Denenberg, V. H., and R. W. Bell. Critical periods for the effects of infantile experience on adult learning. *Science* 131: 227–228, 1960.

DeRenzi, E., and P. Nichelli. Verbal and non-verbal short-term memory impairment following hemispheric damage. *Cortex* 11: 341–354, 1975.

Deutsch, J. A. The cholinergic synapse and the site of memory. *Science* 174: 788–794, 1971.

de Wied, D. Influence of anterior pituitary on avoidance learning and escape behavior. *Am J. Physiol.* 207: 255–59, 1964.

Diamond, R. and P. Rozin. Activation of existing memories in anterograde amnesia. *J. Abnorm. Psychol.* 93: 98–105, 1984.

Disterhoft, J. F., M. T. Shipley, and N. Kraus. Analyzing the rabbit NM conditioned reflex arc. In: *Conditioning: Representation of Involved Neural Functions,* edited by C. D. Woody. New York: Plenum, 1982, 433–449.

Donegan, N. H., R. W. Lowry, and R. F. Thompson. Effects of lesioning cerebellar nuclei on conditioned leg-flexion responses. *Soc. Neurosci. Abstr.* 9: 331, 1983.

Drachman, D. A., and J. Arbit. Memory and the hippocampal complex. II. Is memory a multiple process? *Arch. Neurol.* 15: 52–61, 1966.

Drachman, D. A., and J. Leavitt. Human memory and the cholinergic system: A relationship to aging? *Arch. Neurol.* 30: 113–121, 1974.

Dunn, A. J. Neurochemistry of learning and memory: An evaluation of recent data. *Annu. Rev. Psychol.* 31: 343–390, 1980.

Dunnett, S. B., W. C. Low, S. D. Iversen, U. Stenevi, and A. Bjorklund. Septal transplants restore maze learning in rats with fornix-fimbria lesions. *Brain Res.* 251: 335–348, 1982.

Durkovic, R. G., and D. H. Cohen. Effects of caudal midbrain lesions on conditioning of heart and respiratory rate responses in the pigeon. *J. Comp. Physiol. Psychol.* 69: 329–338, 1969.

Dyal, J. A. Transfer of behavioral bias: Reality and specificity. In: *Chemical Transfer of Learned Information,* edited by E. J. Fjerdingstad. New York: Elsevier, 1971.

Eccles, J. C. *The neurophysiological basis of mind: the principles of neurophysiology.* Oxford, Clarendon Press, 1953.

Eccles, J. C. The modular operation of the cerebral neocortex considered as the material basis of mental events. *Neuroscience* 6: 1839–1856, 1981.

Edelman, G. M., and G. N. Reeke, Jr. Selective networks capable of representative transformations, limited generalizations, and associative memory. *Proc. Natl. Acad. Sci. USA,* 79: 2091–2095, 1982.

Eich, J. M. A composite holographic associative recall model. *Psychol. Rev.* 89: 627–661, 1982.

Ericsson, K. A., W. G. Chase, and S. Faloon. Acquisition of a memory skill. *Science* 208: 1181–1182, 1980.

Evans, F. J. and W. A. F. Thorn. Two types of posthypnotic amnesia: Recall amnesia and source amnesia. *Int. J. Clin. Exp. Hypn.* 14: 162–179, 1966.

Fabiani, M., D. Karis, and E. Donchin. P300 and recall in an incidental memory paradigm. *Psychophysiol.* 23: 298–308, 1986.

Ferguson, S. M., M. Rayport, E. Gardner, W. Kass, H. Weiner, and M. F. Reiser. Similarities in mental content of psychotic states, spontaneous seizures, dreams, and responses to electrical brain stimulation in patients with temporal lobe epilepsy. *Psychosom. Med.* 31: 479–498, 1979.

Ferrier, D. *The Functions of the Brain.* London: Smith, Elder, 1876.

Fibiger, H. C. Drugs and reinforcement mechanisms: A critical review of the catecholamine theory. *Annu. Rev. Pharmacol. Toxicol.* 18: 37–56, 1978.

Fjerdingstad, E. J. *Chemical Transfer of Learned Information* New York: Elsevier, 1971.

Fjerdingstad, E. J., T. Nissen, and H. H. Roigaard-Petersen. Effect of ribonucleic acid (RNA) extracted from the brains of trained animals on learning in rats. *Scand. J. Psychol.* 6: 1–6, 1965.

Flourens, P. *Researches experimentales sur les proprietes et les fonctions du systeme nerveux dans les Animaux Vertebres.* Paris: Balliere, 1824.

Fodor, J. *Modularity of Mind.* Cambridge, MA: MIT Press, 1983.

Foote, S. L., F. E. Bloom, and G. Aston-Jones. Nucleus Locus Ceruleus: New evidence of anatomical and physiological specificity. *Physiol. Rev.* 63: 844–914, 1983.

Foote, S. L., and J. H. Morrison. Postnatal development of laminar innervation patterns by monoaminergic fibers in monkey (Macaca Fascicularis) primary visual cortex. *J. Neurosci.* 4: 2667–2680, 1984.

Forbes, A., and C. S. Sherrington. Acoustic reflexes in the decerebrate cat. *Am. J. Psychol.* 35: 367–376, 1914.

Freed, D. M., N. J. Cohen, and S. Corkin. Rate of forgetting in H.M.: A reanalysis. *Soc. Neurosci. Abstr.* 10: 383, 1984.

Freud, S. S. *The Psychopathology of Everyday Life.* Standard Edition, vol. 6. London: Hargrath Press (1960), 1901.

Freud, S. S. *Civilization and Its Discontents.* Standard Edition XXI. London: Hargrath Press, 1930.

Fuster, J. M. *The Prefrontal Cortex: Anatomy, Physiology, and Neuropsychology of the Frontal Lobe.* New York: Raven Press, 1980.

Fuster, J. M. and J. P. Jervey. Inferotemporal neurons distinguish and retain behaviorally relevant features of visual stimuli. *Science* 212: 952–955, 1981.

Gabor, D. A new microscopic principle. *Nature* 161: 777–778, 1948.

Gabriel, M., Miller, J. D., and S. E. Saltwich. Multiple-unit activity of the rabbit medial geniculate nucleus in conditioning, extinction, and reversal. *Physiol. Psychol.* 4: 123–134, 1976.

Gaffan, D. Recognition impaired and association intact in the memory of monkeys after transection of the fornix. *J. Comp. Physiol. Psychol.* 86: 1100–1109, 1974.

Gaffan, D., E. Gaffan, and S. Harrison. Effects of fornix transection on spontaneous and trained non-matching by monkeys. *Q. J. Exp. Psychol.* 36B: 285–303, 1984.

Gaffan, D., R. C. Saunders, E. A. Gaffan, S. Harrison, C. Shields, and M. J. Owen. Effects of fornix transection upon associative memory in monkeys: Role of the hippocampus in learned action. *Q. J. Exp. Psychol.* 36B: 173–221, 1984.

Gaffan, D., C. Shields, and S. Harrison. Delayed matching by fornix-transected monkeys: The sample, the push, and the bait. *Q. J. Exp. Psychol.* 36B: 305–317, 1984.

Gage, F. H., S. B. Dunett, and P. A. T. Kelley. Intrahippocampal septal grafts ameliorate learning impairments in aged rats. *Science* 225: 533–535, 1984.

Gall, F. J. *Sur les fonction du cerveau et sur celles de chacune des ses parties,* vol. 6, Bailliere, Paris, 1822–1825, 1825.

Gallagher, M., R. A. King, and N. B. Young. Opiate antagonists improve spatial memory. *Science* 221: 975–976, 1983.

Galton, F. *Inquiries into Human Faculty and Its Development.* New York: Macmillan, 1883.

Gardner, H. *Frames of Mind.* New York: Basic Books, 1983.

Gardner, H., F. Boller, J. Moreines, and N. Butters. Retrieving information from Korsakoff patients: Effects of categorical cues and reference to the task. *Cortex* 9: 165–175, 1973.

Gaze, R. M., M. J. Keating, G. Szekely, and L. Beazley. Binocular interaction in the formation of specific intertectal neuronal connexions. *Proc. R. Soc. Lond. [Biol.]* 175: 107–147, 1970.

Gellman, R. S., and F. A. Miles. A new role for the cerebellum in conditioning? *Trends in Neurosci.* 8: 181–182, 1985.

Gerard, R. W. Physiology and psychiatry. *Am. J. Psychiatry* 105: 161–173, 1949.

Ghent, L., M. Mishkin, and H. L. Teuber. Short-term memory after frontal lobe injury in man. *J. Comp. Physiol. Psychol.* 55: 705–709, 1962.

Gibbs, M., and K. T. Ng. Psychobiology of memory: Towards a model of memory formation. *Biobehav. Rev.* 1: 113–136, 1977.

Glanzer, M., and A. R. Cunitz. Two storage mechanisms in free recall. *J. Verb. Learn. Verb. Behav.* 5: 351–360, 1966.

Glickman, S. E. Perseverative neural processes and consolidation of the memory trace. *Psychol. Bull.* 58: 218–233, 1961.

Glickstein, J., and R. W. Sperry. Intermanual somesthetic transfer in split-brain rhesus monkeys. *J. Comp. Physiol. Psychol.* 53: 322–327, 1960.

Glisky, E., D. Schacter, and E. Tulving. Computer learning by memory-impaired patients: Acquisition and retention of complex knowledge. *Neuropsychologia,* 24: 313–328, 1986.

Gloor, P., A. Olivier, L. F. Quesney, F. Andermann, and S. Horowitz. The role of the limbic system in experiential phenomena of temporal lobe epilepsy. *Ann Neurol.* 12: 129–144, 1982.

Gold, P. E., and R. L. Delanoy. ACTH modulation of memory storage processing. In: *Endogenous Peptides and Learning and Memory Processes,* edited by J. C. Martinez, Jr., R. A. Jensen, R. B. Messing, H. Rigter, J. L. McGaugh, New York: Academic Press, 79–98, 1981.

Gold, P. E., and J. L. McGaugh. A single-trace, two process view of memory processes. In: *Short-Term Memory,* edited by D. Deutsch and J. A. Deutsch. New York: Academic Press, 1975, 355–378.

Gold, P. E., and R. van Buskirk. Facilitation of time-dependent memory processes with posttrial epinphrine injections. *Behav. Biol.* 13: 145–153, 1975.

Gold, P. E., and R. van Buskirk. Effects of posttrial hormone injections on memory processes. *Horm. Behav.* 7: 509–517, 1976.

Goldberg, E., S. P. Antin, R. M. Bilder, L. J. Gerstman, J. E. O. Hughes, and S. Mattis. Retrograde amnesia: Possible role of mesencephalic reticular activation in long-term memory. *Science* 213: 1392–1394, 1981.

Goldman, P. S., and W. J. H. Nauta. Columnar distribution of cortico-cortical fibers in the frontal association, limbic, and motor cortex of the developing rhesus monkey. *Brain Res.* 393–413, 1977.

Goldman, P. S., and H. E. Rosvold. Localization of function within the dorsolateral prefrontal cortex of the rhesus monkey. *Exp. Neurol.* 27: 291–304, 1970.

Goldman-Rakic, P. Circuitry of the prefrontal cortex: Short-term memory and the regulation of behavior by representational knowledge. In: *Handbook of Physiology: Higher Functions of The Nervous System,* edited by F. Plum. Bethesda, MD: American Physiological Society, 1987, in press.

Goldman-Rakic, P. S., and M. L. Schwartz. Interdigitation of contralateral and ipsilateral columnar projections to frontal association cortex in primates. *Science* 216: 755–757, 1982.

Goltz, F. Uberdie verrichtungen des Grosshirns. *Pfluger's Arch. Ges. Physiol.* 13, 14, 20, 26, 1876–1884.

Graf, P., and D. Schacter. Implicit and explicit memory for new associations in normal and amnesic subjects. *J. Exp. Psychol. [Learn, Mem. Cog.]* 11: 501–518, 1985.

Graf, P., and D. Schacter. Selective effects of interference on implicit and explicit memory for new associations. *J. Exp. Psychol [Learn. Mem. Cog.],* 1987, in press.

Graf, P., A. P. Shimamura, and L. R. Squire. Priming across modalities and across category levels: extending the domain of preserved function in amnesia. *J. Exp. Psychol. [Learn. Mem. Cog.]* 11: 386–396, 1985.

Graf, P., L. R. Squire, and G. Mandler. The information that amnesic patients do not forget. *J. Exp. Psychol. [Learn. Mem. Cog.]* 10: 164–178, 1984.

Graff-Radford, N., H. Damasio, T. Yamada, P. J. Eslinger, and A. R. Damasio. Nonhaemorrhagic thalamic infarction. *Brain* 108: 485–516.

Greenough, W. T. Possible structural substrate of plastic neural phenomena. In: *Neurobiology of Learning and Memory*, edited by G. Lynch, J. L. McGaugh, and N. M. Weinberger. New York: Guilford Press, 1984a, 470–478.

Greenough, W. T. Structural correlates of information storage in the mammalian brain: A review and hypothesis. *Trends in Neurosci.* 7: 229–233, 1984b.

Gross, C. G. Visual functions of inferotemporal cortex. In: *Handbook of Sensory Physiology*, edited by R. Jung. Berlin: Springer-Verlag, 1973, 451–452.

Gross, C. G., Bender, D. B., and G. L. Gerstein. Activity of inferior temporal neurons in behaving monkeys. *Neuropsychologia* 17: 215–229, 1979.

Gross, C. G., and F. M. Carey. Transfer of learned response by RNA injection: Failure of attempts to replicate. *Science* 150: 1749, 1965.

Gross, C. G., S. I. Chorover, and S. M. Cohen. Caudate, cortical, hippocampal and dorsal thalamic lesions in rats; alternation and Hebb-Williams maze performance. *Neuropsychologia* 3: 53–68, 1965.

Gross, C. G., C. E. Roche-Miranda, and D. B. Bender. Visual properties of neurons in inferotemporal cortex of the Macaque. *J. Neurophysiol.* 35: 96–111, 1972.

Grossberg, S. *Studies of mind and brain.* Dordrecht, Holland; D. Reidel, 1982.

Groves, P. M., and R. F. Thompson. Habituation: A dual-process theory. *Psychol. Rev.* 77: 419–450, 1970.

Groves, P. M. Wilson, C. J., and S. W. Miller, Habituation of the acoustic startle response: A neural systems analysis of habituation in the intact animal. In: *Advances in Psychobiology*, vol. 3, edited by A. H. Riesen and R. F. Thompson. New York: Wiley, 1976.

Gruner, J. E. Sur la pathologie des encephalopathies alcooliques. *Rev. Neurol. (Paris)* 94: 682–689, 1956.

Grunthal, E. Veber das Corpus mamillare und den Korsakowschen Symtomen Komplex. *Confin. Neurol.* 2: 65–95, 1939.

Gudden, H. Klinische und anatomische Beitrage zur Kenntniss der multiplen Alkoholneuritis nebst Bemerkungen uber die Regenerationsvorgange im peripheren Nervensystem. *Arch. für Psychiatr. und Nerven-krank-heiten.* 28: 643–741, 1896.

Halgren, E. Human hippocampal and amygdala recording and stimulation: evidence for a neural model of recent memory. In: *The Neuropsychology of Memory*, edited by L. R. Squire and N. Butters. New York: Guilford Press, 1984, 165–182.

Halgren, E., R. D. Walter, A. G. Cherlow, and P. H. Crandall. Mental phenomena evoked by electrical stimulation of the human hippocampal formation and amygdala. *Brain* 101: 83–117, 1978.

Hamburger, V. Cell death in the development of the lateral motor column of the chick embryo. *J. Comp. Neurol.* 160: 535–546, 1975.

Harley, C. Arm choices in a sunburst maze: effects of hippocampectomy in the rat. *Physiol. and Behav.* 23: 283–290, 1979.

268

Hassler, R., and T. Riechert. Ueber einen Fall von doppelseitiger Forniocotomie bei sogenannter temporaler Epilepsie. *Acta. Neurochir. (Wien)* 5: 330–340, 1957.

Haug, H., U. Barmwater, R. Eggers, D. Fischer, S. Kuhl, and N. L. Sass. Anatomical changes in aging brain; Morphometric analysis of the human prosencephalon. In: *Brain Aging: Neuropathology and Neuropharmacology (Aging, vol. 21),* edited by J. Cervos-Navarro and H. I. Sarkander. New York: Raven Press, 1983, 1–12.

Hawkins, R. D., and E. R. Kandel. Is there a cell-biological alphabet for simple forms of learning? *Psychological Review* 91: 375–391, 1984.

Hawkins, R. D., T. W. Abrams, T. J. Carew, and E. R. Kandel. A cellular mechanism of classical conditioning in Aplysia: Activity-dependent amplification of presynaptic facilitation. *Science* 219: 400–405, 1983.

Haymaker, W., and F. Schiller. *The Founders of Neurology,* 2d ed. Springfield, IL: Thomas, 1970, 461.

Hearst, E. (Ed.) *The First Century of Experimental Psychology.* Hillsdale, NJ: Erlbaum, 1979.

Hebb, D. O. *The organization of behavior.* New York: Wiley, 1949.

Hebb, D. O. Neuropsychology: Retrospect and prospect. *Can. J. Psychol.* 37: 4–7, 1983.

Hecaen, H., and W. L. Albert. *Human Neuropsychology.* New York: Wiley, 1978.

Hilgard, E. R., and D. G. Marquis. *Conditioning and Learning.* New York: Appleton-Century-Crofts, 1940.

Hillyard, S. A., and M. Kutas. Electrophysiology of cognitive processing. *Ann. Rev. Psychol.* 34: 33–61, 1983.

Hinton, G. E. Implementing semantic networks in parallel hardware. In: *Parallel Models of Associative Memory,* edited by G. E. Hinton and J. A. Anderson. Hillsdale, NJ: Erlbaum, 1981, 161–188.

Hirsch, H. V. B., and D. N. Spinelli. Visual experience modifies distribution of horizontally and vertically oriented receptive fields in cats. *Science* 168: 869–871, 1970.

Hirsch, R. The hippocampus and contextual retrieval of information from memory: A theory. *Behav. Biol.* 12: 421–444, 1974.

Hoffman, T. J., C. L. Sheridan, and D. M. Levinson. Interocular transfer in albino rats as a function of forebrain plus midbrain commissurotomy. *Physiol. Behav.* 27: 279–285, 1981.

Hopfield, J. J., and D. W. Tank. Computing with neural circuits: a model. *Science* 233: 625–633.

Hopkins, W. F., and D. Johnston. Frequency-dependent noradrenergic modulation of long-term potentiation in the hippocampus. *Science* 226: 350–352, 1984.

Horel, J. A. The neuroanatomy of amnesia: A critique of the hippocampal memory hypothesis. *Brain* 101: 403–445, 1978.

Horn, G. Changes in the structure of synapses associated with learning. *J. Neurosci.* 5: 3161–3168, 1985.

REFERENCES

Horn, G. *Memory, Imprinting, and the Brain.* Oxford: Clarendon Press, 1985.

Horn, G. Neural mechanisms of learning: An analysis of imprinting in the domestic chick. *Proc. R. Soc. Lond. [Biol.]* 213: 101–137, 1981.

Horn, G., B. J. McCabe, and J. Cipolla-Neto. Imprinting in the domestic chick: The role of each side of the hyperstriatum ventrale in acquisition and retention. *Exp. Brain Res.* 53: 91–98, 1983.

Horowitz, M. J., J. E. Adams, and B. B. Rutkin. Visual imagery on brain stimulation. *Arch. Gen. Psychiat.* 19: 469–486, 1968.

Hoyle, G. Instrumental conditioning of the leg lift in the locust. *Neurosci. Res. Program Bull.* 17: 577–586, 1979.

Hubel, D. H., and T. N. Wiesel. Receptive fields, binocular interaction, and functional architecture in the cat's visual cortex. *J. Physiol.* London 160: 106–154, 1962.

Hubel, D. H., and T. N. Wiesel. Binocular interaction in striate cortex of kittens reared with artificial squint. *J. Neurophysiol.* 29: 1041–1059, 1965.

Hubel, D. H., and T. N. Wiesel. Brain mechanisms of vision. *Scientific Amer.* September, 84–97, 1979.

Hunt, T., T. Hunter, and A. Munro. Control of hemoglobin synthesis: Rate of translation of the messenger RNA for the A and B chains. *J. Mol. Biol.* 43: 123–133, 1969.

Hunter, W. S. The delayed reaction in animals and children. *Behav. Monogr.* 2: 1–86, 1913.

Hunter, W. S. A consideration of Lashley's theory of the equipotentiality of cerebral action. *J. Gen. Psychol.* 3: 455–468, 1930.

Huppert, F. A., and M. Piercy. Normal and abnormal forgetting in organic amnesia: effects of locus of lesion. *Cortex* 15: 385–390, 1979.

Hyden, H., and P. Lange. A differentiation in RNA response in neurons early and late in learning. *Proc. Nat. Acad. Sci. USA* 53: 946–952, 1965.

Hyman, B. T., G. W. Van Hoesen, A. R. Damasio, and C. L. Barnes. Alzheimer's disease: Cell specific pathology isolates the hippocampal formation. *Science,* 225: 1168–1170, 1984.

Imig, T. J., and J. F. Brugge. Sources and terminations of callosal axons related to binaural frequency maps in primary auditory cortex of the cat. *J. Comp. Neurol.* 182: 637–660, 1978.

Isseroff, A., H. E. Rosvold, T. W. Galkin, and P. S. Goldman-Rakic. Spatial memory impairments following damage to the mediodorsal nucleus in the thalamus of rhesus monkeys. *Brain Res.* 232: 97–113, 1982.

Ito, M. Cerebellar control of the vestibulo-ocular reflex: Around the flocculus hypothesis. *Annu. Rev. Neurosci.* 5: 275–296, 1982.

Ito, M., and Y. Miyashita. The effect of chronic destruction of inferior olive upon visual modification of the horizontal vestibulo-ocular reflex of rabbits. *Proc. Jpn. Acad.* 51: 716–760, 1975.

Ito, M., T. Shiida, N. Yagi, and M. Yamamoto. Visual influence on rabbit horizontal vestibulo-ocular reflex presumably effected via the cerebellar flocculus. *Brain Res.* 65: 170–174, 1974.

Iversen, S., and M. Mishkin, Perseverative interference in monkeys following selective lesions of the inferior prefrontal convexity. *Exp. Brain Res.* 11: 376–386, 1970.

Iwai, E. and M. Mishkin. Two visual foci in the temporal lobe of monkeys. In: *Neurophysiological Basis of Learning and Behavior,* edited by N. Yoshii and N. A. Buchwald. Osaka: Osaka University Press, 1968, 1–11.

Izquierdo, I. Effect of naloxone and morphine on various forms of memory in the rat: Possible role of endogenous opiate mechanisms in memory consolidation. *Psychopharmacology* 66: 199–203, 1979.

Jacobsen, C. F. Functions of the frontal association area in primates. *Arch. Neurol. Psychiatry* 33: 558–569, 1935.

Jacobsen, C. F. Studies of cerebral functions in primates: I. The functions of the frontal association areas in monkeys. *Comp. Psychol. Monogr.* 13: 3–60, 1936.

Jacobsen, C. F., and H. W. Nissen. Studies of cerebral function in primates: IV. The effects of frontal lobe lesions on the delayed alternation habit in monkeys. *J. Comp. Physiol. Psychol.* 23: 101–112, 1937.

Jacobson, A. L., C. Fried, and S. D. Horowitz. Planarians and memory. I. Transfer of learning by injection of ribonucleic acid. *Nature* 209: 599–601, 1966.

Jacoby, L. L., and M. Dallas. On the relationship between autobiographical memory and perceptual learning. *J. Exp. Psychol. [Gen.]* 3: 306–340, 1981.

Jacoby, L. L., and D. Witherspoon. Remembering without awareness. *Can. J. Psychol.* 32: 300–324, 1982.

James, W. *Principles of Psychology.* New York: Holt, 1890.

Jenkins, W. M., M. M. Merzenich, and M. T. Ochs. Behaviorally controlled differential use of restricted hand surfaces induce changes in the cortical representation of the hand in area 3b of adult owl monkeys. *Soc. Neurosci. Abstr.* 10(1): 665, 1984.

John, E. R. Switchboard versus statistical theories of learning and memory. *Science* 177: 850–864, 1972.

John, E. R., F. Bartlett, M. Shimokochi, and D. Kleinman. Neural readout from memory. *J. Neurophysiol.* 36: 893–924, 1973.

John, E. R., and P. P. Morgades. Neural correlates of conditioned responses studied with multiple chronically implanted moving microelectrodes. *Exp. Neurol.* 23: 412–425, 1969.

Jonason, K. R., S. M. Lauber, M. J. Robbins, P. M. Meyer, and D. R. Meyer. Effects of amphetamine upon relearning pattern and black-white discriminations following neocortical lesions in rats. *J. Comp. Physiol. Psycho.* 73: 47–55, 1970.

Jones, B., and M. Mishkin. Limbic lesions and the problem of stimulus-reinforcement associations. *Exp. Neurol.* 36: 362–377, 1972.

Jones, E. G., and T. P. S. Powell. An anatomical study of converging sensory pathways within the cerebral cortex of the monkey. *Brain* 93: 793–820, 1970.

Jones, G. M. Plasticity in the adult vestibulo-ocular reflex arc. *Philos. Trans. R. Soc. Lond. [Biol.]* 278: 319–334, 1977.

Jones-Gotman, M., and B. Milner, Right temporal-lobe contribution to image mediated verbal learning. *Neuropsychologia* 16: 61–71, 1978.

Kahn, E. A., and E. C. Crosby. Korsakoff's syndrome associated with surgical lesions involving the mammillary bodies. *Neurology* 22: 117–125, 1972.

Kahneman, D. Method, findings, and theory in studies of visual masking. *Psychol. Bull.* 70: 404–425, 1968.

Kandel, E. R. *Cellular Basis of Behavior*. San Francisco: Freeman, 1976.

Kandel, E. R. Neuronal plasticity and the modification of behavior. In: *Handbook of Physiology. The Nervous System,* vol. I, edited by J. M. Brookhart and V. B. Mountcastle. Bethesda, MD: American Physiological Society, 1977, sect. 1, pt. 2, chapt. 29, 1137–1182.

Kandel, E. R. From metapsychology to molecular biology: explorations into the nature of anxiety. *Am. J. Psychiatry* 140: 1277–1293, 1983.

Kandel, E. R., and J. H. Schwartz. Molecular biology of learning: Modification of transmitter release. *Science* 218: 433–442, 1982.

Kandel, E. R., and W. A. Spencer. Cellular neurophysiological approaches in the study of learning. *Physiol. Rev.* 48: 65–134, 1968.

Kapp, B. S., R. C. Frysinger, M. Gallagher, and J. R. Haselton. Amygdala central nucleus lesions: Effect on heart rate conditioning in the rabbit. *Physiol. Behav.* 23: 1109–1117, 1979.

Kapp, B. S., M. Gallagher, C. D. Applegate, R. C. Frysinger. The amygdala central nucleus: Contributions to conditioned cardiovascular responding during aversive Pavlovian conditioning in the rabbit. In: *Conditioning: Representation of Involved Neural Functions,* edited by C. D. Woody. New York: Plenum Press, 1982, 581–598.

Kasamatsu, T. Neuronal plasticity maintained by the central norepinephrine system in the cat visual cortex. In: *Prog. in Psychobiol. and Physiol. Psychol.,* edited by J. M. Sprague and A. N. Epstein. New York: Academic Press, 1983, 1–83.

Kaushall, P. I., M. Zetin, and L. R. Squire. A psychosocial study of chronic, circumscribed amnesia. *J. Nerv. Ment. Dis.* 169: 383–389, 1981.

Keating, M. J., and J. D. Feldman. Visual deprivation and intertectal inter-ictal neuronal connexions in *Xenopus laevis. Proc. R. Soc. Lond. [Biol.]* 191: 467–474, 1975.

Keppel, G. Consolidation and forgetting theory. In: *Memory Consolidation: Psychobiology of Cognition,* edited by H. Weingartner and E. S. Parker. Hillsdale, NJ: Erlbaum, 1984, 149–161.

Kesner, R. P., and J. M. Novak. Serial position curve in rats: role of the dorsal hippocampus. *Science* 218: 173–175, 1982.

Kettner, R. E., and R. F. Thompson. Auditory signal detection and decision processes in the nervous system. *J. Comp. Physiol. Psychol.* 96: 328–331, 1982.

Kinsbourne, M. and F. Wood. Short-term memory processes and the amnesic syndrome. In: *Short-term Memory,* edited by D. Deutsch and J. A. Deutsch. New York: Academic Pres, 1975, 258–291.

Kintsch, W. *The Representation of Meaning in Memory.* Hillsdale, NJ: Erlbaum, 1974.

Klapp, S. T., E. A. Marshburn, and P. T. Lester. Short-term memory does not involve the "working memory" of information processing: The demise of a common assumption. *J. Exp. Psychol. [Gen.]* 112: 240–264, 1983.

Kluver, H. Functional significance of the geniculo-striate system. In: *Visual Mechanisms,* edited by H. Kluver. Lancaster, PA: Jacques Cattell, 1942, 253–299.

Koffka, K. *Principles of Gestalt Psychology.* New York: Harcourt Brace Jovanovich, 1935.

Kohler, C. L., L. Haglund, and L. W. Swanson. A diffuse alpha-MSH-immunoreactive projection to the hippocampus and spinal cord from individual neurons in the lateral hypothalmic area and zona incerta. *J. Comp. Neurol.* 223: 501–514, 1984.

Kohler, W. *Dynamics in Psychology.* New York: Liveright, 1940.

Kohonen, T. Associative memory: A system theoretical approach. New York: Springer, 1977.

Kolers, P. A. A pattern-analysing basis of recognition. In: *Levels of Processing in Human Memory,* edited by L. S. Cermak and F. I. M. Craik. Hillsdale, NJ: Erlbaum, 1979, 363–387.

Konishi, M. A logical basis for single-neuron study of learning in complex neural systems. In: *The Biology of Learning,* edited by P. Marler and H. Terrace. Dahlem Konferenzen, Berlin: Springer-Verlag, 1984, 311–324.

Konishi, M. Birdsong: From behavior to neuron. *Annu. Rev. Neurosci.* 8: 125–170, 1985.

Konorski, J. *Conditioned Reflexes and Neuron Organization.* Cambridge, England: Cambridge University Press, 1948.

Korsakoff, S. S. Disturbance of psychic function in alcoholic paralysis and its relation to the disturbance of the psychic sphere in multiple neuritis of nonalcoholic origin. *Vestn. Psychiatrii* 4: fascicle 2, 1887.

Kossut, M., and S. P. R. Rose. Differential 2-deoxyglucose uptake into chick brain structures during passive avoidance training. *Neuroscience* 12: 971–977, 1984.

Kovner, R., and J. S. Stamm. Disruption of short-term visual memory by electrical stimulation of inferotemporal cortex in the monkey. *J. Comp. Physiol. Psychol.* 81: 163–172, 1972.

REFERENCES

Kowalska, D. M., J. Bachevalier, and M. Mishkin. Inferior prefrontal cortex and recognition memory. *Soc. Neurosci. Abstr.* 10: 385, 1984.

Krasne, F. B. Extrinsic control of intrinsic neuronal plasticity: an hypothesis from work on simple systems. *Brain Res.* 140: 197–216, 1978.

Krech, D. and E. L. Bennett, Interbrain information transfer: a new approach and some ambiguous data. In: *Chemical Transfer of Learned Information,* edited by E. J. Fjerdingstad. New York: Elsevier, 1971, 143–163.

Lashley, K. S. *Brain Mechanisms and Intelligence: A Quantitative Study of Injuries to the Brain.* Chicago: Chicago University Press, 1929.

Lashley, K. S. In search of the engram. *Symp. Soc. Exp. Biol.* 4: 454–482, 1950.

Lashley, K. S., K. L. Chow, and J. Semmes. An examination of the electrical field theory of cerebral integration. *Psychol. Rev.* 58: 123–136, 1951.

Lavond, D. G., T. L. Hembree, and R. F. Thompson. Effect of kainic acid lesions of the cerebellar interpositus nucleus on eyelid conditioning in the rabbit. *Brain Res.* 326:179–182, 1985.

LeDoux, J. E. A Sakaguchi, and D. J. Reis. Subcortical efferent projections of the medial geniculate nucleus mediate emotional responses conditioned to acoustic stimuli. *J. Neurosci.* 4: 683–698, 1984.

Lee, K., F. Schottler, M. Oliver, and G. S. Lynch. Brief bursts of high-frequency stimulation produce two types of structural change in rat hippocampus. *J. Neurophysiol.* 44: 247–258, 1980.

Lehmann, J., J. I. Nagy, S. Atmadia, and H. C. Fibiger. The nucleus basalis magnocellularis: The origin of a cholinergic projection to the neocortex of the rat. *Neuroscience* 5: 1161–1174, 1980.

Lehtonen, R. Learning, memory, and intellectual performance in a chronic state of amnesic syndrome. *Acta Psychiatr. Neurol. Scand.* 49: Suppl. 54, 1–156, 1973.

Leith, E. N., and J. Upatnicks. Reconstructed wavefronts and communication theory. *J. Opt. Soc. Am.* 52: 1123–1130, 1962.

LeVay, S., and Stryker, M. P. The development of ocular dominance columns in the cat. *Soc. Neurosci. Symp.* 4: 83–98, 1979.

LeVay, S., M. P. Stryker, and C. J. Schatz. Ocular dominance columns and their development in layer IV of the cat's visual cortex. A quantitative study. *J. Comp. Neurol.* 179: 223–244, 1978.

LeVere, T. E., and G. W. Morlock. Nature of visual recovery following posterior neodecortication in the hooded rat. *J. Comp. Physiol. Psychol.* 83: 62–67, 1973.

Liang, K. C., R. G. Juler, and J. L. McGaugh. Modulating effects of posttraining epinephrine on memory: Involvement of the amygdala noradrenergic system. *Brain Res.* 368: 125–133, 1986.

Lichtman, J. W. Reorganization of synaptic connections in the rat submandibular ganglion during postnatal development. *J. Physiol.* 273: 155–177, 1977.

Lindvall, O., and A. Bjorklund. Organization of catecholamine neurons in the rat central nervous system. In: *Handbook of Psychopharmacology. Chemical Pathways in the Brain.* edited by L. L. Iversen, S. D. Iversen, and S. H. Snyder. New York: Plenum, 1978, vol. 9, 139–231.

Lisman, J. E. A mechanism for memory storage insensitive to molecular turnover: Bistable autophosphorylating kinases. *Proc. Natl. Acad. Sci., USA* 82: 3055–3057, 1985.

Livingston, R. B. Reinforcement. In: *The Neurosciences,* edited by G. C. Quarton, T. Melnick, and F. O., Schmitt. New York: Rockefeller University Press, 1967, 568–576.

Livingstone, M. S., and D. H. Hubel. Anatomy and physiology of a color system in the primate visual cortex. *J. Neurosci.* 4: 309–339, 1984.

Loftus, E. F., and G. R. Loftus, On the permanence of stored information in the human brain. *Am. Psychol.* 35: 49–72, 1980.

Lorente de No, R. Cerebral cortex: Architecture, intracortical connections, motor projections. In: *Physiology of the Nervous System,* edited by J. F. Fulton. New York: Oxford University Press, 1938, 291–339.

Lugaro, E. I recenti progressi dell'anatomia del sistema nervoso in rapporto alla psicologia ed alla psichiatria. *Riv. Sper. Freniatr. Med. Leg. Alienazioni Ment.* 26: 831–894, 1900. [Cited in Ramon Y. Cajal, 1911].

Luria, A. R. *Higher Cortical Functions in Man.* London: Tavistock, 1966.

Luria, A. R. Frontal-lobe syndromes. In: *Handbook of Clinical Neurology,* edited by P. J. Vinker and G. W. Bruyn. Amsterdam: North-Holland, 1969, 2: 725–757.

Luria, A. R. *The Working Brain: An Introduction to Neuropsychology.* New York: Basic Books, 1973.

Lynch, G., and M. Baudry. The biochemistry of memory: A new and specific hypothesis. *Science* 224: 1057–1063, 1984.

Lynch, G. Synapses, circuits, and the beginnings of memory. Cambridge: MIT Press, 1986.

Mackintosh, N. J. *Conditioning and associative learning.* New York: Oxford University Press, 1983.

Mackintosh, N. J. Varieties of conditioning. In: *Memory Systems of the Brain,* edited by N. M. Weinberger, G. Lynch, and J. McGaugh. New York: Guilford Press, 1985, 335–350.

McCabe, B. J., J. Cipolla-Neto, G. Horn, and P. Bateson. Amnesic effects of bilateral lesions in the hyperstriatum ventrale of the chick after imprinting. *Exp. Brain Res.* 48: 13–21, 1982.

McCabe, B. J., G. Horn, and P. P. G. Bateson. Effects of restricted lesions of the chick forebrain on the acquisition of filial preferences during imprinting. *Brain Res.* 205: 29–37, 1981.

McConnell, J. V. Memory transfer through cannibalism in planarians. J. Neuropsychiatry 3: Suppl. 1, 542–548, 1962.

McCormick, D. A., G. A. Clark, D. G. Lavond, and R. F. Thompson. Initial localization of the memory trace for a basic form of learning. *Proc. Natl. Acad. Sci. USA* 79: 2731–2735, 1982.

McCormick, D. A., J. E. Steinmetz, and R. F. Thompson. Lesions of the inferior olivary complex cause extinction of the classically conditioned eyeblink response. *Brain Res.,* 332: 120–130, 1985.

McCormick, D. A., and R. F. Thompson. Locus coeruleus lesions and resistance to extinction of a classically conditioned response: Involvement of the neocortex and hippocampus. *Brain Res.* 245: 239–249, 1982.

McCormick, D. A., and R. F. Thompson. Cerebellum: Essential involvement in the classically conditioned eyelid response. *Science* 223: 296–299, 1984.

McEntee, W. J., and R. G. Mair. Memory impairment in Korsakoff's psychosis: A correlation with brain noradrenergic activity. *Science* 202: 905–907, 1978.

McEntee, W. J., and R. G. Mair. Memory enhancement in Korsakoff's psychosis by clonidine: Further evidence of a noradrenergic deficit. *Ann. Neurol.* 7: 466–470, 1980.

McGaugh, J. L. Drug facilitation of learning and memory. *Annu. Rev. Pharmacol. Toxicol.* 13: 229–241, 1973.

McGaugh, J. L. Hormonal influences on memory storage. *Annu. Rev. Psychol.* 34: 297–323, 1983a.

McGaugh, J. L. Preserving the presence of the past: hormonal influences on memory. *Am. Psychol.* 38: 161–174, 1983b.

McGaugh, J. L., and P. E. Gold. Modulation of memory by electrical stimulation of the brain. In: *Neural mechanisms of Learning and Memory,* edited by M. R. Rosenzweig and E. L. Bennett. Cambridge, MA: MIT Press, 1976, 549–560.

McGaugh, J. L., and M. J. Herz. *Memory Consolidation.* San Francisco: Albion, 1972.

McGeoch, J. A. *The Psychology of Human Learning: An Introduction.* New York: Longmans, 1942.

McNaughton, B. L. Long-term synaptic enhancement and short-term potentiation in rat fascia dentata act through different mechanisms. *J. Physiol.* 324: 249–262, 1982.

Mahl, G. F., A. Rothenberg, J. M. R. Delgado, and H. Hamlin. Psychological responses in the human to intracerebral electrical stimulation. *Psychosom. Med.* 26: 337–368, 1964.

Mahut, H. Spatial and object reversal learning in monkeys with partial temporal lobe ablations. *Neuropsychologia* 9: 409–424, 1971.

Mahut, H., and M. Moss. Consolidation of memory: the hippocampus revisited. In: *Neuropsychology of Memory,* edited by L. R. Squire and N. Butters. New York: Guilford Press, 1984, 297–315.

Mahut, H., S. Zola-Morgan, and M. Moss. Hippocampal resections impair associative learning and recognition memory in the monkey. *J. Neurosci.* 2: 1214–1229, 1982.

Mair, W. G. P., E. K. Warrington, and L. Weiskrantz. Memory disorder in Korsakoff psychosis. A neuropathological and neuropsychological investigation of two cases. *Brain* 102: 749–783, 1979.

Malamud, N., and S. A. Skillicorn. Relationship between the Wernicke and Korsakoff syndrome: A clinicopathologic study of seventy cases. *Arch. Neurol. Psychiatry* 76: 585–596, 1956.

Mandler, G. Recognizing: The judgment of previous occurrence. *Psychol. Rev.* 87: 252–271, 1980.

Mandler, J. Representation and recall in infancy. In: *Infant Memory,* edited by M. Moscovitch. New York: Plenum Press, 1984, 75–101.

Markowitsch, H. J. Thalamic mediodorsal nucleus and memory: a critical evaluation of studies in animals and man. *Neurosci. Biobehav. Rev.* 6: 351–380, 1982.

Marler, P. Song learning: Innate species differences in the learning process. In: *The Biology of Learning,* edited by P. Marler and H. Terrace. Dahlem Konferenzen, Berlin: Springer-Verlag, 1984, 289–309.

Marr, D. A theory of cerebellar cortex. *J. Physiol.* 202: 437–470, 1969.

Marslen-Wilson, W. D., and H. L. Teuber. Memory for remote events in anterograde amnesia: Recognition of public figures from news photographs. *Neuropsychologia* 13: 353, 1975.

Martinez, J. L., Jr., R. A. Jensen, R. B. Messing, H. Rigter, and J. L. McGaugh (Eds.). Endogenous peptides and learning and memory processes. New York: Academic Press, 587, 1981.

Martinez, J. L., Jr., R. A. Jensen, R. B. Messing, B. J. Vasquez, B. Soumireu-Mourat, D. Geddes, K. C. Liang, and J. L. McGaugh. Central and peripheral actions of amphetamine on memory storage. *Brain Res.* 182: 157–166, 1980a.

Martinez, J. L., Jr., B. J. Vasquez, H. Rigter, R. B. Messing, R. A. Jensen, K. C. Liang, and J. L. McGaugh. Attenuation of amphetamine-enduced enhancement of learning by adrenal demedullation. *Brain Res.* 195: 443–433, 1980b.

Mason, S. T. Noradrenaline in the brain: Progress in theories of behavioral function. *Prog. Neurobiol.* 16: 263–303, 1981.

Mauk, M. D., J. Steinmetz, and R. F. Thompson. Classical conditioning using stimulation of the inferior olive as the unconditioned stimulus. *Proc. Natl. Acad. Sci. USA.* 83: 5349–5353, 1986.

Mauk, M. D., J. T. Warren, and R. F. Thompson. Selective, naloxone-reversible morphine depression of learned behavioral and hippocampal responses. *Science* 216: 434–435, 1982.

Mayes, A., and P. Meudell. Amnesia in humans and other animals. In: *Memory in Animals and Humans,* edited by A. Mayes. Berkshire, England: Van Nostrand Reinhold, 1983, 203–252.

Meikle, T. H. Failure of interocular transfer of brightness discrimination. *Nature* 202: 1243–1244, 1964.

Meikle, T. H., and J. A. Sechzer. Interocular transfer of brightness discrimination in "split-brain" cats. *Science* 132: 734–735, 1960.

Merzenich, M. M., and J. H. Kaas. Principles of organization of sensory-perceptual systems in mammals. *Prog. Psychobiol. Physiol. Psychol.* 9: 1–42, 1980.

Merzenich, M. M., J. H. Kaas, J. T. Wall, M. Sur, R. J. Nelson, and D. J. Felleman. Progression of change following median nerve section in the cortical representation of the hand in areas 3b and 1 in adult owl and squirrel monkeys. *Neuroscience* 10: 639–665, 1983.

Mesulam, M., and G. W. Van Hoesen. Acetylcholinesterase-rich projections from the basal forebrain of the rhesus monkey to neocortex. *Brain Res.* 109: 152–157, 1976.

Meyer, D. R., and P. M. Meyer. Dynamics and bases of recoveries of functions after injuries to the cerebral cortex. *Physiol. Psychol.* 5: 133–165, 1977.

Michel, D., B. Laurent, N. Foyatier, A. Blanc, and M. Portafaix. Infarctus thalamique paramedian guache. *Rev. Neurol. (Paris),* 138: 533–550, 1982.

Miles, F. A., and S. G. Lisberger. Plasticity in the vestibulo-ocular reflex: A new hypothesis. *Annu. Rev. Neurosci.* 4: 273–300, 1981.

Miller, A. K. H., R. L. Alston, C. Q. Mountjoy and J. A. N. Corsellis. Automated differential cell counting on a sector of the normal human hippocampus: The influence of age. *Neuropathol. Appl. Neurobiol.* 10: 123–141, 1984.

Miller, G. A. The magical number seven: Plus or minus two. Some limits on our capacity for processing information. *Psychol. Rev.* 9: 81–97, 1956.

Miller, N. E. Certain facts of learning relevant to the search for its physical basis. In: *The Neurosciences: First Study Program,* edited by G. C. Quarton, T. Melnechuk, and F. O. Schmitt. New York: Rockefeller University Press, 1967, 643–652.

Miller, R. R., and N. A. Marlin. The physiology and semantics of consolidation. In: *Memory Consolidation,* edited by H. Weingartner and E. Parker. Hillsdale, NJ: Erlbaum, 1984, 85–110.

Miller, R. R. and A. D. Springer. Amnesia, consolidation, and retrieval. *Psychol. Rev.* 80: 69–79, 1973.

Mills, R. P. and P. D. Swanson. Vertical oculomotor apraxia and memory loss. *Ann Neurol.* 4: 149–153, 1978.

Milner, B. Les troubles de la memoire accompagnant des lesions hippocampiques bilaterales. In: *Physiologie de l'hippocampe,* Paris: Centre National de la Recherche Scientifique, 1962, 257–272.

Milner, B. Effects of different brain lesions on card sorting. *Arch. Neurol.* 9: 90–100, 1963.

Milner, B. Some effects of frontal lobectomy in man. In: *The Frontal Granular Cortex and Behavior,* edited by J. M. Warren and K. Akert. New York: McGraw-Hill, 1964, 313–334.

Milner, B. Visually-guided maze learning in man: Effects of bilateral hippocampal, bilateral frontal, and unilateral cerebral lesions. *Neuropsychologia* 3: 317–338, 1965.

Milner, B. Brain mechanisms suggested by studies of temporal lobes. In: *Brain Mechanisms Underlying Speech and Language,* edited by F. L. Darley, New York: Grune and Stratton, 1967, 122–145.

Milner, B. Visual recognition and recall after right temporal-lobe excision in man. *Neuropsychologia* 6: 191–209, 1968.

Milner, B. Interhemispheric differences in the localization of psychological processes in man. *Br. Med. Bull.* 27: 272–277, 1971.

Milner, B. Disorders of learning and memory after temporal lobe lesions in man. *Clin. Neurosurg.* 19: 421–446, 1972.

Milner, B. Hemispheric specialization: Scope and limits. In: *The Neurosciences: Third Study Program,* edited by F. O. Schmitt, and F. G. Worden. Cambridge, MA: MIT Press, 1974, 75–89.

Milner, B. Clues to the cerebral organization of memory. In: *Cerebral Correlates of Conscious Experience,* INSERM Symposium, edited by P. A. Buser and A. Rougeul-Buser. Amsterdam: Elsevier, 1978, 139–153.

Milner, B. Some cognitive effects of frontal-lobe lesions in man. *Philos. Trans. R. Soc. Lond. [Biol.],* 298: 211–226, 1982.

Mishkin, M. Effects of small frontal lesions on delayed alternation in monkeys. *J. Neurophysiol.* 20: 615–622, 1957.

Mishkin, M. Preservation of central sets after frontal lesions in monkeys. In: *The Frontal Granular Cortex and Behavior,* edited by J. M. Warren, and K. Akert. New York: McGraw-Hill, 1964, 219–241.

Mishkin, M. Visual mechanisms beyond the striate cortex. In: *Frontiers in Physiological Psychology,* edited by R. Russell. New York: Academic Press, 1966, 93–119.

Mishkin, M. Memory in monkeys severely impaired by combined but not by separate removal of amygdala and hippocampus. *Nature* 273: 297–298, 1978.

Mishkin, M. Analogous neural models for tactual and visual learning. *Neuropsychologia* 17: 139–151, 1979.

Mishkin, M. A memory system in the monkey. *Philos. R. Soc. Lond. [Biol.]* 298: 85–95, 1982.

Mishkin, M., and J. Delacour. An analysis of short-term visual memory in the monkey. *J. Exp. Psychol. [Anim. Behav.]* 1: 326–334, 1975.

Mishkin, M., B. Malamut, and J. Bachevalier. Memories and habits: Two neural systems. In: *Neurobiology of Learning and Memory,* edited by G. Lynch, J. L. McGaugh, and N. M. Weinberger. New York: Guilford Press, 1984, 65–77.

Mishkin, M., and F. J. Manning. Nonspatial memory after selective prefrontal lesions in monkeys. *Brain Res.* 143: 313–323, 1978.

Mishkin, M., B. J. Spiegler, R. C. Saunders, and B. J. Malamut. An animal model of global amnesia. In: *Toward A Treatment of Alzheimer's Disease,* edited by S. Corkin, K. L. Davis, J. H. Growdon, E. J. Usdin and R. J. Wurtman. New York: Raven Press, 1982, 235–247.

Monsell, S. Components of working memory underlying verbal skills: A "distributed capacities'' view. In: *International Symposium on Attention and Performance, X,* edited by H. Bouma and D. Bouwhuis. Hillsdale, NJ: Erlbaum, 1984, 327–350.

Moore, J. W., C. H. Yeo, D. A. Oakley, and I. S. Russell. Conditioned inhibition of the nictitating membrane response in neodecorticate rabbits. *Behav. Brain Res.* 1: 397–410, 1980.

Morris, R. G. M., P. Garrud, J. N. P. Rawlins, and J. O'Keefe. Place navigation impaired in rats with hippocampal lesions. *Nature* 297: 681–683, 1982.

Morrison, J. H., M. E. Molliver, and R. Grzanna. Noradrenergic innervation of cerebral cortex: Widespread effect of local cortical lesions. *Science* 205: 313–316, 1979.

Moscovitch, M. Multiple dissociations of function in amnesia. In: *Human Memory and Amnesia,* edited by L. Cermak. Hillsdale, NJ: Erlbaum, 337–370, 1982.

Moss, M., H. Mahut, and S. Zola-Morgan. Concurrent discrimination learning of monkeys after hippocampal, entorhinal, or fornix lesions. *J. Neurosci.* 1: 227–240, 1981.

Mountcastle, V. B. Modality and topographic properties of single neurons of cat's somatic sensory cortex. *J. Neurophysiol.* 20: 408–434, 1957.

Mountcastle, V. B. An organizing principle for cerebral function: The unit module and the distributed system. In: *The Neurosciences,* edited by F. O. Schmitt and F. G. Worden. Cambridge, MA: MIT Press, 1979, 21–42.

Muller, G. E., and A. Pilzecker. Experimentelle Beitrage zur Lehre vom Gedachtniss [Experimental contributions to the theory of memory]. *Z. Psychol.* 1: 1–288, 1900.

Murdock, B. B. A theory for the storage and retrieval of item and associative information. *Psychol. Rev.* 89: 609–626, 1982.

Murray, E. A., and M. Mishkin. Severe tactual as well as visual memory deficits following combined removal of the amygdala and hippocampus in monkeys. *J. Neurosci.* 4: 2565–2580, 1984.

Murray, E. A., and M. Mishkin. Amygdalectomy impairs crossmodal association in monkeys. *Science* 228: 604–605, 1985.

Murray, E., and M. Mishkin. Visual recognition in monkeys following rhinal cortical ablations combined with either amygdalectomy or hippocampectomy. *J. Neurosci.,* 6:1991–2003, 1986.

Myers, R. E. Interocular transfer of pattern discrimination in cats following section of crossed optic fibers. *J. Comp. Physiol. Psychol.* 48: 470, 1955.

Nadel, L., and J. Willner. Context and conditioning: A place for space. *Physiol. Psychol.* 8: 218–228, 1980.

Nadel, L., and S. Zola-Morgan. Toward the understanding of infant memory: contributions from animal neuropsychology. In: *Infant Memory,* edited by M. Moscovitch. New York: Plenum Press, 1984, 145–172.

Nakamura, R. K., and M. Mishkin. Blindness in monkeys following non-visual cortical lesions. *Brain Res.* 188: 572–577, 1980.

Nakamura, R. K., and M. Mishkin. Chronic blindness following nonvisual lesions in monkeys: Partial lesions and disconnection effects. *Soc. Neurosci. Abstr.* 8: 812, 1982.

Neisser, U. *Cognitive Psychology.* New York: Appleton-Century-Crofts, 1967.

Neville, H., M. Kutas, G. Chesney, and A. Schmidt. Event-related brain potentials during initial encoding and recognition memory of congruous and incongruous words. *J. Memory and Lang.* 25: 75–92, 1986.

Niki, H., and M. Watanabe. Prefrontal unit activity and delayed response: Relation to cue location versus direction of response. *Brain Res.* 105: 79–88, 1976.

Norman, D. A., and D. E. Rumelhart. *Explorations in Cognition.* San Francisco: Freeman, 1975.

Nottebohm, F. Brain pathways for vocal learning in birds: A review of the first 10 years. In: *Prog. in Psychobiol. and Physiol. Psychol.*, edited by J. M. Sprague and A. N. Epstein. New York: Academic Press, 1980, 86–120.

Oakley, D. A., and I. S. Russell. Neocortical lesions and classical conditioning. *Physiol. and Behav.* 8: 915–926, 1972.

Ojemann, G. A. Brain organization for language from the perspective of electrical stimulation mapping. *Behav. Brain Sci.* 6: 189–230, 1983.

O'Keefe, J., and Nadel, L. *The Hippocampus as a Cognitive Map.* London: Oxford University Press, 1978.

Olton, D. S., J. T. Becker, and G. E. Handelmann. Hippocampus, space, and memory. *Behav. Brain Sci.* 2: 313–365, 1979.

Paivio, A. *Imagery and Verbal Processes.* New York: Holt, Rinehart, and Winston, 1971.

Paller, K. A. Effects of medial temporal lobectomy in monkeys on brain potentials related to memory. Ph.D. Thesis, Univeristy of California, San Diego, 1986.

Paller, K. A., S. Zola-Morgan, L. R. Squire, and S. A. Hillyard. P3-like brain waves in monkeys with bilateral medial temporal lesions. Submitted for publication, 1986.

Papez, J. W. A proposed mechanism of emotion. *Arch. Neurol. Psychiatry* 38: 725–743, 1937.

Parkin, A. J. Residual learning capability in organic amnesia. *Cortex* 18: 417–440, 1982.

Parkin, A. J. Amnesic syndrome: A lesion-specific disorder? *Cortex* 20: 479–508, 1984.

Parkinson, J. K., and M. Mishkin. A selective role for the hippocampus in monkeys: Memory for the location of objects. *Soc. Neurosci. Abstr.* 8: 23, 1982.

Pasik, P., and T. Pasik. Visual functions in monkeys after total removal of visual cerebral cortex. In: *Contributions to Sensory Physiology,* vol 7. New York: Academic Press, 1982, 147–200.

Passingham, R. E. Delayed matching after selective prefrontal lesions in monkeys (Macaca mulatta). *Brain Res.* 92: 89–102, 1975.

Patterson, M. M. Mechanisms of classical conditioning of spinal reflexes. In: *Neural Mechanisms of Goal-directed Behavior and Learning,* edited by R. F. Thompson, L. H. Hicks, and V. B. Shvyrkov. New York: Academic Press, 1980, 263–272.

Pavlov, I. P. *Conditioned Reflexes: An Investigation of the Physiological Activity of the Cerebral Cortex.* London: Oxford University Press, 1927.

Pearson, R. C. A., M. M. Esiri, R. W. Hiorns, G. K. Wilcock, and T. P. S. Powell. Anatomical correlates of the distribution of the pathological changes in the neocortex in Alzheimer disease. *Proc. Natl. Acad. Sci. USA* 82: 4531–4534, 1985.

Peck, C. K., S. G. Crewther, and C. R. Hamilton. Partial interocular transfer of brightness and movement discrimination by split-brain cats. *Brain Res.* 163: 61–75, 1979.

Penfield, W. *The Excitable Cortex in Conscious Man.* Springfield, IL: Thomas, 1958.

Penfield, W. W., and H. Jasper. *Epilepsy and the Functional Anatomy of the Human Brain.* Boston, MA: Little, Brown, 1954.

Penfield, W., and G. Mathieson. Memory: Autopsy findings and comments on the role of hippocampus in experiential recall. *Arch. Neurol.,* Chicago 31: 145–154, 1974.

Penfield, W. and B. Milner. Memory deficit produced by bilateral lesions in the hippocampal zone. *Arch. Neurol. Psychiatry* 79: 475–497, 1958.

Penfield, W., and P. Perot. The brain's record of auditory and visual experience. *Brain* 86: 595–696, 1963.

Petrides, M. Motor conditional associative-learning after selective prefrontal lesions in the monkey. *Behav. Brain Res.* 5: 407–413, 1982.

Petrides, M. Deficits on conditional associative-learning tasks after frontal- and temporal-lobe lesions in man. *Neuropsychologia* 23: 601–614, 1985.

Petrides, M., and B. Milner. Deficits on subject-ordered tasks after frontal- and temporal-lobe lesions in man. *Neuropsychologia* 20 (3): 249–262, 1982.

Poon, L. W., J. Fozard, L. Cermak, D. Avenberg, and L. Thompson (Eds.). *New Directions in Memory and Aging.* Hillsdale, NJ: Erlbaum, 1980.

Potter, M. C., and B. A. Faulconer. Time to understand pictures and words. *Nature* 253: 437–438, 1975.

Powell, P. A., M. Lipkin, and W. L. Milligan. Concomitant changes in classically conditioned heart rate and corneoretinal potential discrimination in the rabbit (Oryctolagus cuniculus). *Learn. Motivation* 5: 532–547, 1974.

Pribram, K. H. Neurophysiology and learning: I. Memory and the organization of attention. In: *Brain Function, Vol. 4: Brain Function and Learning,* edited by D. B. Lindsley and A. A. Lumsdaine. Berkeley: University of California Press, 1967, 79–112.

Pribram, K. H. *Languages of the Brain: Experimental Paradoxes and Principles in Neuropsychology.* Englewood Cliffs, NJ: Prentice-Hall, 1971.

Prosser, C. L., and W. S. Hunter. The extinction of startle responses and spinal reflexes in the white rat. *Am. J. Physiol.* 117: 609–618, 1936.

Purves, D., and J. W. Lichtman. Elimination of synapses in the developing nervous system. *Science* 210: 153–157, 1980.

Quinn, W. G., and R. J. Greenspan. Learning and courtship in Drosophila: Two stories with mutants. *Annu. Rev. Neurosci.* 7: 67–94, 1984.

Rabinowitz, J., F. I. M. Craik, and B. Ackerman. A processing resource account of age differences in recall. *Can. J. Psychol.* 36: 325–344, 1982.

Rakic, P. Prenatal development of the visual system in rhesus monkey. *Philos. Trans. R. Soc. Lond. [Biol.]* 278: 245–260, 1977.

Rakic, P., and K. P. Riley. Overproduction and elimination of retinal axons in the fetus rhesus monkey. *Science* 219: 1441–1449, 1983.

Ramon y Cajal, S. La fine structure des centres nerveux. *Proc. R. Soc. Lond. [Biol.]* 55: 444–468, 1894.

Ramon y Cajal, S. *Histologie du systeme nerveux de L'homme et des vertebres.* Paris: Maloine, vol. 2, 1911.

Ramon y Cajal, S. *Histologie du systeme nerveux de L'homme et des vertebres.* Centenary edition. Madrid: Instituto Ramon y Cajal, vol. 1, 1952.

Ramos, A., E. L. Schwartz, and E. R. John. Stable and plastic unit discharge patterns during behavioral generalization. *Science* 192: 393–396, 1976.

Rauschecker, J. P., and W. Singer. Changes in the circuitry of the kitten visual cortex are gated by postsynaptic activity. *Nature* 280: 58–60, 1979.

Reiff, R., and M. Scheerer. *Memory and Hypnotic Age Regression.* New York: International University Press, 1959.

Reinis, S. The formation of conditioned reflexes in rats after the parenteral administration of brain homogenate. *Act. Nerv. Super. (Praha)* 7: 167–168, 1965.

Remy, M. Contribution a l'etudes de la malade de Korsakow. *Mschr. Psychiast.* 106: 128–144, 1942.

Rescorla, R. A., and A. R. Wagner. A theory of Pavlovian conditioning: variations in the effectiveness of reinforcement and nonreinforcement. In: *Classical conditioning II: current research and theory,* edited by A. H. Black and W. F. Prokasy. New York: Appleton-Century-Crofts, 1972, 64–99.

Ribot, T. *Les Maladies de la Memoire.* Paris: Germer Baillere, 1881. [English Translation: *Diseases of Memory.* New York: Appleton-Century-Crofts, 1882.]

Riley, A. L., D. A. Zellner, and H. J. F. Duncan. The role of endorphins in animal learning and behavior. *Neurosci. Biobehav. Rev.* 4: 69–76, 1980.

Roback, A. A., and T. Kiernan (Eds.) In: *Pictoral History of Psychology and Psychiatry.* New York: Philosophical Library, 1969.

Rolls, E. T. Information representation, processing, and storage in the brain: Analysis at the single neuron level. In: *Neural and Molecular Mechanisms of Learning,* edited by J. P. Changeux and M. Konishi. Berlin: Springer-Verlag, 1986, in press.

Rose, F. C., and C. P. Symonds. Persistent memory defect following encephalitis. *Brain* 83: 195–212, 1960.

Rose, S. P. R. Early visual experience, learning and neurochemical plasticity in the rat and the chick. *Philos. Trans. R. Soc. Lond. [Biol.]* 278: 307–318, 1977.

Rosene, D. L., and G. Van Hoesen. Hippocampal efferents reach widespread areas of cerebral cortex and amygdala in the Rhesus monkey. *Science* 198: 315–317, 1977.

Rosenkilde, C. E. Functional heterogeneity of the prefrontal cortex in the monkey: A review. *Behav. Neural Biol.* 25: 301–345, 1979.

Rosenzweig, M. R. Responsiveness of brain size to individual experience. Behavioral and evolutionary implication. In: *Development and Evolution of Brain Size: Behavioral Implications,* edited by M. E. Hahn, C. Jensen, and B. Dudek. New York: Academic Press, 1979. 263–294.

Rosenzweig, M. R., and E. L. Bennett. Experiential influences on brain anatomy and brain chemistry in rodents. In: *Studies on the Development of Behavior and the Nervous System,* vol. 4, edited by G. Gottlieb. New York: Academic Press, 1978, 289–327.

Ross, R. T., W. B. Orr, P. C. Holland, and T. W. Berger. Hippocampectomy disrupts acquisition and retention of learned conditional responding. *Behav. Neurosci.* 98: 211–225, 1984.

Rosvold, H. E., and B. Zernicki (Eds.). Memorial in honor of Jerzy Konorski. Part A. *Acta Neurobiol. Exp.* 35 (No. 5/6): 488, 1975.

Rozin, P. The evolution of intelligence and access to the cognitive unconscious. *Prog. Psychobiol. Physiol. Psychol.* 6: 245–280, 1976a.

Rozin, P. The psychobiological approach to human memory. In: *Neural Mechanisms of Learning and Memory,* edited by M. R. Rosenzweig and E. L. Bennett. Cambridge, MA: MIT Press, 1976b, 3–48.

Rumelhart, D. E., and J. McClelland (Eds.). *Parallel distributed processing.* 2 vols. Cambridge, MIT Press, 1986.

Rumelhart, D. E., and Norman, D. A. Representation of knowledge. In: *Issues in Cognitive Modeling,* edited by A. Aitkenhead and J. Slack. Hillsdale, NJ: Erlbaum, 1985, 15–62.

Russell, W. R., and P. W. Nathan. Traumatic amnesia. *Brain* 69: 280–300, 1946.

Russo, N. J., B. S. Kapp, B. K. Holmquist, and R. E. Musty. Passive avoidance and amygdala lesions: Relationship with pituitary-adrenal system. *Physiol. Behav.* 16: 191–199, 1976.

Ryle, G. *The Concept of Mind.* San Francisco, CA: Hutchinson, 1949.

Ryugo, D. K., and N. M. Weinberger. Differential plasticity of morphologically distinct neuron populations in the medial geniculate body of the cat during classical conditioning. *Behav. Biol.* 22: 275–301, 1978.

Sakai, M. Prefrontal unit activity during visually guided lever pressing reaction in the monkey. *Brain Res.* 81: 297–309, 1974.

Salmon, D., S. Zola-Morgan, L. R. Squire. Retrograde amnesia following combined hippocampus-amygdala lesions in monkeys. *Physiol. Psych.*, 1986, in press.

Sanders, H. I., and E. K. Warrington. Memory for remote events in amnesic patients. *Brain* 94: 661–668, 1971.

Sanquist, T., J. Rohrbaugh, K. Syndulko, and D. B. Lindsley. Electro-cortical signs of levels of processing: Perceptual analysis and recognition memory. *Psychophysiol.* 17: 568–576, 1980.

Saunders, R. C. Impairment in recognition memory after mammillary body lesions in monkeys. *Soc. Neurosci. Abstr.* 9: 28, 1983.

Scalia, F. The termination of retinal axons in the pretectal region of mammals. *J. Comp. Neurol.* 145: 223–258, 1972.

Schacter, D. L. *Stranger Behind the Engram.* Hillsdale, NJ: Erlbaum, 1982.

Schacter, D. L. Toward the multidisciplinary study of memory: Ontogeny, phylogeny, and pathology of memory systems. In: *Neuropsychology of Memory,* edited by L. R. Squire and N. Butters. New York: Guilford Press, 1984, 13–23.

Schacter, D. L. Multiple forms of memory in humans and animals. In: *Memory Systems of the Brain: Animal and Human Cognitive Processes,* edited by N. Weinberger, G. Lynch, and J. McGaugh. New York: Guilford Press, 1985, 351–379.

Schacter, D. L., and P. Graf. Preserved learning in amnesic patients: Perspectives from research on direct priming. *J. Clin. Exp. Neuropsychol.* 1986, in press.

Schacter, D. L., J. L. Harbluk, and D. R. McLachlan. Retrieval without recollection: An experimental analysis of source amnesia. *J. Verb. Learn. Verb. Behav.* 23: 593–611, 1984.

Schacter, D. L., and M. Moscovitch. Infants, amnesics, and dissociable memory systems. In: *Infant Memory,* edited by M. Moscovitch. New York: Plenum Press, 1984, 173–216.

Schneiderman, N. Response system divergencies in aversive classical conditioning. In: *Classical Conditioning II: Current Research and Theory,* edited by A. H. Black and W. F. Prokasy. New York: Appleton-Century-Crofts, 1972, 341–376.

Schwaber, J. S., B. S. Kapp, G. A. Higgins, and P. R. Rapp. Amygdaloid and basal forebrain direct connections with the nucleus of the solitary tract and the dorsal motor nucleus. *J. Neurosci.* 2: 1424–1438, 1982.

Schwartz, J. H., V. F. Castellucci, and E. R. Kandel. The functioning of identified neurons and synapses in the absence of protein synthesis. *J. Neurophysiol.* 34: 939–953, 1971.

Scoville, W. B., and B. Milner. Loss of recent memory after bilateral hippocampal lesions. *J. Neurol. Neurosurg. Psychiatry.* 20: 11–21, 1957.

Semon, R. *die Mneme als erhaltendes Prinzip im Wechsel des organischen Geschehens.* Leipzig: Wilhelm Engelmann, 1904.

Shallice, T. Specific impairments of planning. *Philos. Trans. Soc. Lond.* 298: 199–209, 1982.

Shatz, C. J., and P. A. Kirkwood, Prenatal development of functional connection in the cat's retinogeniculate pathway. *J. Neurosci.* 4: 1378–1397, 1984.

Shaw, G. L., E. Harth, and A. B. Scheibel. Cooperativity in brain function: assemblies of approximately 30 neurons. *Exp. Neurol.* 77: 324–358, 1982.

Sheridan, C. L. Interocular transfer of brightness and pattern discriminations in normal and corpus-callosum-sectioned rats. *J. Comp. Physiol. Psychol.* 59: 292–294, 1965.

Shimamura, A. P. Priming effects in amnesia: Evidence for a dissociable memory function. *Q. J. Exp. Psychol.*, in press, 1986.

Shimamura, A. P., D. Salmon, L. R. Squire, and N. Butters. Memory dysfunction and word priming in dementia and amnesia. *Behav. Neurosci.*, in press, 1987.

Shimamura, A. P., and L. R. Squire. Paired-associate learning and priming effects in amnesia: a neuropsychological study. *J. Exp. Psychol. [Gen.]* 113: 556–570, 1984.

Shimamura, A. P., and L. R. Squire. Korsakoff's syndrome: A study of the relationship between anterograde amnesia and remote memory impairment. *Behav. Neurosci.* 100: 165–170, 1986a.

Shimamura, A. P., and L. R. Squire. Memory and metamemory: A study of the feeling-of-knowing phenomenon in amnesic patients. *J. Exp. Psychol. [Learn. Mem. Cog.]* 12:452–460, 1986b.

Shimamura, A. P., and L. R. Squire. A neuropsychological study of fact memory and source amnesia. *J. Exp. Psychol. [Learn. Mem. Cog.]*, in press, 1987.

Sidman, M., L. T. Stoddard, and J. P. Mohr. Some additional quantitative observations of immediate memory in a patient with bilateral hippocampal lesions. *Neuropsychologia* 6: 245–254, 1968.

Smith, M. L., and B. Milner. The role of the right hippocampus in the recall of spatial location. *Neuropsychologia* 19: 781–793, 1981.

Smith, M. L., and B. Milner. Differential effects of frontal-lobe lesions on cognitive estimation and spatial memory. *Neuropsychologia* 22: 697–705, 1984.

Smith, O. A., C. A. Astley, J. L. DeVit, J. M. Stein, and K. E. Walsh. Functional analysis of hypothalamic control of the cardiovascular responses accompanying emotional behavior. *Fed. Proc.* 39: 2487–2494, 1980.

Solomon, P. R., and J. W. Moore. Latent inhibition and stimulus generalization of the classically conditioned nictitating membrane response in rabbits (Oryctolagus cuniculus) following dorsal hippocampal ablation. *J. Comp. Physiol. Psychol.* 89: 1192–1203, 1975.

Speedie, L. J., and K. M. Heilman. Amnestic disturbance following infarction of the left dorsomedial nucleus of the thalmus. *Neuropsychologia* 20: 597–604, 1982.

Sperling, G. The information available in brief visual presentations. *Psychol. Monogr.* 74 (Whole No. 498): 1960.

Sperry, R. W. Cerebral regulation of motor coordination in monkeys following multiple transection of sensorimotor cortex. *J. Neurophysiol.* 10: 275–294, 1947.

Sperry, R. W. Physiological plasticity and brain ciricut theory. In: *Biological and Biochemical Bases of Behavior,* edited by H. F. Harlow and C. N. Woolsey. Madison: University of Wisconsin Press, 1958, 401–424.

Sperry, R. W. Preservation of high-order function in isolated somatic cortex in callosum-sectioned cat. *J. Neurophysiol.* 22: 78–87, 1959.

Sperry, R. W. Cerebral organization and behavior. *Science* 133: 1749–1757, 1961.

Sperry, R. W. Chemoaffinity in the orderly growth of nerve fiber patterns and connections. *Proc. Natl. Acad. Sci. USA* 50: 703–710, 1963.

Sperry, R. W., and N. Miner. Pattern perception following insertion of mica plates into visual cortex. *J. Comp. Physiol. Psychol.* 48: 463–469, 1955.

Sperry, R. W., N. Miner, and R. E. Myers. Visual pattern perception following subpial slicing and tantalum wire implantations in the visual cortex. *J. Comp. Physiol. Psychol.* 48: 50–58, 1955.

Spinelli, D. N., and F. E. Jensen. Plasticity: The mirror of experience. *Science* 203: 75–78, 1979.

Squire, L. R. Specifying the defect in human amnesia: Storage, retrieval, and semantics. *Neuropsychologia* 18: 368–372, 1980.

Squire, L. R. Two forms of human amnesia: An analysis of forgetting. *J. Neurosci.* 1: 635–640, 1981.

Squire, L. R. The neuropsychology of human memory. *Annu. Rev. Neurosci.* 5: 241–273, 1982a.

Squire, L. R. Comparisons between forms of amnesia: Some deficits are unique to Korsakoff's syndrome. *J. Exp. Psychol [Learn. Mem. Cog.]* 8: 560–571, 1982b.

Squire, L. R. Mechanisms of memory. *Science* 232: 1612–1919, 1986.

Squire, L. R. The neuropsychology of memory. In: *The Biology of Learning,* edited by P. Marler and H. S. Terrace. Dahlem Konferenzen. Berlin: Springer-Verlag, 1984, 667–685.

Squire, L. R. Memory: Neural systems and behavior. In: *Handbook of Physiology: Higher Functions of the Nervous System,* edited by F. Plum. Bethesda, MD: American Physiological Society, 1987, in press.

Squire, L. R., and N. Cohen. Memory and amnesia: Resistance to disruption develops for years after learning. *Behav. Neural Biol.* 25: 115–125, 1979.

Squire, L. R., and Cohen, N. J. Human memory and amnesia. In: *Neurobiology of Learning and Memory,* edited by G. Lynch, J. L. McGaugh, and N. M. Weinberger. New York: Guilford Press, 1984, 3–64.

Squire, L. R., N. J. Cohen, and L. Nadel. The medial temporal region and memory consolidation: A new hypothesis. In: *Memory Consolidation,* edited by H. Weingartner and E. Parker. Hillsdale, NJ: Erlbaum, 1984, 185–210.

Squire, L. R., N. J. Cohen, and J. A. Zouzounis. Preserved memory in retrograde amnesia: Sparing of a recently acquired skill. *Neuropsychologia* 22: 145–152, 1984.

Squire, L. R., and H. P. Davis. The pharmacology of memory: A neurobiological perspective. *Annu. Rev. Pharmacol. Toxicol.* 21: 323–356, 1981.

Squire, L. R., and M. M. Fox. Assessment of remote memory: Validation of the television test by repeated testing during a seven-day period. *Behav. Res. Meth. Instrum.* 12: 583–586, 1980.

Squire, L. R., and R. Y. Moore. Dorsal thalamic lesion in a noted case of human memory dysfunction. *Ann. Neurol.* 6: 503–506, 1979.

Squire, L. R., and W. T. Schlapfer. Memory and memory disorders: A biological and neurologic perspective. In: *Handbook of Biological Psychiatry,* pt. IV, edited by H. M. van Praag, M. H. Lader, O. J. Rafaelsen, and E. J. Sachar. New York and Basel: Marcel Dekker, 1981, 309–341.

Squire, L. R., and A. P. Shimamura. Characterizing amnesic patients for neurobehavioral study. *Behav. Neurosci.* 1986, in press.

Squire, L. R., A. P. Shimamura, and P. Graf. Independence of recognition memory and priming effects: A neuropsychological analysis. *J. Exp. Psychol. [Learn. Mem. Cog.]* 11: 37–44, 1985.

Squire, L. R., A. P. Shimamura, and P. Graf. Strength and duration of priming effects in amnesic patients and normal subjects. *Neuropsychologia* 1987, in press.

Squire, L. R., and P. C. Slater. Forgetting in very long-term memory as assessed by an improved questionnaire technique. *J. Exp. Psychol. [Human Learn.]* 104: 50–54, 1975.

Squire, L. R., P. C. Slater, and P. M. Chace. Retrograde amnesia: Temporal gradient in very long-term memory following electroconvulsive therapy. *Science* 187: 77–79, 1975.

Squire, L. R., P. C. Slater, and P. L. Miller. Retrograde amnesia following ECT: Long-term follow-up studies. *Arch. Gen. Psychiatry* 38: 89–95, 1981.

Squire, L. R., and C. W. Spanis. Long gradient of retrograde amnesia in mice: continuity with the findings in humans. *Behav. Neurosci.* 98: 345–348, 1984.

Squire, L. R., and S. Zola-Morgan. The neurology of memory: The case for correspondence between the findings for human and nonhuman primate. In: *The Physiological Basis of Memory,* 2d ed., edited by J. A. Deutsch. New York: Academic Press, 1983, 199–268.

Squire, L. R., and S. Zola-Morgan. Neuropsychology of memory: New links between humans and experimental animals. In: *Memory Dysfunctions: An Integration of Animal and Human Research from Preclinical and Clinical Perspectives,* edited by D. Olton, S. Corkin, E. Gamzu. New York: NY Academy of Science, 1985, 137–149.

Srebro, B., E. C. Azmitia, and J. Winson. Effect of 5-HT depletion of the hippocampus on neuronal transmission from perforant path through dentate gyrus. *Brain Res.* 235: 142–147, 1982.

Sretavan, D., and C. J. Shatz. Prenatal development of individual retinogeniculate axons during the period of segregation. *Nature* 308: 845–848, 1984.

Stamm, J. S. Functional dissociation between the inferior and arcuate segments of dorsolateral prefrontal cortex in the monkey. *Neuropsychologia* 11: 181–190, 1973.

Stamm, J. S., and S. C. Rosen. Electrical stimulation and steady potential shifts in prefrontal cortex during delayed response performance by monkeys. *Acta Biol. Exp.* 29: 385–399, 1969.

Stamm, J. S., and S. C. Rosen. The locus and crucial time of implication of prefrontal cortex in the delayed response task. In: *Psychophysiology of the Frontal Lobes,* edited by K. H. Pribram and A. R. Luria. New York: Academic Press, 1973, 139–153.

Staübli, U., D. Fraser, M. Kessler, and G. Lynch. Studies in retrograde and anterograde amnesia after hippocampal denervation by entorhinal lesions. *Behav. Neural Biol.* in press, 1987.

Steinmetz, J. E., D. G. Lavond, and R. F. Thompson. Classical conditioning of the rabbit eyelid response with mossy fiber stimulation as the conditioned stimulus. *Bull. Psychonomic Soc.,* 1985, 23: (3) 245–248.

Stent, G. S. A physiological mechanism for Hebb's postulate of learning. *Proc. Natl. Acad. Sci. USA* 70: 997–1001, 1973.

Stuss, D. T., E. F. Kaplan, D. F. Benson, W. S. Weir, S. Chiulli, and F. F. Sarazin. Evidence for the involvement of orbitofrontal cortex in memory functions: An interference effect. *J. Comp. Physiol. Psychol.* 96 (6): 913–925, 1982.

Sutherland, R. J., and R. H. Dyck. Hippocampal and neocortical contributions to spatial learning and memory. *Soc. Neurosci. Abstr.* 9: 638, 1983.

Swanson, L. W., T. J. Teyler, and R. F. Thompson. Hippocampal long-term potentiation: Mechanisms and implications for memory. *Neurosci. Res. Program Bull.* 20: 613–765, 1982.

Sweet, W. H., G. A. Talland, and F. R. Ervin. Loss of recent memory following section of the fornix. *Trans. Am. Neurol. Assoc.* 84: 876–882, 1959.

Szentagothai, J. The "module-concept" in cerebral cortex architecture. *Brain Res.* 95: 475–496, 1975.

Talland, G. A. *Deranged Memory.* New York: Academic Press, 1965.

Tanzi, E. I fatti e le induzioni nell'odierna istologia del sistema nervosa. *Riv. Sper. Freniatr. Med. Leg. Alienazioni Ment.* 19: 419–472, 1893. [Cited in Ramon y Cajal, 1911].

Teuber, H. L. The riddle of frontal lobe function in man. In: *The Frontal Granular Cortex and Behavior,* edited by J. M. Warren and K. Akert. New York: McGraw-Hill, 1964, 410–477.

Teuber, H. L., B. Milner, and H. G. Vaughan. Persistent anterograde amnesia after stab wound of the basal brain. *Neuropsychologia* 6: 267–282, 1968.

Teyler, T. J., and P. DiScenna. The hippocampal memory indexing theory. *Behav. Neurosci.* 100: 147–154, 1986.

Thomas, G. J. Memory: Time binding in organisms. In: *Neuropsychology of Memory*, edited by L. R. Squire and N. Butters. New York: Guilford Press, 1984, 374–384.

Thompson, R. Retention of a brightness discrimination following neocortical damage in the rat. *J. Comp. Physiol. Psychol.* 53: 212–215, 1960.

Thompson, R. Localization of the visual memory system in the white rat. *J. Comp. Physiol. Psychol. Monogr.* 69: Part 2, 1–29, 1969.

Thompson, R. Neuronal substrates of simple associative learning: Classical conditioning. *Trends in Neurosci.* 6: 270–274, 1983.

Thompson, R. Stereotaxic mapping of brainstem areas critical for memory of visual discrimination habits in the rat. *Physiol. Psychol.* 4: 1–10, 1976.

Thompson, R. *A Behavioral Atlas of the Rat Brain.* New York: Oxford University Press, 1978.

Thompson, R., and J. V. McConnell, Classical conditioning in the planarian, Dugesia Dorotocephala. *J. Comp. Physiol. Psychol.* 48: 65–68, 1955.

Thompson, R., and I. Rich. Differential effects of posterior thalamic lesions on retention of various visual habits. *J. Comp. Physiol. Psychol.* 56: 60–65, 1963.

Thompson, R., and P. H. Spiliotis. Subcortical lesions and retention of a brightness discrimination in the rat: Appetitive vs. aversive motivation. *Psyciol. Psychol.* 9: 63–67, 1981.

Thompson, R. F. The neurobiology of learning and memory. *Science* 233: 941–947, 1986.

Thompson, R. F., T. W. Berger, and J. Madden. Cellular processes of learning and memory in the mammalian CNS. Annu. Rev. Neurosci. 6: 447–491, 1983.

Thompson, R. F., and W. A. Spencer. Habituation: A model phenomenon for the study of neuronal substrates of behavior. *Psychol. Rev.* 173: 16–43, 1966.

Tischler, M. D., and M. Davis. A visual pathway that mediates fear-conditioned enhancement of acoustic startle. *Brain Res.* 276: 55–71, 1983.

Tomlinson, B. E. Morphological brain changes in non-demented old people. In: *Aging of the Central Nervous System, Biological and Psychological Aspects*, edited by H. M. VanPraag and A. F. Kalverbove. Haarlem: De Erven F. Bohn N. V., 1972, 38–57.

Tomlinson, B. E., G. Blessed, and M. Roth. Observations on the brains of non-demented old people. *J. Neurol. Sci.* 7: 331–356, 1968.

Trevarthen, C. B. Double visual learning in split-brain monkeys. *Science* 136: 258–259, 1962.

Tsukahara, N. Synaptic plasticity in the mammalian central nervous system. *Annu. Rev. Neurosci.* 4: 351–379, 1981.

Tsukahara, N., Y. Oda, and T. Notsu. Classical conditioning mediated by the red nucleus in the cat. *J. Neurosci.* 1: 72–79, 1981.

Tulving, E. Episodic and semantic memory. In: *Organization of Memory*, edited by E. Tulving and W. Donaldson. New York: Academic Press, 1972, 381–403.

Tulving, E. *Elements of Episodic Memory.* Oxford: Clarendon Press, 1983.

Tulving, E. Multiple learning and memory systems. In: *Psychology in the 1990's,* edited by K. Lagerspetz and P. Niemi. Amsterdam: North-Holland, 1984, 163–184.

Turner, A. M., and W. T. Greenough. Differential rearing effects on rat visual cortex synapses. I. Synaptic and neuronal density and synapses per neuron. *Brain Res.* 329: 195–203, 1985.

Udin, S. B. Abnormal visual input leads to development of abnormal axon trajectories in frogs. *Nature* 301: 336–338, 1983.

Udin, S. B., and M. J. Keating. Plasticity in a central nervous pathway in Xenopus: Anatomical changes in the isthmotectal projection after larval eye rotation. *J. Comp. Neurol.* 203: 575–594, 1981.

Ungar, G. Molecular mechanisms in information processing. *Int. Rev. Neurobiol.* 13: 223–250, 1970.

Ungar, G. Bioassays for the chemical correlates of acquired information. In: *Chemical Transfer of Learned Information,* edited by E. J. Fjerdingstad. Amsterdam: North-Holland, 1971, 31–49.

Ungar, G., D. M. Desiderio, and W. Parr. Isolation, identification and synthesis of a specific-behavior-inducing brain peptide. *Nature* 238: 198–202, 1972.

Ungar, G., and C. Ocequera-Navarro. Transfer of habituation by material extracted from a brain. *Nature* 207: 301–302, 1965.

Ungerleider, L. G., and R. Desimone. Cortical connections of visual area MT in the macaque. *J. Comp. Neurol.* 248: 190–222, 1986.

Ungerleider, W., and M. Mishkin. Two cortical visual systems. In: *The Analysis of Visual Behavior,* edited by D. J. Ingle, M. A. Goodale, and R. J. W. Mansfield. Cambridge, MA: MIT Press, 198, 549–586.

Uretsky, E., and R. A. McCleary. Effect of hippocampal isolation on retention. *J. Comp. Physiol. Psychol.* 68: 1–8, 1969.

Van Heerden, P. J. A new method of storing and retrieving information. *Appl. Optics* 2: 387–392, 1963.

Van Hoesen, G. W. The parahippocampal gyrus. *Trends in Neurosci.* 5: 345–350, 1982.

Van Hoesen, G. W., D. N. Pandya, and N. Butters. Cortical afferents to the entorhinal cortex of the rhesus monkey. *Science* 175: 1471–1473, 1972.

Van Hoesen, G. W., D. N. Pandya, and N. Butters. Some connections of the entorhinal (area 28) and perirhinal (area 35) cortices of the rhesus monkey. II. Frontal lobe afferents. *Brain Res.* 95: 25–38, 1975.

van Wimersma Greidanus, T. J. B., G. Croiset, E. Bakker, and H. Bowman. Amygdaloid lesions block the effect of neuropeptides (vasopressin and ACTH/4-10) on avoidance behavior. *Physiol. Behav.* 22: 291–295, 1979.

Victor, M., R. D. Adams, and G. H. Collins. *The Wernicke-Korsakoff Syndrome.* Davis: Philadelphia, 1971.

Vincent, S. R., T. Hokfelt, L. R. Skirboll, and J. Y. Wu. Hypothalamic gamma-aminobutyric acid neurons project to the neocortex. *Science* 220: 1309–1310, 1983.

Volpe, B. T., and W. Hirst. The characterization of an amnesic syndrome following hypoxic ischemic injury. *Arch. Neurol.* 40: 436–445, 1983.

von Bechterew, W. V. Demonstration eines Gehirns mit Zerstorung der vorderen und inneren Theile der Hirnrinde beider Schlaferlappen. *Neurologisches Zentpalblatt* 19: 990–991, 1900.

von Bonin, G., and P. Bailey. *The Neocortex of Macaca Mulatta.* Urbana: University of Illinois Press, 1947.

von Cramon, D. Y., N. Hebel, and U. Schuri. A contribution to the anatomical basis of thalamic amnesia. *Brain* 108: 993–1008, 1985.

Walker, A. E. A cytoarchitectural study of the prefrontal area of the macaque monkey. *J. Comp. Neurol.* 73: 59–86, 1940.

Walsh, T. J., and T. Palfai. Peripheral catecholamines and memory: Characteristics of syrosingopine-induced amnesia. *Pharmacol. Biochem. Behav.* 11: 449–52, 1979.

Walters, E. T., and J. M. Byrne. Associative conditioning of single sensory neurons suggests a cellular mechanism for learning. *Science* 219: 405–408, 1983.

Warrington, E. K., and L. Weiskrantz. A new method of testing long-term retention with special reference to amnesic patients. *Nature* 217: 972–974, 1968.

Warrington, E. K., and L. Weiskrantz. Amnesia: A disconnection syndrome? *Neuropsychologia* 20: 233–248, 1982.

Waugh, N. C., and D. A. Norman. Primary memory. *Psychol. Rev.* 72: 89–104, 1965.

Weinberger, N. M. Effects of conditioned arousal on the auditory system. In: *The Neural Basis of Behavior,* edited by A. L. Beckman. New York: Spectrum, 1982, 63–91.

Weinberger, N. M., D. M. Diamond, and T. M. McKenna. Initial events in conditioning: Plasticity in the pupillomotor and auditory systems. In: *Neurobiology of Learning and Memory,* edited by G. Lynch, J. L. McGaugh, and N. M. Weinberger. New York: Guilford Press, 1984, 197–227.

Weiskrantz, L., and E. K. Warrington. Conditioning in amnesic patients. *Neuropsychologia* 17: 187–194, 1979.

Whitehouse, P. J., D. L. Price, R. G. Struble, A. W. Clark, J. T. Coyle, and M. R. DeLong. Alzheimer's disease and senile dementia: Loss of neurons in the basal forebrain. *Science* 215: 1237–1239, 1982.

Wickelgren, W. A. Sparing of short-term memory in an amnesic patient: implications for a strength theory of memory. *Neuropsychologia* 6: 235–244, 1968.

Wickelgren, W. A. The long and the short of memory. In: *Short-term Memory,* edited by D. Deutsch and J. A. Deutsch. New York: Academic Press, 1975, 41–63.

Wickelgren, W. A. Chunking and consolidation: A theoretical synthesis of semantic networks, configuring in conditioning, S-R vs. cognitive learning, normal forgetting, the amnesic syndrome and the hippocampal arousal system. *Psychol. Rev.* 86: 44–60, 1979.

Wiesel, T. Postnatal development of the visual cortex and the influence of environment. *Nature* 299: 583–591, 1982.

Wiesel, T. N., and D. H. Hubel. Single-cell responses in striate cortex of kittens deprived of vision in one eye. *J. Neurophysiol.*, 26: 1003–1017, 1963.

Wiesel, T. N., and D. H. Hubel. Comparison of the effects of unilateral and bilateral eye closure on cortical unit responses in kittens. *J. Neurophysiol.* 28: 1029–1040, 1965.

Williams, M., and J. Pennybacker. Memory disturbances in third ventricle tumours. *J. Neurol. Neurosurg. Psychiatry* 17: 115, 1954.

Winocur, G., S. Oxbury, V. Agnetti, and C. Davis. Amnesia in a patient with bilateral lesions to the thalamus. *Neuropsychologia* 22: 123–144, 1984.

Winograd, T. Frame representations and the declarative-procedural controversy. In: *Representation and Understanding: Studies in Cognitive Science*, edited by D. Bobrow and A. Collins. New York: Academic Press, 1975, 185–210.

Winson, J. Influence of raphe nuclei on neuronal transmission from perforant pathway through dentate gyrus. *J. Neurophysiol.* 44: 937–950, 1980.

Winson, J., and C. Abzug. Neuronal transmission through hippocampal pathways dependent on behavior. *J. Neurophysiol.* 41: 716–732, 1978.

Winston, P. H. *Artificial Intelligence*. Reading, MA: Addison-Wesley, 1977.

Wood, F., V. Ebert, and M. Kinsbourne. The episodic-semantic memory distinction in memory and amnesia: Clinical and experimental observations. In: *Human Memory and Amnesia*, edited by L. Cermak. Hillsdale, NJ: Erlbaum, 1982, 167–194.

Woody, D. D. *Memory, Learning, and Higher Function*. New York: Springer-Verlag, 1982.

Woody, C. D., and F. R. Ervin. Memory function in cats with lesions of the fornix and mammillary bodies. *Physiol. Behav.* 1: 273–280, 1966.

Woolsey, T. A., and H. Van der Loos. The structural organization of layer IV in the somatosensory region (SI) of mouse cerebral cortex. *Brain Res.* 17: 205–242, 1970.

Yeo, C. H., M. J. Hardiman, M. Glickstein, and I. S. Russell. Lesions of cerebellar nuclei abolish the classically conditioned nictitating membrane response. *Soc. Neurosci. Abstr.* 8: 22, 1982.

Yeo, C. H., M. J. Hardiman, and M. Glickstein. Discrete lesions of the cerebellar cortex abolish the classically conditioned nictitating membrane response of the rabbit. *Behav. Brain Res.* 13: 261–266, 1984.

Yin, R. K. Face recognition by brain-injured patients: A dissociable ability? *Neuropsychologia* 8: 395–402, 1970.

Young, J. Z. Learning as a process of selection and amplification. *J. R. Soc. Med.* 72: 801–814, 1979.

Zangwill, O. L. The cerebral localisation of psychological function. *Adv. Sci.* 20: 335–344, 1963.

Zippel, H. P. *Symposium on Memory and Transfer of Information, Gottingen 1972.* New York: Plenum Press, 1973.

Zola-Morgan, S., N. J. Cohen, and L. R. Squire. Recall of remote episodic memory in anmesia. *Neuropsychologia* 21: 487–500, 1983.

Zola-Morgan, S., and L. R. Squire. Preserved learning in monkeys with medial temporal lesions: Sparing of motor and cognitive skills. *J. Neurosci.* 4: 1072–1085, 1984.

Zola-Morgan, S., and L. R. Squire. Medial temporal lesions in monkeys impair memory in a variety of tasks sensitive to human amnesia. *Behav. Neurosci.* 99: 22–34, 1985a.

Zola-Morgan, S., and L. R. Squire. Amnesia in monkeys following lesions of the mediodorsal nucleus of the thalamus. *Ann. Neurol.* 17: 558–564, 1985b.

Zola-Morgan, S., and L. R. Squire. Complementary approaches to the study of memory: Human amnesia and animal models. In: *Memory Systems of the Brain: Animal and Human Cognitive Processes,* edited by N. Weinberger, J. McGaugh, and G. Lynch. New York: Guilford Press, 1985c, 463–477.

Zola-Morgan, S., and L. R. Squire. Memory impairment in monkeys following lesions of the hippocampus. *Behav. Neurosci.,* 100: 155–160, 1986.

Zola-Morgan, S., L. R. Squire, and D. Amaral. Human amnesia and the medial temporal region: Enduring memory impairment following a bilateral lesion limited to the CA1 field of the hippocampus. *J. Neurosci.,* 6: 2950–2967, 1986.

Zola-Morgan, S., L. R. Squire, and M. Mishkin. The neuroanatomy of amnesia: Amygdala-hippocampus vs. temporal stem. *Science* 218: 1337–1339, 1982.

Name Index

Subject Index

AA. *See* Anterograde amnesia
Abstraction
   and prefrontal cortex, 225
Acetylcholine (ACh), 41, 45, 47-49
   neocortical, primary source of, 41
ACh. *See* Acetylcholine
Acoustic startle reflex, 86-88
   habituation of, 86-89, 243
   neural circuit, 87
ACTH, 49, 51, 53
Adrenal demedullation, 51
Adrenal medulla, 49
Adrenal medullary hormones, 53
   and memory, 53
Adrenaline. *See* Epinephrine
After-discharges, 81, 82
Aging and memory, 198-201
Agnosia, 130
Alcohol abuse, 46. *See also* Korsakoff's syndrome
Alertness, effect on memory, 39
Allocortex, 211
Alpha-melanocyte-stimulating hormone, 43
Alpha-receptor agonist, 46
Alzheimer's disease, 48
   and basal forebrain, 197
   and cholinergic neuron lesions, 48
   and olfactory system, 48
   and pathology in entorhinal cortex and hippocampal formation, 48
   priming effects in, 165, 166
   treatment of with cholinergic agonists, 48

Aminergic systems and learning, 44-46
Amnesia, 138
   after bilateral infarction of tuberothalamic or paramedian arteries, 182
   and anoxia, 187, 220
   anterograde (AA), 172, 206, 207
   anterograde and retrograde as linked deficits, 214
   and brain stem damage, 219
   causes of, 206
   and cerebellar damage, 219
   chronic, 213
   and cycloheximide (CXM), 147
   damage to specialized neural system, 179-181
   diencephalic, 180-186, 215, 220
   and encephalitis, 180, 208, 219
   and episodic memory, 171-173
   and functional organization of memory, 202-223
   infantile, 168
   ischemic, 181, 192, 220
   and jigsaw puzzle skills, 152
   medial temporal, 186-94
   and memory failure during normal aging, 199
   and midline thalamic lesions, 183
   and mirror-reading skill, 152
   and neocortex damage, 219-20
   and perceptual and cognitive skills, 152
   post-encephalitic, 156, 180, 208, 219
   and posterior cerebral artery occlusion, 180